# W. I. Thomas

ON SOCIAL ORGANIZATION
AND SOCIAL PERSONALITY

THE HERITAGE OF SOCIOLOGY

*A Series Edited by* Morris Janowitz

# W. I. Thomas

# ON SOCIAL ORGANIZATION
# AND SOCIAL PERSONALITY

Selected Papers

*Edited and with an Introduction by*

MORRIS JANOWITZ

Andrew S. Thomas Memorial Library
MORRIS HARVEY COLLEGE, CHARLESTON, W. VA.

THE UNIVERSITY OF CHICAGO PRESS
CHICAGO AND LONDON

63984

*Library of Congress Catalog Card Number: 66–23701*

THE UNIVERSITY OF CHICAGO PRESS, CHICAGO & LONDON
The University of Toronto Press, Toronto 5, Canada

*© 1966 by The University of Chicago. All rights reserved*
*Published 1966*
*Printed in the United States of America*

*Designed by Andor Braun*

# Contents

INTRODUCTION *by Morris Janowitz*         vii

## I. THE SUBJECT MATTER OF SOCIOLOGY AND SOCIAL PSYCHOLOGY

1. Social Disorganization and Social Reorganization    3
2. Social Personality: Organization of Attitudes    11
3. Rational Control in Social Life    37

## II. SOCIAL ORGANIZATION: INSTITUTIONAL ANALYSIS

4. The Primary Group    57
5. Family and Community    61
6. Leadership, Education, and the Press    87

## III. SOCIAL PERSONALITY: THE DEFINITION OF THE SITUATION

| | | |
|---|---|---|
| 7. | Motivation: The Wishes | 117 |
| 8. | The Unconscious: Configurations of Personality | 140 |
| 9. | Situational Analysis: The Behavior Pattern and the Situation | 154 |
| 10. | Analytical Types: Philistine, Bohemian, and Creative Man | 168 |
| 11. | Social Types: Immigrant Roles | 182 |

## IV. CHANGE: SOCIAL AND PERSONAL

| | | |
|---|---|---|
| 12. | Assimilation: Old World Traits Transplanted | 195 |
| 13. | Conflict: Revolutionary Attitudes | 215 |
| 14. | The Individualization of Behavior | 231 |

## V. METHODOLOGY AND METHOD

| | | |
|---|---|---|
| 15. | Methodological Note: Attitude and Value | 257 |
| 16. | The Relation of Research to the Social Process | 289 |

BIBLIOGRAPHY 307

*Introduction*

THE "CHICAGO SCHOOL" of sociology has come to be viewed as one of the central phases in the historical development of the discipline in the United States. But it is a disputable question whether there was a distinct or unified Chicago approach to sociology. What is not in doubt is that the Department of Sociology at the University of Chicago was among the first and that for a period of almost half a century it dominated the intellectual and professional development of the discipline by the eminence of its faculty and the prominence of its graduates. But during all these years the style of scholarship of the leading members of the Chicago school was exceedingly diverse. The Department of Sociology, like the University as a whole, represented a premeditated construction rather than a gradual evolution of an institution. It was to be expected that no single personality would dominate but rather, as a response to the leadership of the administration, the department was an amalgam of all that seemed intellectually relevant and creative. In fact, at the time of its most intensive activity the Chicago school contained theoretical viewpoints and substantive interests which were extremely variegated.

Despite this real diversity, the sociological world of its day accepted the image of a Chicago school. The image was fashioned by other centers of sociology that competed on both academic and professional grounds. This image was also created by the other disciplines responding to the innovations of their sociological colleagues. And there was an image that emerged in the outside world among journalists, authors, and public leaders who were attracted and repelled by the substantive findings and the social pronouncements of these scholars.

All these images were grounded in reality. In their different ways all the sociologists of the University of Chicago were immensely energetic in their efforts to create a more scientific sociology based on direct empirical observation. They were men who were concerned with the processes of industrialization and urbanization and their attendant social problems. They were professors who were prepared to draw the boundaries of sociology so broad and so vague that the subject matter and theoretical assumptions of the related disciplines—anthropology, economics, psychology (including psychoanalysis), and political science—could be drawn into sociology as their tastes and their problems dictated.

These Chicago sociologists believed that sociological knowledge had an active role to play in solving social problems. But most important was the common concern in their variety of approaches for the study of society as a totality. The decline of the vigor of the Chicago school in its original format was manifested by a shift from what has come to be called macrosociology to an overconcentration of concern upon specific institutions and limited topics of sociological inquiry. Thus, to the extent that there existed a Chicago school, its identifying feature was an empirical approach to the study of the totality of society.

Within the Chicago school, William Isaac Thomas had both his special contributions and his particular contribution to the diversity—his concern with the subjective dimension of social organization, his interests in comparative analysis, and his exploitation of the personal document. Yet W. I. Thomas, like Robert E. Park who followed him, epitomized the basic intellectual outlook of the Chicago school. His outstanding accomplishment, *The Polish Peasant in Europe and America*, and his academic career were both completed before the image of the Chicago school was fully developed. He was not on the scene when his impact on his colleagues was potentially the greatest.

*Introduction* ix

He was dedicated to the belief that sociology had to have a subject matter and a body of empirical findings, but unfortunately, the full significance of his classic writings was obscured by the formal and often sterile controversies about the metatheory and boundaries of sociology and social psychology which came to characterize the later period of the Chicago school. But as the result of a decade of effort, he created in his major work a model which was and still is valid for all those sociologists associated with the Chicago school.

## Thomas' Personal Documents

A biographical account of the man, if available, would be an important document. He was a modern professional sociologist —research grants, large bodies of data, conferences, and the acceptance of the tasks of social policy were part of his life. His style sought to fuse the intellectual and professional roles of the academic and he recognized the different responsibilities of each. Very few biographical materials on W. I. Thomas are available, and only one tiny autobiographical fragment.[1] Not one of his students, and he had many, made the effort to write a social profile. The University of Chicago archives contain only a few administrative letters. The archivist has noted in the record that his inquiries and steps to collect a W. I. Thomas file, to be placed with those of his contemporaries in other disciplines, produced no original papers. It appears to the intellectual historian as if there may have been an effort to obliterate the record of W. I. Thomas as a man. In the absence of documents and documentary materials, a body of lore about Thomas gradually grew and was passed from student generation to student generation, but in time this too has become obliterated.

---

[1] W. I. Thomas prepared a two- or three-page autobiographical statement, "My Life," in response to a request by L. L. Bernard, who was collecting such material on a number of sociologists in the 1930's. The text of Thomas' statement is not to be found in the unpublished collection of these documents. Some fragmentary notes taken by his students are available.

In his introduction to the Social Science Research Council volume on W. I. Thomas edited by Edmund H. Volkart, Donald Young could only write, "The fact that the man who established the personal document and the life history as basic sources in social science has left no such materials about himself explains the absence from this volume of any analysis of his personality and career."[2] The reasons offered seem plausible but not really adequate: "Attempts to obtain biographical statements of an introspective and self-analytic nature were turned aside, less for reasons of modesty than for simple lack of interest. Despite his interest in the human document, Thomas was not an introspective person." Both his modesty and his belief in scholarly impersonality prevented him from producing any substantial autobiography. Moreover, on at least one occasion he actively and successfully objected to the inclusion of biographical materials in an essay about his work written by one of his students.

No doubt the public scandal which caused his removal from the University of Chicago was a further source of inhibition. The strategy for handling Thomas' image was simply to forget about the man as a man. This strategy involved more than self-imposed restraint, for among some it bordered on outright efforts of retaliation. Years after he left the University of Chicago, Thomas' personal behavior was openly offered, by such men as Charles A. Ellwood, as a reason why he should not be elected president of the American Sociological Society; it was inappropriate and most unfortunate for the well-being of the sociological profession.

But the fate of Thomas, from the point of view of the historiography of American sociology, was no different from that of the other central figures in the Chicago school of sociology. They have all disappeared without having caused an adequate

[2] Edmund H. Volkart (ed.), *Social Behavior and Personality* (New York: Social Science Research Council, 1951). This volume was sponsored by the Social Science Research Council's committee on W. I. Thomas' contribution to social science under the chairmanship of Donald Young. It is a careful presentation of selections from W. I. Thomas' work with commentary by the editor. The focus of the volume is on Thomas' concepts and categories.

intellectual and social history to be written.³ The efforts of the Chicago sociologists to create a form of current history in depth and to create new intellectual dimensions apparently had the result of turning them and their students away from a concern with the evolution of their ideas or a recording of the impact of their social environment on themselves. They were empiricists without a strong sense of introspection.

The obvious vita materials about W. I. Thomas are available. Typical of the pioneer American sociologists, he came from a Protestant rural and religious background. He was born on August 13, 1863, in Russell County, Virginia, the son of Thaddeus Peter Thomas, who combined preaching with farming in order to make a living. Except for the fact that his father was affiliated with the Holston Methodist Church Conference, there are no materials about his family. The Thomas home must have had some special vitality and interests, since it produced two sons who completed the Ph.D. degree at a time when that degree was very much more uncommon than it is at present. After spending his youth in Virginia and Tennessee, Thomas enrolled in 1880 at the University of Tennessee and majored in literature and classics. As an undergraduate he not only excelled scholastically but was also ambitious and well-rounded enough to become the equivalent of the "big man on the campus." He won highest honors in oratory, became president of the Literary Society, the most prestigeful academic society on campus, and at the same time was captain of the university officer training unit.

The typical pattern of recruitment into the academic profession in the United States at that time was from a select list of eastern universities such as Harvard and Yale, or from one of the outstanding smaller liberal arts undergraduate schools. But the training of professors was changing as the state universities began to flourish and as new subjects, not well developed in the more traditional universities of the east coast, began to be

---

³ Edward A. Shils, "The Calling of Sociology," in *Theories of Society* (New York: Free Press of Glencoe, 1961), pp. 1405–48. Shils in his essays on the evolution of American sociology has presented important materials for understanding these scholars and their society.

cultivated. W. I. Thomas was at the University of Tennessee during that brief moment when there was enough intellectual ferment in the persons of a few dedicated teachers to stimulate this extremely bright and articulate student to become interested in scholarly research and to pursue an academic career.

It was not a period of high specialization, so that when he stayed on at the University of Tennessee for graduate studies, he worked in English literature and modern languages. In 1886, he was awarded the first doctorate that this university granted. During his graduate studies he was already engaged in teaching and was appointed as an instructor. With the completion of his graduate degree he shifted over to teaching natural history and Greek, and his talents were such that he was immediately awarded the honorific title of Adjunct Professor. The university was apparently flexible about status and the formal definitions of expertise. W. I. Thomas had been trained to be a scholar, and he obviously saw himself as striving to be a learned man.

Therefore the university suggested that he take leave for a year for study in Europe, which in those days, when the German universities were at the height of their eminence, was indispensable for a young man with serious academic aspirations. The year abroad, 1888–89, at Göttingen and Berlin, had an unexpected effect and presaged his capacity for an eclectic response and an omnivorous intellectual appetite. He was exposed to the German folk psychology of Lazarus and Steinthal and to the new subject of ethnology. As a result, his interests began to be redirected. When he returned to the United States, he accepted a professorship in English at Oberlin College and held this post until 1895. At Oberlin, Thomas' interest in the social sciences, and particularly in sociology, deepened, especially because he was at that time "strongly impressed by Spencer's sociology."

Although established as a professor in a traditional subject at one of the outstanding undergraduate colleges in the country, he took steps to retrain himself. During the academic year 1893–94, while on leave from Oberlin, he entered the University of Chicago as one of the first group of graduate sociology students in the newly established Department of Sociology. His studies were directed by Albion W. Small and Charles A. Henderson while he was supported by a full-time fellowship. In the summer of 1894 he offered his first course in the Department of Sociology at Chicago, after having completed what amounted to a year of graduate training. In 1895, he transferred full time to sociology at the University of Chicago with the rank of instructor, giving up his professorship in English; and during the following year, after having completed his doctorate, he became an assistant professor. From then until 1918 he was on the faculty of the University of Chicago, devoting himself to elaborating on his intellectual position and undertaking the research work for his central work on the Polish community. The Department of Sociology at the University of Chicago was a joint Department of Sociology and Anthropology from its founding until 1929. W. I. Thomas taught courses which were designated "purely anthropological," for the two disciplines were and continued to be closely related at the University of Chicago.

Sociology was rapidly emerging as an organized full-fledged discipline at the University, and Thomas was at the center of the effort to create a department which carried on research and trained graduate students. By 1900 he was promoted to associate professor and in 1910 to professor. From 1908 to 1919 Thomas had charge of the Helen Culver Fund for Race Psychology, which by the standards of those days was extremely well endowed. It was by means of these resources that he was able to travel extensively to Europe and collect so much of the material on which *The Polish Peasant in Europe and America* was based. During these travels he met Florian Znaniecki who was to be his active collaborator in preparing this study.

He participated widely in the social and intellectual life of Chicago and was constantly searching for new sources of data. His personal style, interests, and tastes were directly involved in the fashioning of the Chicago emphasis on direct observation and participation in social research. Hardly a staid and reserved professor typical of the period, he dressed with distinction and care, mixed in all social quarters of the city, and enjoyed the life of a bon vivant in the metropolis. He experienced the realities of Chicago life both as an observer and a participant. An active sportsman, he even found time to perfect a more effective golf ball.

At the time Thomas expressed a deep concern with social policy, embodying another of the central themes of the Chicago school. His writing included an analysis of the position of women, and he became a strong advocate of women's rights. He and his wife, Harriet Park, whom he married on June 6, 1888, maintained close connections with social-work circles, and he hoped that his work would supply a sound basis for social policy and practice. Much of the funds for his research came from women who were actively concerned with social reform. He was closely associated with the work of the Chicago Vice Commission and took such "progressive" views of deviant behavior that his activity was abrasive to the commission.

During this period, he enjoyed writing an occasional article for the popular *American Magazine* and held frequent public lectures. His pronouncements were reformist in the extreme, since he believed that suppression of superficial manifestations was pointless. He was a controversial figure not only because of his tolerant views toward deviant behavior but also because of his flamboyant personal manner.

W. I. Thomas' connection with the University of Chicago ended abruptly in 1918, shortly after he was arrested by the Federal Bureau of Investigation on a charge involving alleged violation of the Mann Act and of an act forbidding false hotel registration. These charges were thrown out of court, but there had been extensive publicity because Mrs. Granger, who was involved in the proceedings, reported that she was the wife of an army officer serving in the United States Expeditionary Forces in France. The circumstances surrounding the intervention of federal agents in this case remain unclear. Thomas' wife was active in Henry Ford's peace movement, and her activities had apparently come under official surveillance. It has been asserted that the action against Thomas supplied means for embarrassing and discrediting Mrs. Thomas because of her political activities.

The president of the University of Chicago, Henry Pratt Judson, supported by the trustees, moved directly to dismiss him and thus end the unfavorable publicity, especially that in the *Chicago Tribune*, which was an embarrassment to the administration of the University. The hostility of the administration toward W. I. Thomas as a person and his controversial social outlook speeded the process, but most university personnel did not view it as extraordinary that he should be dismissed. Small, who was chairman of the Department of Sociology at the time, privately sought to protect him; but his case was weakened, since Thomas had had previous personal complications. There was no faculty protest, and there was no particular administrative procedure that had to be observed. Secure academic tenure and the procedures for removal which have come to be taken for granted did not develop until the 1920's and 1930's.

At the time of the most intense newspaper publicity Thomas prepared a long article in his defense which was published by the *Chicago Herald*, the rival of the *Chicago Tribune* at that time, on April 22, 1918. There has grown up a myth about the "brilliant rebuttal" and "profound criticism" Thomas presented in this essay. Unfortunately, the document is of little worth except as it represents a man tragically seeking to defend himself under circumstances of terrific personal pressure and therefore distorting his basic orientation both to social science and to contemporary social problems.

W. I. Thomas was 55 years of age, and he had completed his major work of research. It is difficult, if not impossible, even to speculate about his intellectual future and productivity if he had remained at the University of Chicago. But after his dismissal he never again held a regular university post, and he was thereby deprived of an opportunity to work with and influence directly the rapidly expanding classes of University-of-Chicago-trained sociologists. The personal impact of the event on the man must have been discernible. The University of Chicago Press, which had issued the first two volumes of *The Polish Peasant*, terminated its contractual relations as if to complete the expunging of W. I. Thomas from the Chicago scene. The remaining three volumes were printed by the lesser-known Richard G. Badger publishing house in Boston.

More pressing was Thomas' need for employment, and the next period of his life consisted of a series of research and foundation appointments. He moved to New York City and spent the next year, 1918–19, working on the Americanization studies sponsored by the Carnegie Corporation of New York. With Robert E. Park he collaborated on a manuscript of a book entitled *Old World Traits Transplanted,* which had to appear— so it was conceived—under the authorship of Park and H. A. Miller to protect the reputations of the foundation and of sociology. This episode was personally irritating to Thomas. It was not until 1951 that what was widely known in sociological circles was formally acknowledged—that W. I. Thomas was "primarily responsible" for the book. In *Social Behavior and Personality* an excerpt of a letter from Mr. Allen T. Burns, general director of the project on Americanization studies, to Professor Ernest W. Burgess is reprinted: "The Volume, *Old World Traits Transplanted,* of the Americanization Studies was written primarily by W. I. Thomas, though at the time it was considered by all concerned best to have it appear under the authorship of Park and Miller, who also worked on the volume. I am very glad that Professor Thomas is to receive credit for his invaluable contribution."[4] When Thomas was recommended for a staff appointment to the Americanization project, it was vetoed. After the Americanization study he was supported from 1920 to 1923 by research funds provided by Mrs. W. F. Dummer of Chicago, a wealthy woman interested in sociological inquiry and social welfare problems. He spent the rest of his professional life engaged primarily in research projects, with occasional university appointments. Since he located himself in New York City, it was understandable that he lectured at the New School for Social Research from 1923 to 1928.

During this period he found himself drawn into organizing one of the first social science interdisciplinary conferences. In 1927, with funds supplied by Mrs. Dummer and under the sponsorship of the Illinois Society for Mental Hygiene, a group was

[4] Volkart, p. 258.

assembled under his leadership to probe "the unconscious," and the results were published under the title, *The Unconscious: A Symposium*. This was the first publication to present the approach of social scientists in the United States to the subject of the unconscious. It was during that year that the rehabilitation of W. I. Thomas took another important step. His achievements had made his election to the presidency of the American Sociological Society long overdue, but the belief still persisted that it would be inappropriate to elect him to this office. When his name was entered for nomination, the "old guard" sought to find an appropriate candidate to defeat him. Thomas himself was doubtful about his candidacy and considered withdrawing his name on the pretext that he might be going to India and therefore would not be available to perform the duties of president if elected. Ernest Burgess took it upon himself to persuade him to remain in the race. The "young Turks" organized by Louis Wirth, Kimball Young, George Lundberg, Stuart Chapin, Stuart Rice, and others mobilized their colleagues to elect Thomas, and he won by a wide margin.

The Laura Spelman Rockefeller Memorial subsidized his work from 1926 to 1928, from which appeared in 1928 *The Child in America*, written in collaboration with Dorothy S. Thomas. Subsequently, Thomas undertook some special tasks for Lawrence B. Dunham of the Bureau of Social Hygiene, and he traveled in Western Europe in order to prepare reports on centers engaged in criminological and personality research. From 1930 through 1936 he traveled regularly to Sweden and worked closely with the Social Science Institute of the University of Stockholm. The Social Science Research Council had his services as a staff member for the year 1932–33, and his last academic appointment was as lecturer in sociology at Harvard University in 1936–37. His final publication, *Primitive Behavior: An Introduction to the Social Sciences*, dates from this time. His first marriage, to Harriet Park, was terminated by divorce in 1934, and he married Dorothy Swaine, who had been associated with him in research work for a number of years. The final phase of his career was spent in semiretirement and independent research, first in New Haven until 1939 and then after 1940 in Berkeley, California, where he died at the age of 84 in December, 1947.

## Intellectual Development

W. I. Thomas' sociology was broad in its subject matter, but in retrospect there is a strikingly similar focus in his approach to each new problem. He was not a convert to or from a pre-existing rigid theoretical system. One of his greatest strengths was his pragmatic approach to theory construction. He saw the necessity of theoretical reformulations, and he spent considerable effort at this task in response to the new empirical data that he collected. One can be misled, however, by his constant minor elaboration of categories, when actually rather early in his career he developed a frame of reference which was to dominate the most fruitful period of his scholarship.

It is possible to divide his career into three phases in order to highlight his intellectual growth.[5] The first period carried Thomas from his initial article in the *American Journal of Sociology* in 1896, "The Scope and Method of Folk Psychology," until he took charge of the Helen Culver Research Fund for Race Psychology in 1908. This was the period in which he developed from a traditional ethnographer into an empirical social psychologist and in which he laid the foundation for his approach to social organization and social change. The second period begins with the appearance in 1912 of "Race Psychology: Standpoint and Questionnaire, with Particular Reference to the Immigrant and the Negro."[6] In this paper he set forth basic categories and his proposed "research design" to be followed later in his study of *The Polish Peasant*.

In the second period, the intellectual climax of his career,

5   See Kimball Young, "The Contribution of William Isaac Thomas to Sociology," reprinted from *Sociology and Social Research*, XLVII, Nos. 1, 2, 3, and 6, for a most useful exposition and careful annotation of Thomas' writings.

6   *American Journal of Sociology*, XVII (May, 1912), 725–77.

Introduction    xix

he devoted himself to the preparation of *The Polish Peasant in Europe and America*. Although this work was the high point of his achievements, this phase carried over until approximately 1923, with the publication of *Old World Traits Transplanted* and *The Unadjusted Girl*. This was the period in which Thomas demonstrated his sociological vision. He established his eminence by fusing sociology and social psychology into the analysis of social organization and personality. The third and final period of his work is not easily characterized, but he was deeply involved with "situational analysis" and he became interested in new techniques of research.

When he arrived at the University of Chicago, a turning point in sociology was in the offing. He was immediately exposed to the new empiricism, which reflected his own predilections and which was buttressed by the interests of his teachers, Albion W. Small and Charles R. Henderson. Sociology had been a primitive and diffuse idea and mainly a bookish and speculative subject. To the extent that it was descriptive it relied almost wholly on secondary sources and unsystematically collected data. As final elaboration of this approach, Lester Ward's *The Psychic Factors of Civilization* appeared in 1893, and the third volume of Herbert Spencer's *Principles of Sociology*, on unilinear evolution, was published three years later.

There were a number of intellectual activities to support the new directions in sociology. At the University of Michigan Charles H. Cooley offered his first course in sociology in 1894 and emerged as a transitional figure between the older philosophical tradition and the new orientation. Paralleling the developments at the University of Chicago was the organization of departments of sociology at Columbia by Franklin H. Giddings, who also was trained in economics, and at the University of Kansas by Frank W. Blackman. Most important, the founding of the *American Journal of Sociology* made communication possible among the scattered adherents of the new discipline.

Adjunct disciplines were also experiencing a similar ferment. William James, who was interested in understanding the cultural factors in the formation of personality, had emerged as a dominant figure in the new psychology. At the University of Chicago, W. I. Thomas was exposed to John Dewey and particularly to George Herbert Mead and their ideas about the nature of human nature. He was fully aware of the new work in anthropology, particularly that of Franz Boas, which was leading to a fundamental questioning of simple notions of evolution and producing a more empirically based discipline.

During these early years Thomas read in all the fields that seemed to bear on his boundless interests—sociology, folk psychology, and especially ethnology and folklore studies. He was familiar with the growing body of European literature in these areas. He was a sociological "pack rat," collecting and organizing all sorts of available materials.[7] Kimball Young, who knew of him at first hand, has written, "Statistical reports, case histories, folklore, descriptions of primitive life, illustrative quotations from literary works, and observations of his own were set down for use. His main concern was to bring some scientific order out of these materials; mere theorizing, especially on scanty data, or worse still, on no data whatsoever, seemed to him futile and misleading."[8]

Thomas' research and writing during this first period can best be described as a self-education through which he freed himself from existing forms. Although it was a period of intense productivity, there is, in fact, no single essay from that time that warrants inclusion in this volume. It was a period of clearing the underbrush. It was a period of working through existing ideas in order to emerge with modern sociological constructs. The results have importance in the study of the history of ideas, but

[7] W. I. Thomas was a devoted note-taker on slips of paper about four by six inches in size (actually, he used the millimeter system). Notes taken verbatim from books or monographs went on slips of one color, Thomas' own comments on slips of another color, and bibliographic references on slips of a third color. He apparently accumulated an extremely large collection of these slips, which formed the basis for his lectures and books. Students and faculty were impressed with the data which he could quickly mobilize from his primitive "cross-cultural files."

[8] Kimball Young, pp. 4–5.

they are not among the more lasting contributions of W. I. Thomas.

He had first to discover the limitations of simple notions of social evolution which dominated the social sciences. Without this intellectual emancipation his major work would have been impossible. Thomas also had to confront the issues of biological determinism and the biological factors in social behavior. It was inevitable that he would be a leading figure in separating sociology from the crude biological conception of human behavior then current. His criticism of theories of racial and sexual differences alone would have established him as a pioneer figure in sociology. Biology of that period was unable to contribute to sociological analysis. Nevertheless, although Thomas was sensitive to genetic and constitutional factors in social behavior, he had to turn away from these problems. (If he were to have worked in the 1960's, it is likely that he would have found the new developments in human genetics highly relevant and a vindication of his early, but oversimplified, interests in these matters.)

During this period he wrote mainly on the sociological aspects of sexual behavior and on race—a field which he initially called folk psychology, and which was to become the core of his social psychology. Many of his early essays were collected in a volume entitled *Sex and Society*, published in 1907. But his first influential volume appeared in 1908 in a new format under the title, *Source Book for Social Origins: Ethnological Materials, Psychological Standpoint, Classified and Annotated Bibliographies for the Interpretation of Savage Society*. This book represented W. I. Thomas' concern with fusing theory and empirical data. It contained not only a voluminous collection of essential source materials but also his careful introductions to and his comments on each selection and his bibliographic annotations. Thomas was driving intently for sociological explanations, and his writings covered such topics as male and female roles, gambling, and fashion. By the end of the period the main lines of his approach were clear, although not fully integrated. They may be summarized under four heads.

1. In order to explain social change, the central topic of

social theory, it was necessary to use an approach which would encompass both social organization and the subjective aspects of social reality. As early as his second doctoral dissertation (1897), "On a Difference in the Metabolism of the Sexes," he spoke of "social feeling" and "social organization." Thereafter he remained committed to a fusion or unity of sociology and social psychology. With such a framework he rejected single-factor explanations and moved toward a comprehensive system of analysis. "Without ignoring economic determinism or denying the importance of specific race characters, I have assumed that individual variation is of more importance than racial difference, and the main factors in social change are attention, interest, stimulation, imitation, occupational differentiation, mental attitude, and an accessibility to opportunity and copies."[9]

2. He had already confronted the need for a theory of motivation, an issue which continued to be central in his work and which he never was able to handle satisfactorily. Although his descriptive materials on motives and their transformation were rich, their systematic analysis was outside his competence. He was fiercely anti-Freudian but never found or developed an adequate alternative approach. Instead, he grew to rely more and more on "interactional" theories which emphasized the social context rather than motivation.

3. He developed his criteria for empirical research which would be systematic and which would adequately reflect the nature of social data. He identified the types of data that he would require, particularly personal observation and observation from undesigned and designed records. He believed that personal observation was best pursued while living with a group, "preferably in a family." But Thomas was careful to warn against the dangers of the deviant case. "Be suspicious of striking cases; they may be as surprising to the people among whom they occur as they are to you." Thomas' empirical standpoint was intensive. He essentially offered a synthesis of the anthropologist's or ethnographer's participant observations, the case study method of the

[9] *American Journal of Sociology*, XVII (May, 1912), 726.

social worker, and the content analysis procedures of the traditional humanistic disciplines.

4. For Thomas, comparative analysis meant the comparison of cultures and societies. Because of his ethnographic and historical interests he postulated that sociology could not be concerned merely with specific institutions without a central focus on the societal context. This is a thesis which he rigorously pursued and which sociologists have in recent years come to rediscover.

The second period of W. I. Thomas' intellectual life history was the period of *The Polish Peasant in Europe and America.* The scope of the undertaking was immense not only by the standards of his day but even for many years to come. It took more than a decade to gather the source materials, both in the United States and in Europe, and to prepare the final publication, which totaled 2,244 pages. His original goals were even more ambitious, since he hoped to study a variety of Eastern European immigrant groups. As a result of his field trips, Thomas slowly became aware that he had to concentrate his interests if he were to press his study in the depth he required. Subsequently he did further empirical research, but never again on such a grand scale and with such intensity. The effort could not be duplicated in one man's lifetime. A large research team was unthinkable to him.

But the study was not thought of as an empirical undertaking per se. From the very beginning he saw it as a vehicle for developing and presenting his basic ideas. In a letter to Ellsworth Faris, dated April 3, 1928, without inhibition he described his goals for *The Polish Peasant in Europe and America:* "I think you will appreciate that we were both putting into the volume any and everything that we found ourselves able to say."

In the lore about W. I. Thomas that grew up among graduate students at the University of Chicago there was a story of how he came upon the use of letters as a crucial research tool. Thomas had already decided to concentrate on the assimilation of the Poles to test his ideas. Like a professional ethnographer he had mastered the language and made extensive contacts within the

Polish community in Chicago. He was concerned with direct observation and especially with collecting data by participating in Polish family life. But following the ethnographic approach—which was developed mainly for non-literate peoples—he had not as yet explored written documents of Polish-American society, and he was not thinking in terms of written documentation.

One morning, while walking down a back alley in the Polish community on the West Side of Chicago, he had to sidestep quickly to avoid some garbage which was being disposed of by the direct means of tossing it out the window. In the garbage which fell at his feet were a number of packets of letters. Since he read Polish, he was attracted to their contents, and he started to read a bundle which was arranged serially. In the sequence presented by the letters he saw a rich and rewarding account and in time he was led to pursue the personal document as a research tool. Ernest Burgess, who was at the time a graduate student in the Department of Sociology, has attested to the accuracy of the account, although it became embellished as it circulated from one generation of graduate students to the next.

There are many reasons why Thomas selected the Poles for investigation. They were the largest and therefore the most visible ethnic group on the South Side of Chicago, and it was not Thomas' style to select bizarre and minor themes. The choice was a fortunate one because of the extensive materials both primary and secondary he could locate in Poland, but such materials were accumulated after he began to study the Polish-American community.

In addition, the Poles were a "social problem" in Chicago, and Thomas never segregated his intellectual interests from his social concerns. The Polish-American community was beset with the full range of social problems linked to assimilation and urbanization, and in particular with family strife and crime. Polish crime was characterized by its violent and explosive nature, and this fact obviously fascinated Thomas. He was profoundly curious and deeply sympathetic about Polish crime, as it was known to the police. Boys and young men who were law-abiding or at least conforming would suddenly, with little provocation and no forethought, engage in violent and explosive fights, including attacks on police officers. The sheer attraction that the Poles had for this son of a southern rural minister accounted, in part, for his choice of them as a subject of research. Thomas himself described his field trips to Europe as "also exploratory—a wanderlust at first."[10]

The massive collection of materials about the Poles in Chicago and elsewhere in the United States was paralleled by his efforts in Europe. The work of Polish scholars and the existence of immigrant protective associations with elaborate files made this approach particularly fruitful. In 1913 he met the Polish philosopher, Florian Znaniecki, who turned out to be his most useful source and informant and ultimately, his collaborator. Znaniecki, secretary of the Polish Protective Association, had a wide knowledge of Polish society and was one of the few intellectuals who had a realistic understanding of the social life of the Polish peasant. In the following year, 1914, Poland experienced another German invasion. Znaniecki left Poland and on his own went to Chicago, where he sought out Thomas. Thomas had neither invited him nor encouraged him to come. In fact, Thomas was completely unaware of his journey from Poland until he actually arrived penniless at Thomas' home. Because he had funds at his disposal, Thomas was able to appoint him as a research worker. Since Znaniecki had no formal academic background in sociology, this was a bold step in that time. Thomas eventually made him co-author of the published work. After the completion of the enterprise Znaniecki and Thomas drifted apart. But their personal relations were always cordial and intimate, despite the marked differences in their personal and intellectual styles.

There was never any question about the part each played in the intellectual collaboration. Znaniecki labored diligently in collecting empirical materials and in the role of a knowledgeable informant. He was clearly the junior partner in the research team, but a research collaborator who made a meaningful contribution.

[10] From a student's notes on "My Life" (see n. 1, above).

Thomas had developed his basic ideas before he launched on *The Polish Peasant*, although he continuously sought to reformulate them. This was before Znaniecki arrived in Chicago. Znaniecki brought strong philosophical and methodological interests to the undertaking and he injected them into the collaboration. But his own theoretical position, as it emerged after their joint work, reflected an aspiration for complete explanations. His formulations were formalistic and more categorical in contrast to Thomas' concern with specific testable hypotheses.[11] His style of theory construction was much more prolix and involved.

It was of decisive importance that Thomas visited Poland repeatedly before the outbreak of World War I. It was a period of the re-emergence of a "larger" Polish community and the strengthening of society-wide institutions. Economic, cultural, and political organizations had been devastated by national partition in the nineteenth century. Stagnation and decline ensued as the divided society lived under a colonial type of rule. In the late 1880's a nationalistic revival in which Polish intellectuals had a major role began to develop. Nationalism, as an idea and an organizing concept, was being transformed from a purely ethnic notion into a political form, as had been the case earlier in Western Europe. In this process contact with America was an important stimulus. Poland was taking the first halting steps toward modernization. It was in the throes of national liberation—seeking to become a "new nation." The tensions in Poland were those associated with the process of integration of communal life into a society experiencing urbanization.

Thomas did not observe a nationality group weakening under social change; but rather through its intellectuals, co-operative movements, and political agitation it was demonstrating considerable vitality. These events sharpened the contrast with the social disruption that the Polish community was experiencing at the same time in the United States. They helped fashion Thomas' comparative outlook, without forcing him to assume or

---

[11] In a thoughtful unpublished paper by Ethel Shanas the details of this notion are carefully developed. A copy is available in the archives of the Center for Social Organization Studies, University of Chicago.

Introduction    xxvii

to conclude that the outcome of social change was inevitably social disorganization.

During this second period Thomas worked on studies of immigration, *Old World Traits Transplanted,* and of female delinquency, *The Unadjusted Girl: With Cases and Standpoint for Behavior Analysis.* Both followed much of the format of *The Polish Peasant* but without similar scope. *Old World Traits Transplanted* presented variegated and almost undigested materials; yet it contained the germ of a systematic analysis of the strength and vulnerability of different minority groups in the process of assimilation. In the aftermath of World War I Americanization was a highly charged political issue. The volume anticipated stubborn resistance to "Americanization" as it was then conceived by educators. For Thomas the Old World identifications, institutions, and organizations which expressed themselves in mutual assistance and social solidarity among the immigrant groups were not barriers but advantages in the process of accommodation to the new society. He saw the importance of intermediate "communal" ties—be they ethnic, religious, or residential—as essential components of effective social integration in modern society. The study included, moreover, a most sensitive policy statement about a pluralistic society in that he argued that assimilation took place only when minority groups contributed to and modified the cultural values of the larger society.

*The Unadjusted Girl,* for all its fascinating insight and detailed materials, lacked an explicit concern with social structure and institutional analysis. His theoretical concepts were mainly concerned with situational analysis and the definition of the situation. But the volume is a landmark in the emergence of a sociology of deviant behavior.

Thomas in the third and final period of his work (after 1923) lost control of his intellectual agenda. He was already 60 years of age and had achieved renown. As a person, he was immensely vigorous and stimulating. He maintained a wide circle of contacts with intellectual leaders in the other disciplines and thereby helped to disseminate the kind of interdisciplinary thinking out of which he grew. He continued to expose himself to new literature, new ideas, and new research methodology, including statistical modes of analysis. In his written work he seemed more to be reacting to external pressures than to be pursuing his older pattern of self-directed exploration.

He had a strong desire to elaborate *The Polish Peasant* by extending the analysis to include crucial comparisons. In 1918 as the manuscript was sent to the printer, Thomas started to work on a study of the Jews in Europe and America. For him the Jews with their low incidence of disorganization were to be the "control" group for comparison with the Poles. He believed that the family dynamics and the solidarity of the Jewish family were crucial in understanding their successful accommodation to the American scene. In addition, there was brought to his attention the personal documents of the *bintl brief*, a bundle of letters from immigrants which appeared in the Yiddish-language newspaper, the *Forward*. These would supply him with data comparable to the letters he had collected among the Poles. Although some of these letters appeared in the printed columns of the *Forward*, the newspaper had a large library of similar materials and continually received new documents. It was a grave disappointment to Thomas that he did not receive permission to analyze these letters. Nevertheless, during the 1920's and 1930's, while he worked as a wandering sociologist on his various research and foundation projects, he spent spare moments on his study of Jewish assimilation. From the correspondence in the archives of the University of Chicago, it appears that by the mid-1930's he believed that his manuscript was near completion. He received a grant of $900 from the Social Science Research Council to finish the preparation of the manuscript, and he even started to negotiate with publishers, but the study was never really pursued, never completed, and never published.[12]

During this third period his work turned toward the evaluation of other people's efforts, a concern he had always felt but which he did not allow to dominate his written work. In a decisive break with his earlier style, and perhaps reflecting the pressures of his

---

12 Some of the materials are presented in Marvin Bressler's "Selected Family Patterns" in W. I. Thomas' "Unfinished Study of the Bintl Brief," *American Sociological Review*, XVII (October, 1952), 563–71.

assignments, he undertook to prepare programmatic statements of desired directions for sociology and related social science disciplines. Thomas' more usual approach was to proceed by demonstration and example rather than to draw attention to problems by plans and proposals.

But he continued to be very active, for that was the nature of the man. In one sense, 1928 was the climax of his career, for then he delivered his presidential address at the American Sociological Society entitled "The Behavior Pattern and the Situation," which best characterized his thinking of the period of "situational analysis." His later essay, *The Relation of Research to the Social Process*, prepared for a Brookings Institution conference, was a restatement of some of his basic ideas but recast in the newer language of social research of the day. In 1933 he prepared for the Social Science Research Council a memorandum on "The Organization of a Program in the Field of Personality and Culture." Although it circulated only as an unpublished document until it was printed in 1951, this statement attracted considerable attention. Finally, it is noteworthy that in his last volume, *Primitive Behavior: An Introduction to the Social Sciences* (1937), he returned to comparative ethnography and the source book style that had characterized his initial writings. These final pieces have value mainly because they underline Thomas' pragmatic rather than dogmatic approach to his own theoretical constructs.

## *The Subject Matter of Sociology and Social Psychology*

While W. I. Thomas rejected "mere" system building, he sought to cast his research in highly general terms. But his position was not that of a narrow empiricism such as later characterized much of American sociology. He was a man genuinely interested in broad explanations, but prepared to confront social reality at each point in the research process.

He always had a frame of reference, but he was insistent that his categories should not become detached from concrete social reality. To be sure, there were many missing links in his frame of reference, and often the level of empirical proof was, at best, limited. Nevertheless, the contemporary dispute about grand theory and middle level theory would seem meaningless to him. There could be no social theory without broad and generally applicable assumptions and concepts; yet there could be no sociology without testable propositions based on concrete observation.

The range of specific topics with which he dealt was indeed diverse, but there was a strong element of unity in his work because he was concerned with social control and social change. He was writing about the consequences of industrialization—or modernization, as it has come to be more precisely defined. He believed that human behavior was controlled and had to be controlled. His biological and environmental assumptions made him a sociological realist. Yet, rather explicitly, his work was directed by underlying philosophical and value-oriented questions. Traditional and older forms of social control based on forbidding and ordering were outmoded. They no longer operated effectively. Thomas saw sociology and social psychology as identifying the factors which either increased or decreased the effectiveness of institutions as agencies of social control.

There was also a powerful element of unity in his orientations because of what he rejected. He was extensively exposed to the ideas of social evolution, but he quickly rejected a linear notion of progress and change. He never became a devotee of the position represented by Ferdinand Toennies in German sociology which conceptualized society as undergoing a transformation from "Gemeinschaft" to "Gesellschaft." Thomas appears to have rejected such an approach as too simple and too narrow, although there were members of the Chicago school who incorporated elements of Toennies' thinking. Thomas was too familiar with the original ethnographical writings of the period to accept Toennies' view of primitive society. He was much too detached an observer to accept the value-laden implications of an approach which saw social change as inevitably producing impersonalization and disorganization. He did not conform to the pattern of the rural-born sociologists—moralizers who abhorred the culture of the city; he was too urbane and sophisticated to long for the values of primitive and rural society.

Thomas rejected simple technological and economic determinism, but he did not emerge with a simple normative approach. Instead, he committed himself to a sociological system which, despite its lack of elegance and logical rigor, was a striking parallel to contemporary social system analysis and, alternatively, the formulations of "social structure and personality," or "culture and personality." It had the added advantage of being more than a social interaction theory, for he incorporated both ecological and environmental factors. But in his effort to be comprehensive he now appears excessively eclectic and his views too open-ended.

Social control and the process of social change, the core concepts, were for Thomas the result of the "reciprocal dependence between social organization and individual life organization,"[13] or social personality, as he was prone to call it. Sociology was the study of social organization, namely, the "socially systematized schemes of behavior imposed as rules upon individuals." The key concept was values, "the more or less explicit and formal rules of behavior by which the group tends to maintain, to regulate, and to make more general and more frequent the corresponding type of actions among its members."[14] Thus the organization of these values constituted social organization: "The rule of behavior, and the actions viewed as conforming or not conforming with these rules, constitute with regard to their objective significance a certain number of more or less connected and harmonious systems which can be generally called social institutions, and the totality of institutions found in a concrete social group constitutes the social organization of this group."[15]

Social personality could be thought of as the patterns of attitudes which an individual holds, and social psychology was basically the study of these attitudes or the subjective aspects of social organization. "Social personality as a whole manifests itself only in the course of its total life and not at any particular moment of

[13] *The Polish Peasant*, II, 1128.
[14] *Ibid.*, I, 31.
[15] *Ibid.*, I, 32–33.

its life and that its life is not a mere empirical manifestation of a timeless metaphysical essence, always the same, but is a continuous evolution in which nothing remains unchanged." The analysis of attitudes and social personality required investigation of types, just as the study of values and social organization proceeded by the investigation of institutions.

In W. I. Thomas' writings there was a set of postulates, relatively explicit, for developing an empirically based social theory dealing with the reciprocal relation between social organization and social personality.[16]

First, the process of social change was a continuous process involving both adaptation and disruption. Social organization could be followed by social disorganization, but this was hardly the end state, for social disorganization could give way to social reorganization. In the essay on "Social Disorganization and Social Reorganization,"[17] social organization was defined in terms of the effectiveness of social norms, and alternatively, social disorganization implied the "decrease in the influence of existing social rules of behavior upon individual members of the group."[18]

Second, while social institutions appeared to be in a state of equilibrium at any specific moment, the task of social theory was to account for the processes of social change in developmental terms. Thomas focused on the importance of crisis, technological, personal, social, and political, as creating the preconditions for response. "But crisis, as I am employing the term is not to be regarded as habitually violent. It is simply a disturbance of habit."[19]

16   The presentation of W. I. Thomas' writings in this volume has not been arranged chronologically but rather in a format closely linked to his major categories and interests. His writings were interspersed with ample and full illustrative materials. I have tried to include these materials, but I have taken the liberty of reducing their amount in the interest of covering a wider range of topics.

17   Reprinted in this volume (pp. 3–10).

18   *The Polish Peasant*, II, 1128.

19   W. I. Thomas, *Source Book for Social Origins*, 4th ed. (Boston: Richard G. Badger, 1909), p. 18.

*Introduction xxxiii*

The response of institutions to crisis was not the same as that of the social personalities. The rules for governing social institutions never coincided with the schemes for individual life organization. To state the issue in different terms, social disorganization never exactly corresponded with personal disorganization.

Third, because social change involved the interaction of values (social organization) and attitudes (social personality), the sociologist must have a separate and individual standpoint for observing both elements. Thomas saw no special problems involved in the empirical study of the "objective cultural elements" of institutions. But he dwelt extensively on the "subjective characteristics of the members of the group," which he believed required a standpoint as intensive as that used in the study of institutions, and at the same time independent of the study of institutions. As an introduction to the long life record of an immigrant, Thomas wrote about "social personality" and set forth the empirical requirements for the study of social personality.[20] He concluded that the life history which dealt not with specific attitudes but with the total pattern of predispositions was the appropriate approach.

Fourth, for W. I. Thomas the subject matter of sociology and social psychology did not flow mainly from these formal considerations, but rather from the belief that common sense knowledge was not an adequate basis for organizing social control. If his categories had meaning, it was because they would develop a set of scientific principles which would be relevant for producing more effective patterns of social control. "Rational Control in Social Life"[21] was a theme with which he started *The Polish Peasant* and which was always in the forefront of his thinking. This is not to say that Thomas had an effective conception of the consequences of systematic knowledge for social action. (Znaniecki appears to have been deeply moved by Thomas' persistent interest in these matters. After their collaboration ended, Znaniecki, de-

[20] See "Social Personality: Organization of Attitudes," pp. 11–36 of this volume.

[21] See "Rational Control in Social Life," pp. 37–53 of this volume.

parting from his methodological interests and under the stimulation of Thomas, produced his most significant contribution in his semiempirical writing on *The Social Role of the Man of Knowledge*.[22])

But Thomas did not merely focus on the limitations of common sense knowledge, for he posed evaluative questions concerning social organization and social personality for social research to answer. He posed them in a fashion which is completely compatible with contemporary functional analysis and, even more pertinent, which converges with contemporary policy sciences.

In his view, the result was not that social research would contribute to maintenance of the status quo or that sociology would be an instrument of conservatism. The pressures for social change were too great to permit such an outcome. On the contrary, he was optimistic that the result would be contributions to social reorganization in which authority relations were based on a higher degree of co-operation and would operate "not only to prevent the social group from being disorganized but to increase its cohesion by opening new fields for social co-operations."[23]

## Social Organization: Institutional Analysis

The real world of immigrants, prostitutes, and intellectuals was too exciting for W. I. Thomas to remain fixed on the problems of formal delimitation of the "subject matter of sociology and social psychology." But the genius of the man was that he really made use of his categories as he collected his voluminous empirical materials. He fitted his categories into an over-all schema which gave significance to each of the elements. Following the strategy of the ethnographer, he started with the smallest social units, particularly the family, and extended his analysis to the more inclusive institutions of society. He did not engage in a purely ad hoc series of observations. Instead, he had a set of as-

[22] Florian Znaniecki, *The Social Role of the Man of Knowledge* (New York: Columbia University Press, 1940).
[23] *The Polish Peasant*, II, 1303.

sumptions as to what structures had to be included in a configurational analysis of a society or cultural group. In *The Polish Peasant* this institutional analysis proceeded first in terms of the basic units of the primary group, then the community, and finally a selected series of large-scale organizations, which included such elements as the educational system, the press, and co-operative and voluntary associations.

Thomas grappled with the issues of identifying the essential formal properties in each institution. Thus, in his discussion of primary groups he contended that primary groups were essential aspects of larger social organizations which were viable and effective.[24] They were not mere residual categories. The forms and content of primary groups were numerous, but they were crucial aspects of human behavior and prerequisites for the maintenance of group norms. Much of the subject matter of his research dealt with the disruptive impact of technological change, urbanization, and migration on personal organization. But he saw no process of social reconstruction which did not deal explicitly with primary relations. Thus, when writing an essay entitled "The Persistence of Primary Group Norms in Present Day Society,"[25] he was not only arguing the theoretical necessity of primary groups but also seeking to describe their impact on the educational process.

Perhaps Thomas' real contribution to primary group analysis, aside from his empirical observations, was his insistence on linking the study of primary groups to the larger society, especially to the community context. At the level of community analysis, he identified both the spatial and interactional dimensions of community in a manner which loosely combined the ecological and the normative approaches.[26] He focused on the community of residence, both because of his interest in the Polish village and his attention to the residential communities of Chicago. He was aware that modern society separated place of work from place of residence, but he never fully developed the links between the occu-

[24] See "The Primary Group," pp. 57–60 of this volume.
[25] Reprinted in this volume (pp. 168–81).
[26] See "Family and Community," pp. 61–86 of this volume.

pational community and the residential community. The sense of social solidarity that occupations and professions might develop never figures prominently in his analysis.

He followed an ethnographic approach as he linked family directly to residential community. The community had vitality to the extent that it could organize family life. When personal disorganization took place in the rural communities of Poland, and more extensively in the urban communities of Chicago, it originated precisely in the absence of mediating community institutions for linking the family effectively to the large society. Size was a relevant dimension in that small isolated communities had certain built-in advantages for regulating family dynamics. But, as mentioned previously, Thomas did not use a simple-minded theory of *Gemeinschaft* and *Gesellschaft*. In agrarian societies, local villages had to have essential linkages with the large society if they were to be effective in managing their internal affairs and developing integrated value systems. This was clearly not the case in Poland during the nineteenth century when rural life fell into decay. The process of social reorganization was one in which new institutions or revitalized old ones linked the village to the large society. In a parallel but less effective way the immigrant community in the United States at the time of his investigation was striving to develop such institutional linkages. The analysis of these societywide institutions, therefore, became the final and crucial step in the analysis of social organization.

Leadership, education, press, and co-operative institutions were the suprainstitutional elements that were selected for analysis by Thomas and Znaniecki in Poland.[27] In the United States special attention was paid to "superterritorial" associations designed to bridge the gap between the immigrant community and the larger American society.

The materials on Poland parallel many contemporary analyses of the so-called new nations in nation-building. Thomas, however, resisted an explicit analysis of elites, with the exception of the intellectuals. By contrast, his analyses of the social aspects of

[27] See "Leadership, Education, and the Press," pp. 87–114 of this volume.

education and the role of the press were penetrating. He clearly saw that the role of the educational system in the emergence of an integrated Polish society was not primarily to transmit technical education, important though that may have been, but rather to create a national identity by developing a historical and cultural context. In this process the intellectuals of Polish society were important but Thomas gave no explanation of how this came to be. What happened in Poland is in contrast to the experiences of the new nations where the intellectuals are generally attracted to the main urban centers and avoid involvement in the rural and wider society.

His discussion of the press was perhaps the most trenchant. He observed that the characteristics of the mass media were such that for an emerging nation or for an immigrant group in the United States they could serve as symbolic devices for societal integration. There was no assumption that the mass media must inevitably be socially disruptive. The concept of the opinion leader was clearly present without designation, although Thomas was not so naïve as to overlook the direct confrontation between the audience and the press. He remarked that "small groups of such enlightened peasants scattered through the country but concentrated by means of indirect communication around some leaders acting through the popular press have constituted a continually growing nucleus of the wider community with which, through various direct personal bonds, an increasing circle of the population was more or less closely associated."[28] These leaders appealed to and worked through primary group sentiments.

Thomas was at his best at the micro level of the family and the community. By contrast, there is much that is unsatisfactory in his macrosociological analysis of the integration of institutions. First, like much of the writing that was to come from the Chicago school, his work neglects the political process per se as if it were a derivative aspect of society. There is little analysis of the over-all structure of politics in Poland and none for the United States. But the national political system has a crucial impact in regulating

[28] *The Polish Peasant*, II, 1393.

social change. Second, there is a neglect of the positive role of tradition and traditional authority. He did not probe the extent to which integration in Poland was assisted by the fact that the intellectuals could draw on a Polish tradition which gave them a basis of legitimate authority. This asset was relatively absent in the United States among the transplanted immigrants. Third, as a result, there are few sharp comparisons and no real explanation of the differences between the secondary institutions of Poland and the United States. His analysis is strongest in describing value differences and weakest in probing organizational elements.

## Social Personality: Definition of the Situation

W. I. Thomas devoted as much energy to thinking about personal organization as he did to the study of social organization. He was a direct forerunner in what has come to be called the study of personality and culture. Although his writing on this subject was never as clear and precise or as rewarding as in the area of institutional analysis, it may well be judged to have had greater impact. As in the case of his institutional analysis, if one looks at his definitions rather than his research, it appears that his thinking underwent constant modification, whereas in reality he was focusing repeatedly on two central themes. First, he was seeking to develop a theory of motivation, rooted in biology but manifesting the consequences of social experience, which would be broadly applicable and relevant for his comparative analysis. Second, he was seeking to formulate typologies of social personalities through which different patterns of motives could be seen as influencing social organization and social change.

Thomas used the primitive and somewhat undifferentiated idea of wishes as the basic elements of his postulates about social personality. The wishes derived from the elemental appetites for food and sex. These were the persistent emotional predispositions of man. He was clear as he developed the four wishes—new experience, security, response, and recognition—that these were arbitrary categories. But, like his other taxonomies, they were de-

*Introduction* xxxix

signed to fuse a sense of social reality into his theoretical schema. The ideas of the four wishes were first presented in 1917 in "The Persistence of Primary Group Norms in Present Day Society."[29] They were further developed about the same time in *The Polish Peasant* ("Life Record of an Immigrant"), and the fullest exposition, elaborated with autobiographical and biographical materials, is contained in *The Unadjusted Girl*.[30] But the notion of the four wishes never succeeded in fulfilling his own aspirations and must be considered one of the weaker aspects of his work.

These categories were sociological in the sense that they reflected an interactional point of view. But they must also be thought of as W. I. Thomas' efforts to come to terms with psychoanalysis. It is not true that psychoanalysis had no impact on Thomas; he was constantly reacting against it. He never understood the technique of free association or psychoanalytic treatment. In fact, he was hostile to these approaches as contributions to field-work methodology, since he believed they excessively manipulated the subject. But he was fully aware of the substantive aspects of psychoanalytic theory and Freud's formulation of human motives and of the unconscious. In part the four wishes were his own independent formulation, and in part they were a reactive posture against the issues raised by psychoanalytic concepts of motivation. It is important, however, to point out a convergence of his view with psychoanalysis in that he saw the "wishes" not as particularistic traits but rather as a basis for developing a configurational or Gestalt type of analysis. In *The Unadjusted Girl* he used the term character, which was later to figure so prominently in the study of personality and culture. He described character as "an expression of the organization of the wishes resulting from temperament and experience."[31]

Another example of Thomas' response to psychoanalysis appears in "The Configurations of Personality."[32] In this essay he

[29] See pp. 168–81 of this volume.
[30] See "Motivation: The Wishes," pp. 117–39 of this volume.
[31] *The Unadjusted Girl*, p. 39.
[32] See "The Unconscious: Configurations of Personality," pp. 140–53 of this volume.

set a pattern of sociological thinking which was to become widespread and influential. He sought to demonstrate that intellectual progress could be made by recasting psychological phenomena into sociological categories. He chose the unconscious precisely because it was central to Sigmund Freud's thinking, and to be able to handle this difficult subject matter was to deal effectively, in his view, with the problems of social personality. He identified three types of unconscious, or rather described the unconscious as having three regions: (1) the visceral unconscious, where aversions and preferences were to be found; (2) the lapsed unconscious, which consisted of a body of habit traditionally perpetuated; and (3) the critical unconscious, the region of fantasy where the individual was in psychic intimacy with himself. Even the most casual observer would note that these three categories bear a resemblance to the id, ego, and superego, and to the more contemporary formulation of Talcott Parsons' categories of affective, cognitive, and evaluative.

In the final phase of his work, Thomas felt pressed to restate his concepts of social personality in abstract and formal terms and in a fashion unrelated to his basic mode of linking theory to data. The result was a type of analysis which he called situational analysis, but which in effect was a continuation of the influence of pragmatism and the interactional social psychology of George Herbert Mead. Much of this later work by Thomas was encapsulated in his phrase, "If men define situations as real, they are real in their consequences," as stated in *The Child in America*. The most explicit statement of this approach for handling social personality is to be found in his presidential address entitled "Situational Analysis: The Behavior Pattern and the Situation."[33] Thomas sought to use this as an opportunity to explicate his ideas, but the essay is devoid of empirical content.

But aside from these excursions into situational analysis, the main core of his writings on social personality is to be found in his discussion and research into types and typologies. Types, analytic and social (concrete), were seen by him as the co-ordinating

[33] See "Situational Analysis: The Behavior Pattern and the Situation," pp. 154–67 of this volume.

concepts for linking social organization to social personality. Types were dependent on the "different temperament dispositions and on the degree and steadiness of the pressure exercised by the given social organization."[34] The subtle and wide-ranging mind of W. I. Thomas generated typologies of different sorts and on different levels of abstraction. His three types, the Philistine, the Bohemian, and the Creative Man, constituted a kind of analytic typology, since they were not linked to any specific social situation.[35]

The "Philistine" was the individual who adapted his activities completely to the prevailing definitions and norms; he chose security at the cost of new experience and individuality. The "Bohemian" was unable to fit into any frame, social or personal, because his life was spent trying to escape definitions and avoid suppressions instead of building up a positive organization of ends and attitudes. He had avoided Philistinism at the cost of character and success because he had a strong personal tendency to revolt against social pressures which were not strong or consistent enough. In contrast to these two types—the Philistine tending to accept all the definitions and the Bohemian tending to reject them—the Creative Man reconciled his desire for new experience with the desire of society for stability by redefining situations and creating new norms of superior social value. He disorganized the old system momentarily but provided the elements for a more efficient organization.

In addition, Thomas proceeded to construct a set of concrete typologies applicable to specific social situations. In his view, social psychology had to confront historical reality and had to have substantive content. Thus, for example, in *Old World Traits Transplanted* he dealt with variations in immigrants: the settler, the colonist, and the political idealist. Succeeding generations of sociologists invented typologies to cover subjects as diverse as minority group leaders and types of boxers. For W. I. Thomas social

[34] "The Persistence of Primary Group Norms in Present Day Society" (see pp. 168–81 of this volume).
[35] *Ibid.*

personality and social types were not merely response patterns to external changes in the environment. Although he never developed an adequate theory of motivation and socialization, he saw social change as involving leadership and ideology which were expressions of social personality.

## Change: Social and Personal

The chroniclers of sociology generally describe W. I. Thomas as a social psychological sociologist. He probably would have thought such a label a verbal barbarism and of little relevance. He did not think of social psychology as a separate discipline, and he launched his research with a concern for institutional structures which separated him from those social psychologists who focus on patterns of "human interaction." But there is one sense in which a "social psychological" outlook served to introduce an imbalance into his work rather than to enrich it.

In effect, he handled the outcome of social change (the reciprocal relationship between social organization and social personality) mainly in terms of attitudes and attitude transformation. He never developed an adequate set of categories for institutional change, and in particular for dealing with societywide political institutions. To some degree, this was the result of his interest in observing the raw materials of the social scene. His direct observations made it more feasible for him to chart changes in social personality rather than changes in institutions—a state of affairs which still dominates sociology. As a result, he concentrated on a series of processes, such as assimilation, co-operation, rebellion, and revolution, which applied more adequately to attitude patterns than to institutional change. He is explicit on this point.

Nevertheless, Thomas used his framework effectively. He did not arbitrarily categorize human response to change. Paralleling Freud, he emphasized the continuity between the normal and the abnormal. He proceeded, for example, as if there were a spectrum from criminal attitudes to interest in new fashions to religious revivals to a revolutionary conspiratorial outlook. In one form or

*Introduction* xliii

another, these were group and individual responses to crisis. While he hoped for rational control of social and personal change, he did not fear some turmoil, since he assumed that there were social situations under which such behavior was the basis for constructive change. Unfortunately, as in many other formulations about conflict, his writings were hardly precise about these conditions.

If the task of comparative analysis is to explicate the conditions under which social change produces attitudes which are integrative in contrast to those which are disruptive, it can hardly be said that Thomas succeeded. But he was able to pose the central problems, namely those of explaining differential responses to social change. In a grand manner he took the first steps in collecting comparative materials.

Thomas' materials are most useful if they are evaluated as examples of the formation of attitude patterns involved in collective problem-solving—successful or unsuccessful. The case of immigrant groups in the United States is one of attitude formation conducive to adjustment and of assimilation leading to relatively effective social and political change. Peasant resistance to feudal rule in Poland was an expression of conflict and rebellion which remained relatively limited in consequences compared with other types of attitude change, especially the formation of national consciousness.

The process of assimilation as presented by Thomas and his associates in *Old World Traits Transplanted* centers on the observation that immigration to the United States did not involve highly individualized persons.[36] First, primary group relations and the survival of Old World community features assisted the transition. Those immigrant groups which were the most individualized and had the lowest degree of group solidarity encountered the greatest degree of disruption. But Thomas and his associates did not probe the conditions under which solidarity among immigrant groups could be so strong as to be excessive and interfere with assimilation in the larger society. Second, Thomas was fully aware

[36] See "Assimilation: Old World Traits Transplanted," pp. 195–214 of this volume.

of the fact that the value assumptions of the larger society—the pluralism, achievement orientation, and group tolerance ethic—set the crucial context of the assimilation process. Thomas was relatively optimistic about the processes of assimilation, although he emphasized the profound barriers confronting the Negro. He did not hold that assimilation would produce a homogeneous melting-pot culture but anticipated a contemporary theme, namely, a society in which there would be important residues of ethnic culture.

In contrast, primary group solidarity and increased community integration led to initial conflict and rebellion in Poland because of the moral order and social institutions, particularly the church. In his analysis of "Revolutionary Attitudes,"[37] he presents one of the most brilliant sections in *The Polish Peasant* and sets the framework for what is later to be called collective behavior. He emphasized the distinction between revolt, an outburst against the social order, and revolution, a premeditated effort to transform radically the social order along some ideological concept. In Poland revolt took place mainly in the rural areas as sporadic and direct outbursts. Revolutionary movements were to be found throughout the entire society. In urban areas there was class conflict, while in the rural areas there was religious conflict about social organization of the church, but not about its dogma.

Thomas was particularly sensitive to the role of the intellectual in these processes of change. He pointed out that intellectuals come from outside the peasant segments of Polish society; they often come from the nobility. He offered the intriguing proposition that the intellectual was less important in fashioning revolutions than in the reorganization process. Intellectual leaders could help convert revolt into revolution, but their efforts were secondary to other, underlying conditions. In the process of reconstruction, however, the intellectuals had a wide range of potential influence.

Because of his concern with the intimate details of personal experience, the materials and the analysis of the sporadic revolt

37  See "Conflict: Revolutionary Attitudes," pp. 215–30 of this volume.

were most fully developed. Thomas was obviously fascinated by the social and personal conditions producing revolts that did not have the slightest chance of success. This was a form of human response which shaded off into sheer resistance to the system, without the benefit of mediating institutional structures.

Thomas extended his observations of social change to include those attitude formations in which the process of social change was so profound and so disruptive that the consequence was extreme and self-destructive individual behavior without any group problem-solving implications. *The Unadjusted Girl,* particularly the prostitute, became the prime example, and was described in detail under the rubric "The Individualization of Behavior."[38] The unadjusted girl was not, in Thomas' terms, revolting against an established order, but rather was deviating because she had never been effectively integrated into a social order. Because he was unable to press his empirical research to the point of comparing systematically different types of female deviant behavior, the results were highly fragmentary. Furthermore, since he rejected psychoanalytic theory and did not have an alternative view of family dynamics, he overlooked those family constellations which contribute to specific types of deviant behavior. But his case method of studying deviant behavior became a standard research tool.

## *Methodology and Method*

In assessing W. I. Thomas' work, there is some point in making a distinction between methodology and method. Methodology refers to the broad and fundamental questions of theory construction, explanation, and proof, whereas method involves the specific and technical problems of data collection. Thomas was aware of the difference and he addressed himself to both sets of problems. Yet it is a mistake to evaluate Thomas in terms of methodology and method aside from the contents and problems with which he dealt. Because of the strong interest in methodological

[38] See "The Individualization of Behavior," pp. 231–53 of this volume.

issues in American sociology, the contributions of W. I. Thomas in particular have been distorted and obscured by repeated efforts to transform him into a methodologist.

Thomas resisted involvement in "pure" methodological questions. Nevertheless, he progressively participated in the transformation of his own interest. But it was, of course, some of his successors who made it appear that Thomas concentrated on these issues. When asked to prepare a chapter on his method for a case book on *Methods in Social Science,* to be edited by Stuart A. Rice for the committee on scientific method in the social sciences of the Social Science Research Council, he simply refused to cooperate and instead suggested Robert A. Park.[39] Park asked for comments from Thomas as he started to write the chapter, and he received the oversimplified, but revealing answer from Thomas that "it is my experience that formal methodological studies are relatively unprofitable. . . . Progress in method is made from point to point by setting up objectives, employing certain techniques, then resetting the problems with the introduction of still other objectives and the modification of techniques."[40]

After Thomas departed from the University of Chicago campus, successive classes of graduate students, preparing for preliminary doctoral examinations, were directed to the "Methodological Note"[41] of *The Polish Peasant* and subsequently to Herbert Blumer's critique rather than to the substantive and problematic aspects of the work. The Social Science Research Council, through its committee of appraisal of research, commissioned Herbert Blumer to engage in a more extensive and thoroughgoing critique of *The Polish Peasant,* since it was judged to be the most impor-

[39] Robert E. Park, "The Sociological Methods of William G. Sumner and of William I. Thomas and Florian Znaniecki" in Stuart A. Rice (ed.), *Methods in Social Science* (Chicago: University of Chicago Press, 1931), p. 174.
[40] Letter from W. I. Thomas to Robert E. Park in 1928, reproduced in Herbert Blumer, *An Appraisal of Thomas and Znaniecki: The Polish Peasant in Europe and America* (New York: Social Science Research Council, 1946), p. 166.
[41] Reprinted in this volume (pp. 257–88).

*Introduction xlvii*

tant contribution to American sociology. There were few sociological volumes which could bear the weight of such repeated critiques. Blumer's appraisal, which was published in 1939, made some relevant observations about the difficulty of proof and verification in sociology. But the volume seemed to approach *The Polish Peasant* in narrow epistemological terms with little regard for its substantive issues.

W. I. Thomas was reluctant to prepare the "Methodological Note," and it was Znaniecki who called for an explicit statement of the book's methodology. The fact that the note was written at all was clearly the result of Znaniecki's initiative and Thomas' encouragement of him to take a significant role in the preparation of the work. The note did reflect Thomas' thinking, and there was probably nothing in it with which he would have taken issue. However, parts of it were drafted by Znaniecki and therefore reflected his concern with methodological studies in a manner which digressed from Thomas' style and outlook. It separated theory from data in a way not characteristic of Thomas. Thomas, for example, had many years before committed himself to the notion of the reciprocal interaction of social organization and individual organization. One of the main themes of the "Methodological Note" was the effort by Znaniecki to formalize this idea under the terms of reference, value and attitude. The result was to produce such sociological axioms as "the cause of a value or an attitude is never an attitude or a value alone but always a combination of an attitude and a value." It is most doubtful whether this type of theorizing had any effect on the actual gathering of data or on their interpretation. By contrast, Thomas' actual methodology emerges directly and simply from his writing and can be summarized so as to reflect his no-nonsense mind.

First, Thomas rejected simple analogies with the natural sciences because he viewed these as excessively rigid and distorted. He was interested in various types of holistic analysis, although he was not stimulated by biological analogies. He also rejected mechanistic notions of causality and single-variable explanations. His conclusions on these matters paralleled the position presented subsequently by Talcott Parsons in *The Structure of Social Action*.

Second, he believed that the accumulation of rational knowledge was to be desired as an end in itself, but its main purpose was for human betterment. He subscribed to the idea of an imaginative application of the scientific method to the subject of human behavior. Yet his humanistic background never allowed him to lose sight of the complexity of his subject matter. This meant he was dedicated to hypothesis formulation, objective data collection, and verification. He was clear that the special character of the data of sociology would deeply influence the way in which the scientific method could be applied. In particular, the experimental method had only limited application. But he was not greatly interested in the complex problems of the form that sociological generalization would take. Nevertheless, if one considers the period in which he was writing, he did reasonably well in integrating his specific hypotheses with his larger theoretical framework.

Third, because he was oriented to the study of total societies and their comparative analysis, he had to comment on the methodology of such comparisons. His position was problem-oriented and best summarized by the statement "and we are not obliged even to wait until all the societies have been studied monographically in their whole concrete reality before beginning the comparative study of particular problems."[42]

Fourth, and most important, Thomas was a "functionalist" in the sense that he believed that hypothetical and value-oriented questions had to be asked about the conditions under which optimum social relations would occur. The type and range of questions he offered put him in the main line of the development of sociology as a "policy science." Many of his formulations, especially his typologies, were concerned with the interplay of means and ends. The analysis of acceptance and rejection of instrumental means and social ends has become a central issue of contemporary sociological theory. Thomas' analysis is still highly rele-

[42] *The Polish Peasant*, II, 1849.

*Introduction*     xlix

vant however because he did not rely on rigid dichotomies (acceptance-rejection) but was aware of the need for subtle and differentiated criteria for judging the consequences of attitudes and behavior patterns. For Thomas sociological research, in essence, made it possible to give an additional perspective and greater precision to a variety of questions which had been posed and would continue to be posed by social philosophers. The following list of questions which Thomas and Znaniecki offered in *The Polish Peasant* characterized their evaluative standpoint.

1. The problem of individualization. "How far is individualization compatible with social cohesion? What are the forms of individualization that can be considered socially useful or socially harmful? What are the forms of social organization that allow for the greatest amount of individualism?"

2. The problem of efficiency. What is the "relation between individual and social efficiency"?

3. The problem of abnormality—crime, vagabondage, prostitution, alcoholism, etc. "How far is abnormality the unavoidable manifestation of inborn tendencies of the individual, and how far is it due to social conditions?"

4. The occupational problem. "How can work be organized to meet the needs of economic productivity and at the same time to be stimulating to those involved?"

5. The relations of the sexes. "In the relation between the sexes how can a maximum of reciprocal response be obtained with the minimum of interference of personal interest?" and "How is the general social efficiency of a group affected by the various systems of relations between man and woman?"

6. The problem of the fight of races (nationalities) and cultures. "To stop wars one must either stop the fight of races and cultures by the introduction of new schemes of attitudes and values or substitute for the isolated national state as instrument of cultural expansion some other type of organization."

7. The problem of social happiness. No central formulation of the issue is offered. The comment is made that "aside from abstract philosophical discussion and some popular psychological

analysis, the problem of happiness has never been seriously studied since the epoch of Greek hedonism."

8. "Closely connected with the foregoing is the problem of an ideal organization of culture. . . . Is there one perfect form of organization that would unify the widest individualism and the strongest social cohesion, that would exclude any abnormality by making use of all human tendencies, that would harmonize the highest efficiency with the greatest happiness? . . . Perhaps there are many forms of a perfect organization of society, and the differentiation of national cultures being impossible to overcome, every nation should simply try to bring its system to the greatest possible perfection, profiting by the experiences of others, but not imitating them."[43]

At the level of method, Thomas' main interest was in human documents, those self-generated expressions which supply an independent indicator of individual organization. He used letters and other types of written materials, but the life history document was crucial. For a period these materials occupied a central position in sociological research, and they still continue to reappear. However, the natural history of social personality has come generally to be reconstructed by interview techniques, clinical approaches, and participant observation. Therefore, because of changed empirical requirements, the more lasting contribution of Thomas to method was his pointed criticism of the interview, which he felt manipulated the respondent excessively. The interview has emerged as a dominant instrument of social psychology, and the criticism of W. I. Thomas has had its impact only on a minority of sociologists. His point of view has been given recognition in that the interview is no longer thought of as a neutral instrument but is recognized as a social process itself. Therefore, the field worker should seek less to "neutralize" his approach and more to fashion it to meet his research needs and the requirements of the social context.

After the completion of *The Polish Peasant*, and as Thomas' writing became more and more programmatic, he sought to adapt his holistic approach to the new techniques of social re-

[43] *Ibid.*, I, 78–86.

*Introduction* li

search. It was as if he consciously sought not to stand in the way of progress. He sought to explore the manner in which statistical analysis could be used so as to be compatible with his concerns for configurational analysis. Thomas came to give the highest priority to the statistical verification of hypotheses but insisted on interpretation in terms of unmeasured factors and of the total situation.

Because Thomas began to emphasize the notion of situational analysis, his comments on methodology and method were recast to fit this mold but in a fashion that can hardly be called more than relabeling. For the term situational analysis it would be possible, in the contemporary language of social research, to substitute the phrase contextual analysis. He used the title "The Relation of Research to the Social Process"[44] to emphasize his concern that statistical data not lead to sheer manipulation of variables in a fashion detached from social reality. He repeatedly sought to describe the social units that need to be taken into account, such as family, community, and institutions, but he did so as a commentator on statistical analysis rather than as an expert practitioner.

Toward the very end of his intellectual career, among the various documents and memoranda that he prepared on assignment was a statement written under the stimulation of the Social Science Research Council on "personality and culture." This particular document has been described as one of the first crystallizations of the field. Thomas was able to present a continuity in this report, as his central interests fitted under the rubric of personality and culture, and his method, especially his intensive and comparative standpoint, was directly applicable. He incorporated new developments in method, such as the quantification of life history and clinical materials, and emphasized the emerging importance of cross-national studies, a research theme which had to wait almost thirty years to be implemented. But he concluded with his persistent skepticism of system-building, observing that there was not, could not, and should not be a unitary character to the subject matter of personality and culture.

[44] Reprinted in this volume (pp. 289–305).

## Intellectual Impact

W. I. Thomas was a sociologist's sociologist. Among the key figures of the period his impact was immediate and direct. With the publication of *The Polish Peasant* he achieved a commanding intellectual position. It was a comprehensive study with a level of theoretical sophistication and empirical detail which had not yet been achieved. The richness he displayed in explaining the structures and mechanisms of social control and the explication of the personal responses—disruptive and integrative—meant that sociological analysis had been transformed.

In 1922 Henry Pratt Fairchild spoke for the learned society of sociologists when he wrote that "taken as a whole, this work is unique. As far as the present reviewer's knowledge goes, there is nothing like it in American literature."[45] Floyd House, in his *Development of Sociology*, which was published in 1936 and which served for many years as a graduate student handbook, ranked it in importance with Sumner's *Folkways*. The book was widely discussed in both the professional and general journals. In fact, there were some thirty reviews in English, and it was extensively reviewed outside the United States, where it was also instantly acclaimed. In many parts of Asia it raised the contemporary issue of whether modernization could proceed without social disorganization.

Despite the academic recognition he received, much of his long-term impact was indirect and through the work of the core of sociologists whom he influenced. The number of sociologists in the United States during the 1920's was very small, and the number abroad even smaller, and this in part accounts for the limited audience he reached directly. The first edition of 1,500 copies of *The Polish Peasant* was not exhausted until 1926, almost eight years after publication. The sale may well have been inhibited by the interruption in the publication arrangements by the University of Chicago Press and its subsequent distribution by a relatively small house. The second edition, also of

[45] *American Journal of Sociology*, XVII (1922–23), 524.

1,500 copies, appeared in 1927 under Alfred Knopf's imprint, which helped put the volumes back into the mainstream, but this edition was not sold out until 1937. One can argue that 3,000 copies was indeed a respectable sale for a multivolume study, but there is no direct relation between the sale of a book and its intellectual influence. When, after many years of delay, a new edition was prepared by Dover Publications in 1958, it sold more than 1,500 copies in a three-year period, reflecting the great expansion of the sociological audience and continuing interest in the study.

After he left the University of Chicago, many of his books and writings went out of print and were not republished. A number of his writings remained in typescript or mimeographed form during his lifetime. Donald Young has claimed that this state of affairs was of no serious concern to Thomas, but as he has also pointed out, "Sociologists, social psychologists and others working in the field of social behavior, however, were troubled by the lack of ready access to his writing."[46]

Thus, it was through the combination of his teaching and his writings that Thomas had his full impact. He was a campus character who attracted wide attention among students because he performed as an intellectual with broad interests throughout the campus. He drew large undergraduate audiences because of his strong sense of detachment and the materials contained in his courses—primitive societies, the sociology of sexual relations, and the position of women. From its inception, the Department of Sociology developed a strong emphasis on lecturing to undergraduates. Sociological instruction was a kind of extension of the social gospel, spreading knowledge to help men confront and deal with the problems of the day. Thomas was one of four secularized sociological preachers on the University of Chicago campus. Albion Small, coming from a religious background, preached against the sins of capitalism in a polysyllabic language. Charles R. Henderson lectured in the Department of Sociology on social amelioration and also held the post of university chap-

[46] Donald Young, in Volkart, p. v (see n. 2, above).

lain; and George E. Vincent was an eloquent and gifted lecturer on social psychology.

On a visit to Tuskegee Institute, Thomas made personal contact with Robert E. Park and arranged to have him teach at the University of Chicago during the summer of 1914. Thomas became his sponsor and after many years of agitation was able to arrange for a regular appointment in the Department of Sociology. When Park first arrived on the University of Chicago campus, he was 50 years of age and had already actively pursued his sociological writings, although his chief period of productivity and impact came after he joined the University. His contact with Thomas and his appointment to the University of Chicago were crucial in stimulating his subsequent research.

Thomas had a profound influence on Park, both personally and intellectually. They had many common interests and a common concern for direct observation of social change. Thomas encouraged Park to be more explicit and systematic in formulating his point of view. In turn, Robert E. Park carried on and elaborated many of the research interests of Thomas and busied himself with graduate teaching in the tradition of Thomas. With the exception of William F. Ogburn, the new members of the Department of Sociology were trained at the University of Chicago. Ernest Burgess studied directly under both Thomas and Park. Ellsworth Faris, Louis Wirth, Robert Redfield, and Everett Hughes were trained by Park after Thomas left the campus, but they all knew Thomas personally and were strongly influenced by his writings. It was particularly through the efforts of Everett Hughes that W. I. Thomas' tradition of intensive social observation was transmitted to the post–World War II generation of Chicago sociologists.

Subsequently, Samuel Stouffer and Herbert Blumer, after they had been exposed to the same influences, joined the Department of Sociology. Stouffer's interest in attitude research was stimulated by Thomas and supported by the prior work of Thurstone, who had also been exposed to Thomas. The concern of Stouffer was to push the comparison, by statistical analysis, of human documents with questionnaire data. While Blumer departed from the empirical style of Thomas, his basic interest in collective behavior and public opinion was influenced by Thomas. Finally, the line of the Chicago faculty became diffuse and unclear, but such men as Herbert Goldhamer and, especially, Edward A. Shils acknowledged the role of Thomas in fashioning their interests and tastes.

A host of graduate students from the period of Thomas and Park produced the empirical monographs about the city of Chicago which characterized the Chicago school. Other graduate students emphasized Thomas' formulations of social personality and produced such works as *The Jackroller* by Clifford Shaw. A group of figures who either were students at Chicago or were influenced by Thomas' writings emerged as the academic leaders of sociology: Donald Young, Kimball Young, Leonard Cottrell, Jr., Edward Reuter, and Stuart Queen, for example. Park and Burgess, building on the Thomas source book format, prepared the influential *Introduction to the Science of Sociology*, while other writers produced a flood of textbooks on social disorganization which spread out through the undergraduate culture.

The circles of impact grew wider and more diffuse through Thomas' personal activity and the work of his students. He came into close contact with some of the leaders of the newer psychoanalytic movement seeking to put personality theory into a social and interactional framework, in particular Harry Stack Sullivan. He knew Edward Sapir and others in social anthropology who were concerned with language. Many of the followers of George Herbert Mead found in Thomas an empirical interest which propelled them into field work. Even the notion of the "opinion leader" found one origin in the work of Thomas as it was passed down through Douglas Waples and Bernard Berelson, both of whom were saturated in Chicago sociology. The net is wide and encompasses much of sociology before 1940, and to trace out its reticulations would only be to serve antiquarian interests.[47]

---

[47] It is interesting to speculate about the link between W. I. Thomas' types and the parallel constructions of David Riesman (other directed, inner directed, and autonomous). There is evidence that David Riesman, while at the University of Chicago, developed his categories without

It would be rewarding to have an account of his activities and interest in social policy and social action, but the full record is not available. Thomas must have speculated on the consequences and worth of these endeavors. In contrast to Robert E. Park, who later became outright hostile to social work, Thomas remained sympathetic, although critical. Many of his concepts found their way into the training and ideology of the social service profession. His essential point of view emphasized the necessity of understanding the values and culture of the immigrant population and the need to strengthen the institutions of self-help and community organization as a bridge for assimilation into the large society.

Thus it is only necessary to substitute the word "Negro" for "immigrant" or "Polish" in the following passage from *The Polish Peasant* to find contemporary issues in social work:

It is a mistake to suppose that a "community center" established by American social agencies can in its present form even approximately fulfill the social function of a Polish parish. It is an institution imposed from the outside instead of being freely developed by the initiative and co-operation of the people themselves and this, in addition to its racially unfamiliar character, would be enough to prevent it from exercising any deep social influence. Its managers usually know little or nothing of the traditions, attitudes, and native language of the people with whom they have to deal and therefore could not become genuine social leaders under any conditions.... Whatever real assistance the American social center gives to the immigrant community is the result of the "case method," which consists in dealing directly and separately with individuals and families. While this method may bring efficient temporary help to the individual it does not contribute to the social progress of the community nor does it possess much preventive

---

explicit knowledge of the work of W. I. Thomas. Riesman presented his materials before publication at a meeting of the Society for Social Research in the period immediately after World War II, at which Ellsworth Faris was present. It was then that Faris introduced Riesman to the writings of W. I. Thomas. But such intellectual influences could have been transmitted indirectly, of course, especially in the intellectual environment of the University of Chicago.

influence in struggling against social disorganization. Both of these purposes can be attained only by organizing and encouraging social self-help on the co-operative basis. Finally, in their relations with immigrants the American social workers usually assume, consciously or not, the attitude of a kindly and protective superiority, occasionally, though seldom, verging on despotism.[48]

This was one of the earliest critiques of social work by a sociologist. One line of descent of this theme is clear. In the 1930's the "Chicago area project," under the active leadership of Clifford Shaw and Henry McKay, and in which Ernest Burgess was also involved, was the first large-scale attempt to throw off in the inner city what was later to be called welfare colonialism. This was an effort of sociologists without benefit of political ideology. The Chicago area project served as the training ground of such men as Joseph Lohman and became one source of intellectual stimulation for federal programs of "community action" through the efforts of such men as Leonard Cottrell, Jr., and Lloyd Ohlin.[49] But the area project was no more than an administrative formulation of the sociological interests and intellectual ferment created by W. I. Thomas. Just as Thomas neglected political process, so did the Chicago area project. And it remained for the civil rights movement to close the gap between political process and the analysis of social organization at the community level.

In summary, W. I. Thomas produced a classic contribution to sociology. To say in sociology that a man's work is classic means that the scientific attitude in the discipline admits its debt to the past. It likewise means that the man's work cannot be read without drawing out its relevance to present sociological problems.

Thomas' work, *The Polish Peasant*, and some of his other writings have significant contemporary relevance. In part this

[48] *The Polish Peasant*, II, 1526–27.
[49] It may be noted that Saul K. Alinsky, social critic and consultant, studied sociology at the University of Chicago at the time of the Chicago area project, and some of his notions of community action and organization are strikingly parallel to those developed in this project.

is so because he was comprehensive (although he also tended to be eclectic). It is so also because he had a powerful sense of the important, although he recognized that the most minor detail was a composite aspect of basic issues. His relevance rests mainly, however, on his formulation of the substantive problems of sociology, namely, those of social change associated with urbanization—or modernization, as it has come to be called. He was one of the first American social scientists to deal intensively with the issues of acculturation and cultural change. These problems have become even more central intellectual issues since Thomas wrote.

With the passage of time, it is understandable that Thomas' contribution has come to be equated with selected key concepts which have become the common currency of sociology. But this is a most truncated view of the man and his accomplishments, for his treatment of concrete problems made his contributions truly classic. The organizing principle for presenting the writings of W. I. Thomas in this volume is to encompass the wide range of his work by including both his key concepts and a sampling of his empirical observations and conclusions.

*Morris Janowitz*

# I. The Subject Matter of Sociology and Social Psychology

# 1

# SOCIAL DISORGANIZATION AND SOCIAL REORGANIZATION

THE CONCEPT of social disorganization as we shall use it refers primarily to institutions and only secondarily to men. Just as group-organization embodied in socially systematized schemes of behavior imposed as rules upon individuals never exactly coincides with individual life-organization consisting in personally systematized schemes of behavior, so social disorganization never exactly corresponds to individual disorganization. Even if we imagined a group lacking all internal differentiation, *i.e.*, a group in which every member would accept all the socially sanctioned and none but the socially sanctioned rules of behavior as schemes of his own conduct, still every member would systematize these schemes differently in his personal evolution, would make a different life-organization out of them, because neither his temperament nor his life-history would be exactly the same as those of other members. As a matter of fact, such a uniform group is a pure fiction; even in the least differentiated groups we find socially sanctioned rules of behavior which explicitly apply only to certain classes of individuals and are not supposed to be used by others in organizing their conduct, and

Reprinted from *The Polish Peasant in Europe and America* (New York: Alfred A. Knopf, 1927; New York: Dover Publications, 1958), II, 1127–32, 1303–6.

we find individuals who in organizing their conduct use some personal schemes of their own invention besides the traditionally sanctioned social rules. Moreover, the progress of social differentiation is accompanied by a growth of special institutions, consisting essentially in a systematic organization of a certain number of socially selected schemes for the permanent achievement of certain results. This institutional organization and the life-organization of any of the individuals through whose activity the institution is socially realized partly overlap, but one individual cannot fully realize in his life the whole systematic organization of the institution since the latter always implies the collaboration of many, and on the other hand each individual has many interests which have to be organized outside of this particular institution.

There is, of course, a certain reciprocal dependence between social organization and individual life-organization. We shall discuss the influence which social organization exercises upon the individual; we shall see in this and in the following volumes how the life-organization of individual members of a group, particularly of leading members, influences social organization. But the nature of this reciprocal influence in each particular case is a problem to be studied, not a dogma to be accepted in advance.

These points must be kept in mind if we are to understand the question of social disorganization. We can define the latter briefly as a *decrease of the influence of existing social rules of behavior upon individual members of the group*. This decrease may present innumerable degrees, ranging from a single break of some particular rule by one individual up to a general decay of all the institutions of the group. Now, social disorganization in this sense has no unequivocal connection whatever with individual disorganization, which consists in a decrease of the individual's ability to organize his whole life for the efficient, progressive and continuous realization of his fundamental interests. An individual who breaks some or even most of the social rules prevailing in his group may indeed do this because he is losing the minimum capacity of life-organization required by social conformism; but he may also reject the schemes of behavior im-

## Social Disorganization and Reorganization 5

posed by his milieu because they hinder him in reaching a more efficient and more comprehensive life-organization. On the other hand also, the social organization of a group may be very permanent and strong in the sense that no opposition is manifested to the existing rules and institutions; and yet, this lack of opposition may be simply the result of the narrowness of the interests of the group-members and may be accompanied by a very rudimentary, mechanical and inefficient life-organization of each member individually. Of course, a strong group organization may be also the product of a conscious moral effort of its members and thus correspond to a very high degree of life-organization of each of them individually. It is therefore impossible to conclude from social as to individual organization or disorganization, or vice versa. In other words, social organization is not coextensive with individual morality, nor does social disorganization correspond to individual demoralization.

Social disorganization is not an exceptional phenomenon limited to certain periods or certain societies; some of it is found always and everywhere, since always and everywhere there are individual cases of breaking social rules, cases which exercise some disorganizing influence on group institutions and, if not counteracted, are apt to multiply and to lead to a complete decay of the latter. But during periods of social stability this continuous incipient disorganization is continuously neutralized by such activities of the group as reinforce with the help of social sanctions the power of existing rules. The stability of group institutions is thus simply a dynamic equilibrium of processes of disorganization and *reorganization.* This equilibrium is disturbed when processes of disorganization can no longer be checked by any attempts to reinforce the existing rules. A period of prevalent disorganization follows, which may lead to a complete dissolution of the group. More usually, however, it is counteracted and stopped before it reaches this limit by a new process of reorganization which in this case does not consist in a mere reinforcement of the decaying organization, but in a production of new schemes of behavior and new institutions better adapted to the changed demands of the group; we call this production of new schemes and institutions *social reconstruction*. Social reconstruction is possible only because and in so far as, during the period of social disorganization a part at least of the members of the group have not become individually disorganized, but, on the contrary, have been working toward a new and more efficient personal life-organization and have expressed a part at least of the constructive tendencies implied in their individual activities in an effort to produce new social institutions.

In studying the process of social disorganization we must, of course, in accordance with the chief aim of all science, try to explain it causally, *i.e.*, to analyze its concrete complexity into simple facts which could be subordinated to more or less general laws of causally determined becoming. We have seen in our Methodological Note that in the field of social reality a causal fact contains three components, *i.e.*, an effect, whether individual or social, always has a composite cause, containing both an individual (subjective) and a social (objective) element. We have called the subjective socio-psychological elements of social reality *attitudes* and the objective, social elements which impose themselves upon the individual as given and provoke his reaction *social values*. If we want to explain causally the appearance of an attitude, we must remember that it is never produced by an external influence alone, but by an external influence plus a definite tendency or predisposition, in other words, by a social value acting upon or, more exactly, appealing to some preexisting attitude. If we want to explain causally the appearance of a social value—a scheme of behavior, an institution, a material product—we cannot do it by merely going back to some subjective, psychological phenomenon of "will" or "feeling" or "reflection," but we must take into account as part of the real cause the preexisting objective, social data which in combination with a subjective tendency gave rise to this effect; in other words, we must explain a social value by an attitude acting upon or influenced by some preexisting social value.

As long as we are concerned with disorganization alone, leaving provisionally aside the following process of reconstruction, the phenomenon which we want to explain is evidently the appearance of such attitudes as impair the efficiency of existing rules of behavior and thus lead to the decay of social institutions. Every social rule is the expression of a definite combination of certain attitudes; if instead of these attitudes some others appear, the influence of the rule is disturbed. There may be thus several different ways in which a rule can lose its efficiency, and still more numerous ways in which an institution, which always involves several regulating schemes, can fall into decay. The causal explanation of any particular case of social disorganization demands thus that we find, first of all, what are the particular attitudes whose appearance manifests itself socially in the loss of influence of the existing social rules, and then try to determine the causes of these attitudes. Our tendency should be, of course, to analyze the apparent diversity and complexity of particular social processes into a limited number of more or less general causal facts, and this tendency can be realized in the study of disorganization if we find that the decay of *different rules* existing in a given society is the objective manifestation of *similar attitudes,* that, in other words, many given, apparently different phenomena of disorganization can be causally explained in the same way. We cannot reach any laws of social disorganization, *i.e.,* we cannot find causes which always and everywhere produce social disorganization; we can only hope to determine laws of socio-psychological becoming, *i.e.,* find causes which always and everywhere produce certain definite attitudes, and these causes will explain also social disorganization in all those cases in which it will be found that the attitudes produced by them are the real background of social disorganization, that the decay of given rules or institutions is merely the objective, superficial manifestation of the appearance of these attitudes. Our task is the same as that of the physicist or chemist who does not attempt to find laws of the multiform changes which happen in the sensual appearance of our material environment, but searches for laws of the more fundamental and general processes which are supposed to underlie those directly observable changes, and explains the latter causally only in so far as it can be shown that they are the superficial manifestations of certain deeper, causally explicable effects. . . .

## The Concept of Social Reorganization

The decay of the traditional social organization is due to the appearance and development of new attitudes leading to activities which do not comply with the socially recognized and sanctioned schemes of behavior. The problem of social reconstruction is to create new schemes of behavior—new rules of personal conduct and new institutions—which will supplant or modify the old schemes and correspond better to the changed attitudes, that is, which will permit the latter to express themselves in action and at the same time will regulate their active manifestations so as not only to prevent the social group from becoming disorganized but to increase its cohesion by opening new fields for social cooperation.

In this process of creating new social forms the role of the individual, the inventor or leader, is much more important than in the preservation and defense of the old forms or in revolutionary movements which tend merely to overthrow the traditional system, leaving the problem of reconstruction to be solved later. For even when the defense of the traditional organization is assumed by particular individuals the latter act merely as official or unofficial representatives of the group; they may be more or less original and efficient in realizing their aim, but their aim has been defined for them entirely by social tradition. In revolution, as we have seen, the individual can generalize and make more conscious only tendencies which already exist in the group. Whereas, in social reconstruction his task is to discover and understand the new attitudes which demand an outlet, to invent the schemes of behavior which would best correspond to these attitudes, and to make the group accept these schemes as social rules or institutions. More than this, he must usually develop the new attitudes in certain parts of society which have been evolving more slowly and are not yet ready for the reform; and often

## Social Disorganization and Reorganization

he has to struggle against obstinate defenders of the traditional system.

We are not concerned here with the methods by which the social leader discovers the new needs of society and invents new forms of social organization; this would lead us far beyond the study of the peasant class. What interests us is, how are new forms imposed upon the peasant communities and what is the social organization resulting? Now, it is clear that in order to have a peasant community consciously accept any institution different from the traditional ones it is indispensable to have this community intellectually prepared to meet new problems. Education of the peasant is thus the first and indispensable step of social reconstruction.

Further, we have seen that social disorganization came as a consequence of the breakdown of the old isolation of peasant communities; the contacts between each community and the outside social world have been continually increasing in number, variety and intensity. It is evident that any attempt of social reconstruction must take this fact into account; a social organization based exclusively upon such interests and relations as bind together the members of an isolated community would have no chance to last and to develop. But, on the other hand, in constructing a new social system those attitudes of social solidarity which are indispensable to assure a harmonious cooperation of individuals in the active realization of their new tendencies cannot be created out of nothing; use must be made of the attitudes on which the unity of the old community rested. Though no longer sufficient in their old form to organize socially the new interests, they can be changed by proper influences into somewhat different, more comprehensive and more conscious attitudes which are better suited to the new conditions. In other words, the principle of the community has to be modified and extended so as to apply to all those social elements with which the peasant primary group is or soon will be in contact—to the whole peasant class, or even to the whole nation. A wider community is thus gradually evolved, and the instrument through which its opinion is formed and its solidarity promoted is the press.

The social system which develops on this basis naturally tends to reconcile, by modifying them, the two originally contradictory principles—the traditional absorption of the individual by the group and the new self-assertion of the individual against or independently of the group. The method which, after various trials, proves the most efficient in fulfilling this difficult task is the method of conscious cooperation. Closed social groups are freely formed for the common pursuit of definite positive interests which each individual can more efficiently satisfy in this way than if he worked alone. These organized groups are scattered all over the country in various peasant communities, but know about one another through the press. The further task of social organization is to bring groups with similar or supplementary purposes together for common pursuit, just as individuals are brought together in each particular group.

The more extensive and coherent this new social system becomes, the more frequent, varied and important are its contacts with the social and political institutions created by other classes and in which the peasants until recently had not actively participated (except, of course, those individuals who became members of other classes and ceased to belong to the peasant class). The peasant begins consciously to cooperate in those activities by which national unity is maintained and national culture developed. This fact has a particular importance for Poland where for a whole century national life had to be preserved by voluntary cooperation, not only without the help of the state but even against the state, and where at this moment the same method of voluntary cooperation is being used in reconstructing a national state system. The significance of such a historical experiment for sociology is evident, for it contributes more than anything to the solution of the most essential problem of modern times—how to pass from the type of national organization in which public services are exacted and public order enforced by coercion to a different type, in which not only a small minority, but the majority which is now culturally passive will voluntarily contribute to social order and cultural progress.

# 2

# SOCIAL PERSONALITY:

# ORGANIZATION OF ATTITUDES

THE PRESENT problem is the application of the methods of social psychology to an evolving human personality.

Elsewhere we have outlined the standpoint that a nomothetic social science is possible only if all social becoming is viewed as the product of a continual interaction of individual consciousness and objective social reality. In this connection the human personality is both a continually producing factor and a continually produced result of social evolution, and this double relation expresses itself in every elementary social fact; there can be for social science no change of social reality which is not the common effect of pre-existing social values and individual attitudes acting upon them, no change of individual consciousness which is not the common effect of pre-existing individual attitudes and social values acting upon them. When viewed as a factor of social evolution the human personality is a ground of the causal explanation of social happenings; when viewed as a product of social evolution it is causally explicable by social happenings. In the first case individual attitudes toward pre-existing social values serve to explain the appearance of new social values; in the second case social values acting upon pre-existing individual at-

---

Reprinted from *The Polish Peasant in Europe and America* (New York: Alfred A. Knopf, 1927; New York: Dover Publications, 1958), II, 1831–63.

titudes serve to explain the appearance of new individual attitudes.

The study of human personalities, both as factors and as products of social evolution, serves first of all the same purpose as the study of any other social data—the determination of social laws. A personality is always a constituted element of some social group; the values with which it has to deal are, were and will be common to many personalities, some of them common to all mankind, and the attitudes which it exhibits are also shared by many other individuals. And even if the values as viewed by a given individual, and the attitudes assumed by this individual present peculiarities distinguishing them to some extent from values given to and attitudes assumed by all other individuals, we can ignore these peculiarities for the purposes of scientific generalization, just as the natural scientist ignores the peculiarities which make each physical thing or happening in a sense unique. In analyzing the experiences and attitudes of an individual we always reach data and elementary facts which are not exclusively limited to this individual's personality but can be treated as mere instances of more or less general classes of data or facts, and can thus be used for the determination of laws of social becoming. Whether we draw our materials for sociological analysis from detailed life-records of concrete individuals or from the observation of mass-phenomena, the problems of sociological analysis are the same. But even when we are searching for abstract laws life-records of concrete personalities have a marked superiority over any other kind of materials. We are safe in saying that personal life-records, as complete as possible, constitute the *perfect* type of sociological material, and that if social science has to use other materials at all it is only because of the practical difficulty of obtaining at the moment a sufficient number of such records to cover the totality of sociological problems, and of the enormous amount of work demanded for an adequate analysis of all the personal materials necessary to characterize the life of a social group. If we are forced to use mass-phenomena as material, or any kind of happenings taken without regard to the life-histories of the individuals who participate in them, it

## Social Personality

is a defect, not an advantage, of our present sociological method.

Indeed it is clear that even for the characterization of single social data—attitudes and values—personal life-records give us the most exact approach. An attitude as manifested in an isolated act is always subject to misinterpretation, but this danger diminishes in the very measure of our ability to connect this act with past acts of the same individual. A social institution can be fully understood only if we do not limit ourselves to the abstract study of its formal organization, but analyze the way in which it appears in the personal experience of various members of the group and follow the influence which it has upon their lives. And the superiority of life-records over every other kind of material for the purposes of sociological analysis appears with particular force when we pass from the characterization of single data to the determination of facts, for there is no safer and more efficient way of finding among the innumerable antecedents of a social happening the real causes of this happening than to analyze the past of the individuals through whose agency this happening occurred. The development of sociological investigation during the past fifteen or twenty years, particularly the growing emphasis, which under the pressure of practical needs, is being put upon special and actual empirical problems as opposed to the general speculations of the preceding period, leads to the growing realization that we must collect more complete sociological documents than we possess. And the more complete a sociological document becomes the more it approaches a full personal liferecord. The ultimate aim of social science, like that of every other science, is to reconcile the highest possible exactness and generality in its theoretic conclusions with the greatest possible concreteness of the object-matter upon which these conclusions bear. Or, in other words, to use as few general laws as possible for the explanation of as much concrete social life as possible. And since concrete social life is concrete only when taken together with the individual life which underlies social happenings, since the personal element is a constitutive factor of every social occurrence, social science cannot remain on the surface of social becoming, where certain schools wish to have it float, but must reach the actual human experiences and attitudes which constitute the full, live and active social reality beneath the formal organization of social institutions, or behind the statistically tabulated mass-phenomena which taken in themselves are nothing but symptoms of unknown causal processes and can serve only as provisional ground for sociological hypotheses.

But in order to be able to use adequately personal life-records for the purposes of nomothetic generalizations social science must have criteria permitting it to select at once from a mass of concrete human documents, those which are likely to be scientifically valuable for the solution of a given general problem. We cannot study the life-histories of all the individuals participating in a certain social happening, for then our task would be inexhaustible. We must limit ourselves, just as the natural scientist does, to a few *representative* cases whose thorough study will yield results as nearly applicable as possible to all other cases concerned. But the problem of selecting representative cases is much less easy in social than in natural science because the greater complexity and variety which human personalities present as compared with natural things makes their classification more difficult. When the mineralogist has studied the chemical composition of a stone it is easy for him to ascertain to what other stones the results of his investigation will apply, for the class of which this stone was chosen as representative is distinguishable by certain superficial physical features, and the scientist can assume without too much risk that any stone presenting the same physical features belongs to the same class and has approximately the same chemical composition. But up to the present the sociologist lacks really efficient heuristic devices of this kind. When he has studied the process of the appearance of a certain attitude or a certain value in the life-history of one social personality he is taking a serious risk when he provisionally assumes that this case is representative of a certain general class—that the process is the same, for example, in all the individuals who belong to a certain community, nation, profession, religious denomination, etc. Of course any error which he commits can be corrected by further research, but the question is, how to diminish in advance the chances of such errors, how to find criteria which will permit us, after having investigated one human being, to tell more or less exactly to what class of human beings the results of this investigation are applicable.

Such criteria can be given only by a theory of human individuals as social personalities. The use of individual life-records as material for the determination of abstract social laws must be supplemented by a sociological study of these individuals themselves in their entire personal evolution, as concrete components of the social world. The tendency of such a study is exactly opposite to that of a search for general laws. Its task is the *synthesis* of the concrete from its abstract elements, not the analysis of the concrete into abstract elements. If the ideal of nomothetic research is to analyze the whole conscious life going on in a society into elementary facts and to subordinate these to general laws, the ideal of the theory of social personalities is to reconstruct the entire process of every personal evolution from single facts, each of which should be perfectly explicable on the basis of a general law. And such a synthetic investigation, in addition to being an indispensable auxiliary of nomothetic sociological generalization, has also an important theoretic and practical interest of its own, as is indicated in the attention which has always been paid to biography and to questions of temperament and character. There has been, however, a striking lack of progress in these investigations; they still remain approximately on the level which they reached in antiquity. The reason of this stagnation is evident. Almost all the studies of temperament and character have been constructed on the ground of individual, not of social psychology, and since personal evolution can be understood only in connection with social life these theories were unable to take into adequate consideration the whole wealth of important problems bearing on personal evolution, and had to limit themselves to a mere abstract description and classification of statically considered formal types.

Before proceeding, therefore, to the investigation of the present problem we must discuss the standpoint from which every synthetic study of a human individual as social personality should be made. This implies a complete revision of the problem of *type*, for the concept of type plays the same part in social synthesis as the concept of the causal fact plays in social analysis, the aim of the former being to find classes, just as the aim of the latter is to find laws. Our present discussion will be, of course, merely formal and methodological; we do not aim to establish in advance a complete classification of human personalities—this must be the result of long studies—but to show in what way such a classification can be reached. We shall be forced, indeed, to characterize several ideal types which social personalities tend to assume, but our characterization will be purely formal and based upon relations between the individual and his social environment whose essential features are the same in all societies, whatever may be the content of the personal and social life. Our classification will, therefore, claim to be only a starting-point for researches whose aim must consist in a synthetic characterization of human types precisely with regard to the content of the attitudes and values which constitute their social personalities.

The essential points, which cannot be here sufficiently emphasized, are that the social personality as a whole manifests itself only in the course of its total life and not at any particular moment of its life, and that its life is not a mere empirical manifestation of a timeless metaphysical essence, always the same, but is a continuous evolution in which nothing remains unchanged. This evolution often tends toward a stabilization as its ultimate limit, but never attains this limit completely; and even then it is not this limit as such, but the very course of evolution tending to this limit, that constitutes the main object-matter of socio-psychological synthesis.

If we wish, therefore, to use the concept of type as applied to social personalities, we must, first of all, extend this concept to the process of personal evolution. Now this implies a special problem. A personal evolution taken in its totality is certainly a unique occurrence; no individual develops in the same way as any other individual. On the other hand, from the standpoint of nomothetic social science this total development should be entirely analyzable into elementary facts, each indefinitely repeatable and subordinated to a general law. But the possibility of subordinating single isolated facts of individual life to general laws of becoming is evidently not sufficient to justify any generalizations concerning personalities for the combination of these elementary facts in the evolution of each individual may be so different from what it is in the life of others that no comparison of any two personalities is possible. We must therefore assume—and social observation certainly corroborates this assumption—that not only single attitudes and values, not only single elementary facts, but more or less complete combinations, series of facts, present a certain similarity from individual to individual. This similarity cannot be assumed to go as far as absolute identity; the identity is always only approximate. Nor is any such combination of facts universal; it is not a matter of a single abstract law, but of a concrete co-operation of many laws, and is therefore usually common to only a certain number of individuals. But the concept of type, unlike the concept of law, needs only an approximate identity of individual cases, and a class is supposed to possess only a relative generality.

The application of sociological generalization to social personalities requires thus, first of all, the admission of what we may call *typical lines of genesis*.[1] A line of genesis is a series of facts through which a certain attitude is developed from some other attitude (or group of attitudes), a value from some other value (or group of values), when it does not develop directly, and the process cannot be treated as a single elementary fact. For example there is probably no social influence that could produce directly an attitude of appreciation of science from the parvenu's pride in his wealth, no intellectual attitude that could directly lead an untrained individual to produce a scientifically valid concept from the data of common-sense observation; but by a series of intermediary stages the parvenu can become a sincere protector of science, by a more or less long training in theoretic research a student learns to produce scientific values. In such a series every

---

[1] The existence of typical lines of genesis has a fundamental importance for problems concerning the general types of individual development in any particular field—intellectual, moral, religious, aesthetic, economic. It is, in fact, a conscious or unconscious basis of all special education and professional training.

single link is a fact of the type: attitude—value—attitude, or: value—attitude—value, and as such, if properly analyzed, can always be explained by sociological law (or lead to the discovery of a sociological law), but the series as a whole cannot be subject to any law, for there are many possible ways in which an attitude can be developed out of another attitude, a value out of another value; all depends on the nature of the intermediary data. Thus, if we have as starting-point an attitude $a$ and as result an attitude $m$, the evolution may have gone on in such a way that out of $a$, under the influence of a value $B$, is evolved the attitude $d$; out of $d$, under the influence of $J$, the attitude $k$, and $k$, under the influence of a value $N$, was changed into the attitude $m$. But it may have happened also that $a$ was influenced not by $B$, but by $C$, and the result was a different attitude $e$, which again under the influence not of $F$, but of $G$, gave $i$, and $i$, when influenced by $L$, also produced $m$. And the same can be said of values. To take well-known examples, there is probably usually one and the same primary attitude—a particular form of the desire for excitement, which we shall analyze in a later volume—out of which habitual drinking develops, and yet there are many possible ways of becoming a drunkard. The history of inventions shows that many inventors working independently on the same practical problem may produce the same invention, but their procedure may be completely different. And of course it is hardly necessary to say that from a given attitude or value many different lines of evolution may start and reach quite different results, and that a given attitude or value may have been reached from many different starting-points by different lines of evolution. Moreover in the development of a human personality there are many and various divergent lines of genesis, since at any moment of his life the individual not only presents many attitudes acquired during his past development and produces many values which he has learned to produce, but this acquired set of attitudes and abilities is more or less different from moment to moment. Viewed therefore from the standpoint of particular lines of genesis the human personality in its total evolution might appear as too complex to be the object-matter of scientific generalization. But the theoretically limitless variety of lines of genesis is really limited in practice. There are only a few typical ways in which an attitude is developed out of a determined other attitude or a value out of a determined other value. More than this, when an attitude or a value becomes the starting-point of a line of evolution we can assume that there are only a few different results which this evolution may reach, and when an attitude or a value is given, we can assume that there are only a few different starting-points from which such a result might have been reached. As long as the attitudes of the individual are unsettled and unorganized, as in the child, a new attitude can be developed out of a pre-existing one in many ways, because the individual is open to many and various influences; there is in him little to interfere with a given influence. This gives, of course, many opportunities to educational endeavors tending to produce certain values; and for the same reason a determined influence exercised upon the child may open the way to almost any line of genesis and lead to any new ultimate results. On the contrary, when the individual has acquired a more or less rich stock of stabilized attitudes, a certain influence may not be accepted because in disagreement with this stock. Therefore the way in which a given new attitude can develop is limited, and it may be difficult, sometimes even practically impossible, to produce it because the necessary influences to which the individual would react in the desired way may not be available. Thus the stabilization of individual attitudes diminishes the probability that his future development will assume an unforeseen direction.

And there is a further limitation of the possible lines of genesis in the stability and limited variety of external conditions. First of all there is a general negative limitation of external influences by the fact that the milieu in which the individual lives includes only a limited variety of values. But much more important is the positive limitation of evolution which society imposes upon the individual by putting him into a determined frame of organized activities which involves in advance a general succession of influences—early family education, beginning of a definite career with determined openings, marriage, etc.—establishes a regularity of periodical alternations of work and play, food and sleep, etc., and with the help of economic, legal and moral sanctions prescribes and excludes certain forms of behavior. The more uniform and steady this frame, the greater the relative parallelism of evolution between individuals; similar lines of genesis repeat themselves in many members of the group, for the individual cannot find around him influences which would make him take a course different from other members of the group in acquiring a new attitude. Of course this means also a limitation of the variety of possible attitudes or values that can develop from a given starting-point; given a certain material in the form of an individual disposition or of a social value, it is probable that the group will make of it something very definite, and the same in every case, particularly where the social framework is little varied and flexible.

Still more extensive uniformities of development are found in connection with temperament and character. Not only single attitudes or values but wide and organized groups of attitudes and groups of values are found developing in a similar way in many personalities and certain of these organized groups assume such prevalence in personal life that the individual taken in his entire evolution may be approximately characterized by the prominence of a few such groups. *Temperament* and *character* are the concepts in which has been expressed the common-sense realization that there are always a few organized groups of attitudes in a personality which pay a predominant part in its activity, so that for practical purposes any attitudes outside of those groups can be neglected as inconspicuously manifesting themselves in personal behavior. The concept of individual *life-organization* may be used to indicate the existence, within the sphere of experience of an individual, of a limited number of selected and organized groups of social values which play a predominant part in his life both as partial causes and partial effects of his more or less organized attitudes.

We must here investigate the methodological significance of these concepts and attempt to give them more exact and more productive meanings than those they have had in popular psychology and in half-literary reflection about human life. It must be remembered in particular that the fundamental problems of the synthesis of human personalities are not problems of a personal *status* but problems of personal *becoming*, that the ultimate question is not what temperaments and characters there are but what are the ways in which a definite character is developed out of a definite temperament, not what life-organizations exist but by what means a certain life-organization is developed. It is relatively easy to classify temperaments and characters, but this classification is entirely unproductive unless it is used as a mere preparation for the study of their evolution, where the aim is to determine human types as *dynamic* types, as types of development. Similarly with regard to personal life-organization, we find in any society ready models of organization with which individuals are expected to comply; but the analysis of these models does not constitute a study of personalities—it is merely its starting-point. After learning what models the group proposes to its members, we must learn by what typical means those members gradually realize or fail to realize these models. In other words, the concepts of temperament, character, life-organization mark only the starting-point and the limit of the evolution which is the real object-matter of the study of human personalities. It becomes, therefore, a point of essential importance to frame definitions of temperament, character and life-organization which may be used in the study of personal evolution.

We may call temperament the fundamental original group of attitudes of the individual as existing independently of any social influences; we may call character the set of organized and fixed groups of attitudes developed by social influences operating upon the temperamental basis. The temperamental attitudes are essentially instinctive, that is, they express themselves in biological action but not in reflective consciousness; the attitudes of the character are intellectual, that is, they are given by conscious reflection. This does not mean that the temperamental attitude cannot be experienced; it usually is experienced when for some reason the activity is inhibited. But with the temperamental attitude there is no conscious connection between the separate actions in which it expresses itself; every single feeling and satisfaction (e.g., hunger), is for the individual a separate entity; the living being does not generalize these feelings as forming one series, one permanent attitude. On the contrary, every manifestation of a character-attitude is given to the subject as a single expression of a more or less general tendency; a helpful or harmful action is accompanied by a consciousness of sympathy or hate, that is, by a conscious tendency to the repetition (or remembrance) of actions with an analogous meaning; the attitude accompanying the actual production of some piece of work is given as one element of a series that may be willingness or unwillingness to do such work, desire to realize a plan, to earn money, etc. This consciousness need not be always explicit, but it must be implicitly present and become explicit from time to time if the attitude is to be defined as a character-attitude.

Correspondingly, the temperamental attitudes are not systematically organized and co-ordinated among themselves in the whole course of personal life but are only associated with each other by being repeatedly used together for the production of certain common results in certain conditions provided by the organism and its environment. If a certain group of temperamental attitudes reappears from case to case in such activities as the satisfaction of hunger or of the sexual appetite, it is not because these attitudes have been consciously subordinated to a predominant attitude, but because their association has habitually brought the desired result in the given conditions. And, on the other hand, there is no conscious tendency to establish harmony and to avoid contradictions between separate groups of temperamental attitudes manifested at various moments of individual life. A group of temperamental attitudes either finds its expression at a given moment by pushing others aside, or is pushed aside by some other group and is not expressed at all. Thus, hunger and sexual desire, fear and anger manifest themselves independently of each other without any conscious attempt at co-ordination. In character, on the contrary, attitudes are more or less systematized; their continuity through many manifestations makes this indispensable. Thus, hunger or sexual desire becomes a permanent basis of a conscious and systematic organization of a large group of economic, social, hedonistic, intellectual, aesthetic attitudes, and this organization works continuously, independently of the actual association of these attitudes from case to case; the attitudes organized for the permanent satisfaction of hunger or sexual desire manifest themselves even while no hunger or sexual desire is actually felt and while the actual material conditions do not suggest them in any way. Moreover, between the system of attitudes subordinated to hunger and the system of attitudes subordinated to sexual desire, between a general policy of prudence having the attitude of fear as its basis and a general system of aggressive tendencies rooted ultimately in the attitude of anger, permanent relations are usually established, either by subordinating the conflicting attitudes to some more general attitude—desire for happiness, for social success, etc.—or by giving priority to one of them.

These differences between temperament and character find their expression on the objective side in matters of life-organization. But in order to understand this side of the question we must get rid of the whole schematic conception of the world assimilated from common-sense reflection and from science. We must put ourselves in the position of the subject who tries to find his way in this world, and we must remember, first of all, that the environment by which he is influenced and to which he adapts himself, is *his* world, not the objective world of science—is nature and society as he sees them, not as the scientist sees them. The individual subject reacts only to his experience, and his experience is not everything that an absolutely objective observer might find in the portion of the world within the individual's reach, but only what the individual himself finds. And what he finds depends upon his practical attitudes toward his environment, the demands he makes upon it and his control over it, the wishes he seeks to satisfy and the way in which he tries to satisfy them. His world thus widens with the development of his demands and his means of control, and the process of this widening involves two essential phases—the introduction of new complexities of data into the sphere of his experience and the definition of new situations within those complexities.

The first phase is characterized by an essential vagueness. The situation is quite undetermined; even if there are already in the individual wishes which will give significance to the new data, they are not sufficiently determined with regard to these data, and the complexity is not ordered, values are not outlined, their relations are not established. In the second phase the situation becomes definite, the wish is crystallized and objectified, and the individual begins to control his new experience. Now, the sphere of experience in which new situations can be defined by the temperament alone does not include social life at all. It includes only internal organic processes and such external experiences as are directly connected with the satisfaction of organic needs and the avoidance of physical danger. Of course this sphere is also continually extended, chiefly during the period between birth and maturity, and its extension, as we know from observation and from direct consciousness of such processes as the development and satisfaction of sexual instincts, has also the two periods of vague perception of a chaos of new data and gradual definition of new situations. But all the material with which the temperament deals has one essential limitation: it includes only natural objects, whose significance for the individual is determined by their sensual content. Meanwhile the social values are significant as much or more because of the meaning they have for other individuals or for the group. For example, a material object outside of social life and in relation to organic needs may be significant on account of its sensual qualities, as food, as shelter, as source of possible pain, etc. In social life it acquires through its meaning for others ideal qualities which make it an economic value (object of exchange), a source of vanity, a weapon in a fight for some other value, etc. A word outside of social life is a mere sound, perhaps helping to foresee possible danger or satisfaction; in social life it has a meaning, it points to experiences common to many individuals and known as common by all of them. A painting as natural object is a piece of canvas with colors, perhaps suggesting by association the things represented; in social life it has a new meaning; it stands for the ideas and emotions of the painter himself, the critics, the crowd of observers, etc. An individual of the other sex is naturally chiefly a body, object of physical satisfaction; socially it is also a conscious being with an experience of its own and a personality which has to be adapted to the subject's own personality or to which the subject has to adapt himself. And so on. This is why social psychology, while rejecting the old conception of individual consciousness as closed receptacle or series of conscious data or happenings, cannot accept as its methodological basis the principles recently developed by the behavioristic school. The behavior of an individual as social personality is not scientifically reducible to sensually observable movements and cannot be explained on the ground of the direct experience of the observing psychologist; the movements (including words) must be interpreted in terms of intentions, desires, emotions, etc.—in a word, in terms of attitudes—and the explanation of any particular act of personal behavior must be sought on the ground of the experience of the behaving individual which the observer has indirectly to reconstruct by way of conclusions from what is directly given to him. We cannot neglect the meanings, the suggestions which objects have for the conscious individual, because it is these meanings which determine the individual's behavior; and we cannot explain these meanings as mere abbreviations of the individual's past acts of biological adaptation to his material environment—as manifestations of organic memory—because the meanings to which he reacts are not only those which material things have assumed for him as a result of his own past organic activities, but also those which these things have acquired long ago in society and which the individual is taught to understand during his whole education as conscious member of a social group.

The biological being and his behavior represent therefore nothing but the limit dividing natural from social life; the individual is an object-matter of social psychology only in so far as his activities are above this limit, imply on his part a conscious realization of existing social meanings and require from the scientist an indirect reconstruction of his attitudes. Therefore this limit itself must be defined by social psychology in terms of attitudes, and the concept of temperamental attitudes serves precisely this purpose. An individual with nothing but his biological formation, or—in social terms—with nothing but his temperamental attitudes, is not yet a social personality, but is able to become one. In the face of the world of social meanings he stands powerless; he is not even conscious of the existence of this reality, and when the latter manifests itself to him in changes of the material reality upon which his instincts bear, he is quite lost and either passively submits to the unexpected, or aimlessly revolts. Such is the position of the animal or the infant in human society; and a similar phenomenon repeats itself on a smaller scale whenever an individual on a low level of civilization gets in touch with a higher civilized environment, a worldling with a body of specialists, a foreigner with an autochthonic society, etc. In fact, human beings for the most part never suspect the existence of innumerable meanings—scientific, artistic, moral, political, economic—and a field of social reality whose meanings the individual does not know, even if he can observe its sensual contents, is as much out of the reach of his practical experience as the other side of the moon.

In order to become a social personality in any domain the individual must therefore not only realize the existence of the social meanings which objects possess in this domain, but also learn how to adapt himself to the demands which society puts upon him from the standpoint of these meanings and how to control these meanings for his personal purposes; and since meanings imply conscious thought, he must do this by conscious reflection, not by mere instinctive adaptations of reflexes. In order to satisfy the social demands put upon his personality he must reflectively organize his temperamental attitudes; in order to obtain the satisfaction of his own demands, he must develop intellectual methods for the control of social reality in place of the instinctive ways which are sufficient to control natural reality. And this effective reorganization of temperamental attitudes leads, as we have seen, to character, while the parallel development of intellectual methods of controlling social reality leads to a life-organization, which is nothing but the totality of these methods at work in the individual's social career.

The practical problem which the individual faces in constructing a life-organization has only in so far a similarity with the problem of biological control of the living being's natural environment as the solution of both implies a certain stabilization of individual experiences, the realization of a certain more or less permanent order within that sphere of reality which the individual controls. But the nature of this stability, of this permanent order, is essentially different in both cases—a difference which has been obliterated by the indistinct use of the term "habit" to indicate any uniformities of behavior. This term should be restricted to the biological field. A habit, inherited or acquired, is the tendency to repeat the same act in similar material conditions. The stabilization reached through habit involves no conscious, purposeful regulation of new experiences, but merely the tendency to find in new experiences old elements which will enable the living being to react to them in an old way. This tendency is unreflective; reflection arises only when there is disappointment, when new experiences cannot be practically assimilated to the old ones. But this form of stability can work only when the reality to which the individual has to adjust is entirely constituted by sensually given contents and relations. It is evidently insufficient when he has to take social meanings into account, interpret his experience not exclusively in terms of his own needs and wishes, but also in terms of the traditions, customs, beliefs, aspirations of his social milieu. Thus the introduction of any stable order into experience requires continual reflection, for it is impossible even to realize whether a certain experience is socially new or old without consciously interpreting the given content—an object, a movement, a word—and realizing what social meaning it possesses. However stable a social milieu may be, its stability can never be compared with that of a physical milieu; social situations never spontaneously repeat themselves, every situation is more or less new, for every one includes new human activities differently combined. The individual does not find passively ready situations exactly similar to past situations; he must consciously define every situation as similar to certain past situations, if he wants to apply to it the same solution applied to those situations. And this is what society expects him to do when it requires of him a stable life-organization; it does not want him to react instinctively in the same way to the same material conditions, but to construct reflectively similar social situations even if material conditions vary. The uniformity of behavior it tends to impose upon the individual is not a uniformity of organic habits but of consciously followed *rules*. The individual, in order to control social reality for his needs, must develop not series of uniform reactions, but general *schemes* of situations; his life-organization is a set of rules for definite situations, which may be even expressed in abstract formulas. Moral principles, legal prescription, economic forms, religious rites, social customs, etc., are examples of schemes.

The definiteness of attitudes attained in character and the corresponding schematization of social data in life-organization admit, however, a wide scale of gradation with regard to one point of fundamental importance—the range of possibilities of further development remaining open to the individual after the stabilization. This depends on the nature of the attitudes involved in the character and of the schemes of life-organization, and also on the way in which both are unified and systematized. And here three typical cases can be distinguished.

The set of attitudes constituting the character may be such as practically to exclude the development of any new attitude in the given conditions of life, because the reflective attitudes of an individual have attained so great a fixity that he is accessible to only a certain class of influences—those constituting the most permanent part of his social milieu. The only possibilities of evolution then remaining open to the individual are the slow changes brought by age in himself and by time in his social milieu, or a change of conditions so radical as to destroy at once the values to whose influence he was adapted and presumably his own character. This is the type which has found its expression in literature as the "Philistine." It is opposed to the "Bohemian," whose possibilities of evolution are not closed, simply because his character remains unformed. Some of his temperamental attitudes are in their primary form, others may have become intellectualized but remain unrelated to each other, do not constitute a stable and systematized set, and do not exclude any new attitude, so that the individual remains open to any and all influences. As opposed to both these types we find the third type of the individual whose character is settled and organized but involves the possibility and even the necessity of evolution, because the reflective attitudes constituting it include a tendency to change, regulated by plans of productive activity, and the individual remains open to such influences as will be in line of his preconceived development. This is the type of the creative individual.

A parallel distinction must be made with regard to the schemes of social situations constituting the life-organization. The ability to define every situation which the individual meets in his experience is not necessarily a proof of intellectual superiority; it may mean simply a limitation of claims and interests and a stability of external conditions which do not allow any radically new situations to be noticed, so that a few narrow schemes are sufficient to lead the individual through life, simply because he does not see problems on his way which demand new schemes. This type of schemes constitutes the common stock of social traditions in which every class of situation is defined in the same way once and forever. These schemes harmonize perfectly with the Philistine's character and therefore the Philistine is always a conformist, usually accepting social tradition in its most stable elements. Of course every important and unexpected change in the conditions of life results for such an individual in a disorganization of activity. As long as he can he still applies the old schemes, and up to a certain point his old definition of new situations may be sufficient to allow him to satisfy his claims if the latter are low, although he cannot compete with those who have higher claims and more efficient schemes. But as soon as the results of his activity become unsuccessful even in his own eyes, he is entirely lost; the situation becomes for him completely vague and undetermined, he is ready to accept any definition that may be suggested to him and is unable to keep any permanent line of activity. This is the case with any conservative and intellectually limited member of a stable community, whatever may be his social class, when he finds himself transferred into another community or when his own group undergoes some rapid and sudden change.

Opposed to this type we find an undetermined variation of schemes in the life of all the numerous species of the Bohemian. The choice of the scheme by a Bohemian depends on his momentary standpoint, and this may be determined either by some outburst of a primary temperamental attitude or by some isolated character-attitude which makes him subject to some indiscriminately accepted influence. In either case inconsistency is the essential feature of his activity. But on the other hand he shows a degree of adaptability to new conditions quite in contrast with the Philistine, though his adaptability is only provisional and does not lead to a new systematic life-organization.

But adaptability to new situations and diversity of interest are even compatible with a consistency of activity superior to that which tradition can give if the individual builds his life-organization not upon the presumption of the immutability of his sphere of social values, but upon the tendency to modify and to enlarge it according to some definite aims. These may be purely intellectual or aesthetic, and in this case the individual searches for new situations to be defined simply in order to widen and to perfect his knowledge or his aesthetic interpretation and appreciation; or his aims may be "practical," in any sense of the term—hedonistic, economical, political, moral, religious— and then the individual searches for new situations in order to widen the control of his environment, to adapt to his purposes a continually increasing sphere of social reality. This is the creative man.

The Philistine, the Bohemian and the creative man are the three fundamental forms of personal determination toward which social personalities tend in their evolution. None of these forms is ever completely and absolutely realized by a human individual in all lines of activity; there is no Philistine who lacks completely Bohemian tendencies, no Bohemian who is not a Philistine in certain respects, no creative man who is fully and exclusively creative and does not need some Philistine routine in certain lines to make creation in other lines practically possible, and some Bohemianism in order to be able to reject occasionally such fixed attitudes and social regulations as hinder his progress, even if he should be unable at the time to substitute for them any positive organization in the given line. But while pure Philistinism, pure Bohemianism and pure creativeness represent only ideal limits of personal evolution, the process of personal evolution grows to be more and more definite as it progresses, so that, while the form which a human personality will assume is not determined in advance, either by the individual's temperament or by his social milieu, his future becomes more and more determined by the very course of his development; he approaches more and more to Philistinism, Bohemianism or creativeness and thereby his possibilities of becoming something else continually diminish.

These three general types—limits of personal evolution—include, of course, an indefinite number of variations, depending on the nature of the attitudes by which characters are constituted and on the schemes composing the life-organization of social individuals. If we wished therefore to classify human personalities on the ground of the limits of development to which they tend, our task would be very difficult, if not impossible, for we should have to take characters and life-organizations separately in all their varieties into account. In each of these three fundamental types similar characters may correspond to indefinitely varying life-organizations and similar life-organizations to indefinitely varying characters. But, as we have seen, the problem is to study characters and life-organizations not in their static abstract form, but in their dynamic concrete development. And both character and life-organization—the subjective and the objective side of the personality—develop together. For an attitude can become stabilized as a part of the reflective character only under the influence of a scheme of behavior, and *vice versa*, the construction or acceptance of a scheme demands that an attitude be stabilized as a part of character. Every process of personal evolution consists, therefore, in a complex evolutionary series in which social schemes, acting upon pre-existing attitudes, produce new attitudes in such a way that the latter represent a determination of the temperamental tendencies with regard to the social world, a realization in a conscious form of the character-possibilities which the individual brings with him; and these new attitudes, with their intellectual continuity, acting upon preexisting sets of social values in the sphere of individual experiences produce new values in such a way that every production of a value represents at the same time a definition of some vague situation, and this is a step toward the constitution of some consistent scheme of behavior. In the continual interaction between the individual and his environment we can say neither that the individual is the product of his milieu nor that he produces his milieu; or rather, we can say both. For the individual can indeed develop only under the influence of his environment, but on the other hand during his development he modifies this environment by defining situations and solving them according to his wishes and tendencies. His influence upon the environment may be scarcely noticeable socially, may have little importance for others, but it is important for himself, since, as we have said, the world in which he lives is not the world as society or the scientific observer sees it but as he sees it himself. In various cases we may find various degrees of dependence upon the environment, conditioned by the primary qualities of the individual and the type of social organization. The individual is relatively dependent upon society in his evolution, if he develops mainly such attitudes as lead to dependence, which is then due both to his temperamental dispositions and to the fact that the organization of society is such as to enforce by various means individual subjection; he is relatively independent if in his evolution he develops attitudes producing independence, which again results from certain primary tendencies determined by a social organization which favors individual spontaneity. And thus both dependence and independence are gradual products of an evolution which is due originally to reciprocal interaction; the individual cannot become exclusively dependent upon society without the help of his own disposition, nor become independent of society without the help of social influences. The fundamental principles of personal evolution must be sought therefore both in the individual's own nature and in his social milieu.

## Social Personality   33

We find, indeed, two universal traits manifested in all individual attitudes, instinctive or intellectual, which form the condition of both development and conservatism. In the reflex system of all the higher organisms are two powerful tendencies which in their most distinct and explicit form manifest themselves as curiosity and fear. Without curiosity, that is, an interest in new situations in general, the animal would not live; to neglect the new situation might mean either that he was about to be eaten or that he was missing his chance for food. And fear with its contrary tendency to avoid certain experiences for the sake of security is equally essential to life. To represent these two permanent tendencies as they become parts of character in the course of the social development of a personality we shall use the terms *"desire for new experience"* and *"desire for stability."* These two tendencies in every permanent attitude manifest themselves in the rhythmical form which conscious life assumes in every line. When consciousness embraces only a short span of activities, the rhythm expresses itself in the alternation of single wishes or appetites with repose. The satisfaction of hunger or of sexual desire and the subsequent wish for uninterrupted calm are the most general examples. On a higher level these tendencies manifest themselves with regard to much more complex and longer series of facts. The desire for stability extends to a whole period of regular alternations of activity and rest from which new experiences are relatively excluded; the desire for new experience finds its expression in the break of such a whole line of regulated activities. And the range and complexity of both stability and change may have many degrees. Thus, for example, stability may mean the possibility of a single series of satisfactions of hunger in a certain restaurant, of a week's relation with an individual of the other sex, of a few days' stay in one place during travel, of a certain kind of work in an office; or it may lie in the possibility of such an organization of money-affairs as gives the certainty of always getting food, of a permanent marriage-relation, settling permanently in one place, a life career, etc. And new experience may mean change of restaurant, change of the temporary sexual relation, change of the kind of work within the same office, the resuming of travel, the acquiring of wealth, getting a divorce, developing a Don Juan attitude toward women, change of career or speciality, development of amateur or sporting interests, etc.

On the individual side, then, alternation of the desire for new experience and of the desire for security is the fundamental principle of personal evolution, as including both the development of a character and of a life-organization. On the social side the essential point of this evolution lies in the fact that the individual living in society has to fit into a pre-existing social world, to take part in the hedonistic, economic, political, religious, moral, aesthetic, intellectual activities of the group. For these activities the group has objective *systems,* more or less complex sets of schemes, organized either by traditional association or with a conscious regard to the greatest possible efficiency of the result, but with only a secondary, or even with no interest in the particular desires, abilities and experiences of the individuals who have to perform these activities. The latter feature of the social systems results, of course, from the fact that the systems have to regulate identically the activities of many individuals at once, and that they usually last longer than the period of activity of an individual, passing from generation to generation. The gradual establishment of a determined relation between these systems which constitute together the social organization of the civilized life of a group, and individual character and life-organization in the course of their progressive formation, is the central problem of the social control of personal evolution. And social control—which, when applied to personal evolution, may be called "social education"—manifests itself also in the duality of two opposite tendencies: the tendency to suppress in the course of personal evolution, any attitudes or values which are either directly in disharmony with the existing social organization or seem to be the starting-points of lines of genesis which are expected to lead to socially disharmonious consequences; and the tendency to develop by adequately influencing personal evolution features of character and schemes of situations required by the existing social systems.

There is, of course, no pre-existing harmony whatever between the individual and the social factors of personal evolution, and the fundamental tendencies of the individual are always in some disaccordance with the fundamental tendencies of social control. Personal evolution is always a struggle between the individual and society—a struggle for self-expression on the part of the individual, for his subjection on the part of society—and it is in the total course of this struggle that the personality—not as a static "essence" but as a dynamic, continually evolving set of activities—manifests and constructs itself. The relative degree of the desire for new experience and the desire for stability necessary for and compatible with the progressive incorporation of a personality into a social organization is dependent on the nature of individual interests and of the social systems. Thus, different occupations allow for more or less change, as in the cases of the artist and the factory workman; and a many-sided dilettante needs and can obtain more new experiences than a specialist; single life usually makes more new experiences along certain lines possible and demands less stabilization than married life; political co-operation with the conservative part of a group brings less change than taking part in a revolutionary movement. And in modern society in general there is an increasing tendency to appreciate change, as compared with the appreciation of stability in the ancient and medieval worlds. For every system within a given group and at a certain time there is a maximum and a minimum of change and of stability permissible and required. The widening of this range and the increase of the variety of systems are, of course, favorable to individual self-expression within the socially permitted limits. Thus, the whole process of development of the personality as ruled in various proportions by the desire for new experience and the desire for stability on the individual side, by the tendency to suppress and the tendency to develop personal possibilities on the social side, includes the following parallel and interdependent processes:

(1) Determination of the character on the ground of the temperament;

(2) Constitution of a life-organization which permits a more or less complete objective expression of the various attitudes included in the character;

(3) Adaptation of the character to social demands put upon the personality;

(4) Adaptation of individual life-organization to social organization.

# 3

# RATIONAL CONTROL IN SOCIAL LIFE

ONE OF the most significant features of social evolution is the growing importance which a conscious and rational technique tends to assume in social life. We are less and less ready to let any social processes go on without our active interference and we feel more and more dissatisfied with any active interference based upon a mere whim of an individual or a social body, or upon preconceived philosophical, religious, or moral generalizations.

The marvelous results attained by a rational technique in the sphere of material reality invite us to apply some analogous procedure to social reality. Our success in controlling nature gives us confidence that we shall eventually be able to control the social world in the same measure. Our actual inefficiency in this line is due, not to any fundamental limitation of our reason, but simply to the historical fact that the objective attitude toward social reality is a recent acquisition.

While our realization that nature can be controlled only by treating it as independent of any immediate act of our will or reason is four centuries old, our confidence in "legislation" and

---

Reprinted from *The Polish Peasant in Europe and America* (New York: Alfred A. Knopf, 1927; New York: Dover Publications, 1958), I, 1–20.

in "moral suasion" shows that this idea is not yet generally realized with regard to the social world. But the tendency to rational control is growing in this field also and constitutes at present an insistent demand on the social sciences.

This demand for a rational control results from the increasing rapidity of social evolution. The old forms of control were based upon the assumption of an essential stability of the whole social framework and were effective only in so far as this stability was real. In a stable social organization there is time enough to develop in a purely empirical way, through innumerable experiments and failures, approximately sufficient means of control with regard to the ordinary and frequent social phenomena, while the errors made in treating the uncommon and rare phenomena seldom affect social life in such a manner as to imperil the existence of the group; if they do, then the catastrophe is accepted as incomprehensible and inevitable. Thus—to take an example—the Polish peasant community has developed during many centuries complicated systems of beliefs and rules of behavior sufficient to control social life under ordinary circumstances, and the cohesion of the group and the persistence of its membership are strong enough to withstand passively the influence of eventual extraordinary occurrences, although there is no adequate method of meeting them. And if the crisis is too serious and the old unity or prosperity of the group breaks down, this is usually treated at first as a result of superior forces against which no fight is possible.

But when, owing to the breakdown of the isolation of the group and its contact with a more complex and fluid world, the social evolution becomes more rapid and the crises more frequent and varied, there is no time for the same gradual, empirical, unmethodical elaboration of approximately adequate means of control, and no crisis can be passively borne, but every one must be met in a more or less adequate way, for they are too various and frequent not to imperil social life unless controlled in time. The substitution of a conscious technique for a half-conscious routine has become, therefore, a social necessity, though it is evident that the development of this technique could be only gradual, and that even now we find in it many implicit or explicit ideas and methods corresponding to stages of human thought passed hundreds or even thousands of years ago.

The oldest but most persistent form of social technique is that of "ordering-and-forbidding"—that is, meeting a crisis by an arbitrary act of will decreeing the disappearance of the undesirable or the appearance of the desirable phenomena, and using arbitrary physical action to enforce the decree. This method corresponds exactly to the magical phase of natural technique. In both, the essential means of bringing a determined effect is more or less consciously thought to reside in the act of will itself by which the effect is decreed as desirable and of which the action is merely an indispensable vehicle or instrument; in both, the process by which the cause (act of will and physical action) is supposed to bring its effect to realization remains out of reach of investigation; in both, finally, if the result is not attained, some new act of will with new material accessories is introduced, instead of trying to find and remove the perturbing causes. A good instance of this in the social field is the typical legislative procedure of today.

It frequently happens both in magic and in the ordering-and-forbidding technique that the means by which the act of will is helped are really effective, and thus the result is attained, but, as the process of causation, being unknown, cannot be controlled, the success is always more or less accidental and dependent upon the stability of general conditions; when these are changed, the intended effect fails to appear, the subject is unable to account for the reasons of the failure and can only try by guesswork some other means. And even more frequent than this accidental success is the result that the action brings some effect, but not the desired one.

There is, indeed, one difference between the ordering-and-forbidding technique and magic. In social life an expressed act of will may be sometimes a real cause, when the person or body from which it emanates has a particular authority in the eyes of those to whom the order or prohibition applies. But this does not change the nature of the technique as such. The prestige of rulers, ecclesiastics, and legislators was a condition making an act of will an efficient cause under the old régimes, but it loses its value in the modern partly or completely republican organizations.

A more effective technique, based upon "common sense" and represented by "practical" sociology, has naturally originated in those lines of social action in which there was either no place for legislative measures or in which the *hoc volo, sic jubeo* proved too evidently inefficient—in business, in charity and philanthropy, in diplomacy, in personal association, etc. Here, indeed, the act of will having been recognized as inefficient in directing the causal process, real causes are sought for every phenomenon, and an endeavor is made to control the effects by acting upon the causes, and, though it is often partly successful, many fallacies are implicitly involved in this technique; it has still many characters of a planless empiricism, trying to get at the real cause by a rather haphazard selection of various possibilities, directed only by a rough and popular reflection, and its deficiencies have to be shown and removed if a new and more efficient method of action is to be introduced.

The first of these fallacies has often been exposed. It is the latent or manifest supposition that we know social reality because we live in it, and that we can assume things and relations as certain on the basis of our empirical acquaintance with them. The attitude is here about the same as in the ancient assumption that we know the physical world because we live and act in it, and that therefore we have the right of generalizing without a special and thorough investigation, on the mere basis of "common sense." The history of physical science gives us many good examples of the results to which common sense can lead, such as the geocentric system of astronomy and the mediaeval ideas about motion. And it is easy to show that not even the widest individual acquaintance with social reality, not even the most evident success of individual adaptation to this reality, can offer any serious guaranty of the validity of the common-sense generalizations.

Indeed, the individual's sphere of practical acquaintance with social reality, however vast it may be as compared with that of others, is always limited and constitutes only a small part of the whole complexity of social facts. It usually extends over only one society, often over only one class of this society; this we may call the exterior limitation. In addition there is an interior limitation, still more important, due to the fact that among all the experiences which the individual meets within the sphere of his social life a large, perhaps the larger, part is left unheeded, never becoming a basis of common-sense generalizations. This selection of experiences is the result of individual temperament on the one hand and of individual interest on the other. In any case, whether temperamental inclinations or practical considerations operate, the selection is subjective—that is, valid only for this particular individual in this particular social position—and thereby it is quite different from, and incommensurable with, the selection which a scientist would make in face of the same body of data from an objective, impersonal viewpoint.

Nor is the practical success of the individual within his sphere of activity a guaranty of his knowledge of the relations between the social phenomena which he is able to control. Of course there must be some objective validity in his schemes of social facts—otherwise he could not live in society—but the truth of these schemes is always only a rough approximation and is mixed with an enormous amount of error. When we assume that a successful adaptation of the individual to his environment is a proof that he knows this environment thoroughly, we forget that there are degrees of success, that the standard of success is to a large extent subjective, and that all the standards of success applied in human society may be—and really are—very low, because they make allowance for a very large number of partial failures, each of which denotes one or many errors. Two elements are found in varying proportions in every adaptation; one is the actual control exercised over the environment; the other is the claims which this control serves to satisfy. The adaptation may be perfect, either because of particularly successful and wide control or because of particularly limited claims. Whenever the control within the given range of claims proves insufficient, the individual or the group can either develop a better control or limit the claims.

And, in fact, in every activity the second method, of adaptation by failures, plays a very important rôle. Thus the individual's knowledge of his environment can be considered as real only in the particular matters in which he does actually control it; his schemes can be true only in so far as they are perfectly, absolutely successful. And if we remember how much of practical success is due to mere chance and luck, even this limited number of truths becomes doubtful. Finally, the truths that stand the test of individual practice are always schemes of the concrete and singular, as are the situations in which the individual finds himself.

In this way the acquaintance with social data and the knowledge of social relations which we acquire in practice are always more or less subjective, limited both in number and in generality. Thence comes the well-known fact that the really valuable part of practical wisdom acquired by the individual during his life is incommunicable—cannot be stated in general terms; everyone must acquire it afresh by a kind of apprenticeship to life—that is, by learning to select experiences according to the demands of his own personality and to construct for his own use particular schemes of the concrete situations which he encounters. Thus, all the generalizations constituting the common-sense social theory and based on individual experience are both insignificant and subject to innumerable exceptions. A sociology that accepts them necessarily condemns itself to remain in the same methodological stage, and a practice based upon them must be as insecure and as full of failures as is the activity of every individual.

Whenever, now, this "practical" sociology makes an effort to get above the level of popular generalizations by the study of social reality instead of relying upon individual experience, it still preserves the same method as the individual in his personal reflection; investigation always goes on with an immediate reference to practical aims, and the standards of the desirable and undesirable are the ground upon which theoretic problems are approached. This is the second fallacy of the practical sociology, and the results of work from this standpoint are quite disproportionate to the enormous efforts that have recently been put forth in the collection and elaboration of materials preparatory to social reforms. The example of physical science and material technique should have shown long ago that only a scientific investigation, which is quite free from any dependence on practice, can become practically useful in its applications. Of course this does not mean that the scientist should not select for investigation problems whose solution has actual practical importance; the sociologist may study crime or war as the chemist studies dyestuffs. But from the method of the study itself all practical considerations must be excluded if we want the results to be valid. And this has not yet been realized by practical sociology.

The usual standpoint here is that of an explicit or implicit norm with which reality should comply. The norm may be intrinsic to the reality, as when it is presumed that the actually prevailing traditional or customary state of things is normal; or it may be extrinsic, as when moral, religious, or aesthetic standards are applied to social reality and the prevailing state of things is found in disaccord with the norm, and in so far abnormal. But this difference has no essential importance. In both cases the normal, agreeing with the norm, is supposed to be known either by practical acquaintance or by some particular kind of rational or irrational evidence; the problem is supposed to lie in the abnormal, the disharmony with the norm. In the first case the abnormal is the exceptional, in the second case it is the usual, while the normal constitutes an exception, but the general methods of investigation remains the same.

There is no doubt that the application of norms to reality had a historical merit; investigation was provoked in this way and the "abnormal" became the first object of empirical studies. It is the morally indignant observer of vice and crime and the political idealist-reformer who start positive investigations. But as soon as the investigation is started both indignation and idealism should be put aside. For in treating a certain body of material as representing the normal, another body of material as standing for the abnormal, we introduce at once a division that is necessarily artificial; for if these terms have a meaning it can be determined only on the basis of investigation, and the criterion of normality must be such as to allow us to include in the normal, not only a certain determined stage of social life and a limited class of facts, but also the whole series of different stages through which social life passes, and the whole variety of social phenomena. The definition a priori of a group of facts that we are going to investigate as abnormal has two immediate consequences. First, our attention is turned to such facts as seem the most important practically, as being most conspicuously contrary to the norm and calling most insistently for reform. But the things that are practically important may be quite insignificant theoretically and, on the contrary, those which seem to have no importance from the practical point of view may be the source of important scientific discoveries. The scientific value of a fact depends on its connection with other facts, and in this connection the most commonplace facts are often precisely the most valuable ones, while a fact that strikes the imagination or stirs the moral feeling may be really either isolated or exceptional, or so simple as to involve hardly any problems. Again, by separating the abnormal from the normal we deprive ourselves of the opportunity of studying them in their connection with each other, while only in this connection can their study be fully fruitful. There is no break in continuity between the normal and the abnormal in concrete life that would permit any exact separation of the corresponding bodies of material, and the nature of the normal and the abnormal as determined by theoretic abstraction can be perfectly understood only with the help of comparison.

But there are other consequences of this fallacy. When the norm is not a result but a starting-point of the investigation, as it is in this case, every practical custom or habit, every moral, political, religious view, claims to be *the* norm and to treat as abnormal whatever does not agree with it. The result is harmful both in practice and in theory. In practice, as history shows and as we see at every moment, a social technique based upon pre-existing norms tends to suppress all the social energies which seem to act in a way contrary to the demands of the norm, and to ignore all the social energies not included in the sphere embraced by the norm. This limits still more the practical importance of the technique and often makes it simply harmful instead of useful. In theory, a sociology using norms as its basis deprives itself of the possibility of understanding and controlling any important facts of social evolution. Indeed, every social process of real importance always includes a change of the norms themselves, not alone of the activity embraced by the norms. Traditions and customs, morality and religion, undergo an evolution that is more and more rapid, and it is evident that a sociology proceeding on the assumption that a certain norm is valid and that whatever does not comply with it is abnormal finds itself absolutely helpless when it suddenly realizes that this norm has lost all social significance and that some other norm has appeared in its place. This helplessness is particularly striking in moments of great social crisis when the evolution of norms becomes exceptionally rapid. We notice it, for example, with particular vividness during the present war, when the whole individualistic system of norms elaborated during the last two centuries begins to retreat before a quite different system, which may be a state socialism or something quite new.

The third fallacy of the common-sense sociology is the implicit assumption that any group of social facts can be treated theoretically and practically in an arbitrary isolation from the rest of the life of the given society. This assumption is perhaps unconsciously drawn from the general form of social organization, in which the real isolation of certain groups of facts is a result of the demands of practical life. In any line of organized human activity only actions of a certain kind are used, and it is assumed that only such individuals will take part in this particular organization as are able and willing to perform these actions, and that they will not bring into this sphere of activity any tendencies that may destroy the organization. The factory and the army corps are typical examples of such organizations. The isolation of a group of facts from the rest of social life is here really and practically performed. But exactly in so far as such a system functions in a perfect manner there is no place at all for social science or social practice; the only thing required is a material division and organization of these isolated human actions. The task of social theory and social technique lies outside of these systems; it begins, for example, whenever external tendencies not harmonizing with the organized activities are introduced into the system, when the workmen in the factory start a strike or the soldiers of the army corps a mutiny. Then the isolation disappears; the system enters, through the individuals who are its members, into relation with the whole complexity of social life. And this lack of real isolation, which characterizes a system of organized activity only at moments of crisis, is a permanent feature of all the artificial, abstractly formed groups of facts such as "prostitution," "crime," "education," "war," etc. Every single fact included under these generalizations is connected by innumerable ties with an indefinite number of other facts belonging to various groups, and these relations give to every fact a different character. If we start to study these facts as a whole, without heeding their connection with the rest of the social world, we must necessarily come to quite arbitrary generalizations. If we start to act upon these facts in a uniform way simply because their abstract essence seems to be the same, we must necessarily produce quite different results, varying with the relations of every particular case to the rest of the social world. This does not mean that it is not possible to isolate such groups of facts for theoretic investigation or practical activity, but simply that the isolation must come, not a priori, but a posteriori, in the same way as the distinction between the normal and the abnormal. The facts must first be taken in connection with the whole to which they belong, and the question of a later isolation is a methodological problem.

There are two other fallacies involved to a certain extent in social practice, although practical sociology has already repudiated them. The reason for their persistence in practice is that, even if the erroneousness of the old assumption has been recognized, no new working ideas have been put in their place. These assumptions are: (1) that men react in the same way to the same influences regardless of their individual or social past, and that therefore it is possible to provoke identical behavior in various individuals by identical means; (2) that men develop spontaneously, without external influence, tendencies which enable them to profit in a full and uniform way from given conditions, and that therefore it is sufficient to create favorable or remove unfavorable conditions in order to give birth to or suppress given tendencies.

The assumption of identical reactions to identical influences is found in the most various lines of traditional social activity; the examples of legal practice and of education are sufficient to illustrate it. In the former all the assumptions about the "motives" of the behavior of the parties, all the rules and forms of investigation and examination, all the decisions of the courts, are essentially based upon this principle. Considerations of the variety of traditions, habits, temperaments, etc., enter only incidentally and secondarily, and usually in doubtful cases, by the initiative of the lawyers; they are the result of common-sense psychological observations, but find little if any place in the objective system of laws and rules. And where, as in the American juvenile courts, an attempt is made to base legal practice upon these considerations, all legal apparatus is properly waived, and the whole procedure rests upon the personal qualifications of the judge. In education the same principle is exhibited in the identity of curricula, and is even carried so far as to require identical work from students in connection with the courses they follow, instead of leaving to everyone as much field as possible for personal initiative. Here again the fallaciousness of the principle is corrected only by the efforts of those individual teachers who try to adapt their methods to the personalities of the pupils, using practical tact and individual acquaintance. But as yet no objective principles have been generally substituted for the traditional uniformity.

The assumption of the spontaneous development of tendencies if the material conditions are given is found in the exaggerated importance ascribed by social reformers to changes of material environment and in the easy conclusions drawn from material conditions on the mentality and character of individuals and groups. For example, it is assumed that good housing conditions will create a good family life, that the abolition of saloons will stop drinking, that the organization of a well-endowed institution is all that is necessary to make the public realize its value in practice. To be sure, material conditions do help or hinder to a large extent the development of corresponding lines of behavior, but only if the tendency is already there, for the way in which they will be used depends on the people who use them. The normal way of social action would be to develop the tendency and to create the condition simultaneously, and, if this is impossible, attention should be paid rather to the development of tendencies than to the change of the conditions, because a strong social tendency will always find its expression by modifying the conditions, while the contrary is not true. For example, a perfect family life may exist in a Polish peasant community in conditions which would probably be considered in America as a necessary breeding-place of crime and pauperism, while uncommonly favorable external conditions in the Polish aristocratic class do not hinder a decay of family life. In Southern France and Northern Italy there is less drunkenness with the saloon than in the prohibition states of America. In Russian Poland alone, without a Polish university and with only a private philosophical association, more than twice as much original philosophical literature has been published recently as in Russia with her eleven endowed universities. And innumerable examples could be cited from all departments of social life. But it is easy to understand that in the absence of a science of behavior social reformers pay more attention to the material conditions of the people than to the psychology of the people who live in these conditions; for the conditions are concrete and tangible, and we know how to grasp them and to conceive and realize almost perfect plans of material improvements, while in the absence of a science the reformer has no objective principles on which he can rely, and unconsciously tends to ascribe a preponderating importance to the material side of social life.

And these fallacies of the common-sense sociology are not always due to a lack of theoretic ability or of a serious scientific attitude on the part of the men who do the work. They are the unavoidable consequence of the necessity of meeting actual situations at once. Social life goes on without interruption and has to be controlled at every moment. The business man or politician, the educator or charity-worker, finds himself continually confronted by new social problems which he must solve, however imperfect and provisional he knows his solutions to be, for the stream of evolution does not wait for him. He must have immediate results, and it is a merit on his part if he tries to reconcile the claims of actuality with those of scientific objectivity, as far as they can be reconciled, and endeavors to understand the social reality as well as he can before acting. Certainly social life is improved by even such a control as common-sense sociology is able to give; certainly no effort should be discouraged, for the ultimate balance proves usually favorable. But in social activity, even more than in material activity, the common-sense method is the most wasteful method, and to replace it gradually by a more efficient one will be a good investment.

While, then, there is no doubt that actual situations must be handled immediately, we see that they cannot be solved adequately as long as theoretical reflection has their immediate solution in view. But there is evidently one issue from this dilemma, and it is the same as in material technique and physical science. We must be able to foresee future situations and prepare for them, and we must have in stock a large body of secure and objective knowledge capable of being applied to any situation, whether foreseen or unexpected. This means that we must have an empirical and exact social science ready for eventual application. And such a science can be constituted only if we treat it as an end in itself, not as a means to something else, and if we give it time and opportunity to develop along all the lines of investigation possible, even if we do not see what may be the eventual applications of one or another of its results. The example of physical science and its applications show that the only practically economical way of creating an efficient technique is to create a science independent of any technical limitations and then to take every one of its results and try where and in what way they can be practically applied. The contrary attitude, the refusal to recognize any science that does not work to solve practical problems, in addition to leading to that inefficiency of both science and practice which we have analyzed above, shows a curious narrowness of mental horizon. We do not know what the future science will be before it is constituted and what may be the applications of its discoveries before they are applied; we do not know what will be the future of society and what social problems may arise demanding solution. The only practically justifiable attitude toward science is absolute liberty and disinterested help.

Of course this does not mean that the actual social technique should wait until the science is constituted; such as it is, it is incomparably better than none. But, just as in material technique, as soon as a scientific discovery is at hand an effort should be made to find for it a practical application, and if it can be applied in some particular field a new technique should take the place of the old in this field.

But if no practical aims should be introduced beforehand into scientific investigation, social practice has, nevertheless, the right to demand from social theory that at least some of its results shall be applicable at once, and that the number and importance of such results shall continually increase. As one of the pragmatists has expressed it, practical life can and must give credit to science, but sooner or later science must pay her debts, and the longer the delay the greater the interest required. This demand of ultimate practical applicability is as important for science itself as for practice; it is a test, not only of the practical, but of the theoretical, value of the science. A science whose results can be applied proves thereby that it is really based upon experience, that it is able to grasp a great variety of problems, that its method is really exact—that it is valid. The test of applicability is a salutary responsibility which science must assume in her own interest.

If we attempt now to determine what should be the object-matter and the method of a social theory that would be able to satisfy the demands of modern social practice, it is evident that its main object should be the actual civilized society in its full development and with all its complexity of situations, for it is the control of the actual civilized society that is sought in most endeavors of rational practice. But here, as in every other science, a determined body of material assumes its full significance only if we can use comparison freely, in order to distinguish the essential from the accidental, the simple from the complex, the primary from the derived. And fortunately social life gives us favorable conditions for comparative studies, particularly at the present stage of evolution, in the coexistence of a certain number of civilized societies sufficiently alike in their fundamental cultural problems to make comparison possible, and differing sufficiently in their traditions, customs, and general national spirit to make comparison fruitful. And from the list of these civilized societies we should by no means exclude those non-white societies, like the Chinese, whose organization and attitudes differ profoundly from our own, but which interest us both as social experiments and as situations with which we have to reconcile our own future.

In contrast with this study of the various present civilized societies, the lines along which most of the purely scientific sociological work has been done up to the present—that is, ethnography of primitive societies and social history—have a secondary, though by no means a negligible, importance. Their relation to social practice is only mediate; they can help the practitioner to solve actual cultural problems only to the degree that they help the scientist to understand actual cultural life; they are auxiliary, and their own scientific value will increase with the progress of the main sphere of studies. In all the endeavors to understand and interpret the past and the savage we must use, consciously or not, our knowledge of our civilized present life, which remains always a basis of comparison, whether the past and the primitive are conceived as analogous with, or as different from, the present and the civilized. The less objective and critical our knowledge of the present, the more subjective and unmethodical is our interpretation of the past and the primitive; unable to see the relative and limited character of the culture within which we live, we unconsciously bend every unfamiliar phenomenon to the limitations of our own social personality. A really objective understanding of history and ethnography can therefore be expected only as a result of a methodical knowledge of present cultural societies.

Another point to be emphasized with regard to the question of the object-matter of social theory is the necessity of taking into account the whole life of a given society instead of arbitrarily selecting and isolating beforehand certain particular groups of facts. We have seen already that the contrary procedure constitutes one of the fallacies of the common-sense sociology. It is also a fallacy usually committed by the observers of their own or of other societies—litterateurs, journalists, travelers, popular psychologists, etc. In describing a given society they pick out the most prominent situations, the most evident problems, thinking to characterize thereby the life of the given group. Still more harmful for the development of science is this fallacy when used in the comparative sociology which studies an institution, an idea, a myth, a legal or moral norm, a form of art, etc., by simply comparing its content in various societies without studying it in the whole meaning which it has in a particular society and then comparing this with the whole meaning which it has in the various societies. We are all more or less guilty of this fault, but it pleases us to attribute it mainly to Herbert Spencer.

In order to avoid arbitrary limitations and subjective interpretations there are only two possible courses open. We can study monographically whole concrete societies with the total complexity of problems and situations which constitute their cultural life; or we can work on special social problems, following the problem in a certain limited number of concrete social groups and studying it in every group with regard to the particular form which it assumes under the influence of the conditions prevailing in this society, taking into account the complex meaning which a concrete cultural phenomenon has in a determined cultural environment. In studying the society we go from the whole social context to the problem, and in studying the problem we go from the problem to the whole social context. And in both types of work the only safe method is to start with the assumption that we know absolutely nothing about the group or the problem we are to investigate except such purely formal criteria as enable us to distinguish materials belonging to our sphere of interest from those which do not belong there. But this attitude of indiscriminate receptivity toward any concrete data should mark only the first stage of investigation—that of limiting the field. As soon as we become acquainted with the materials we begin to select them with the help of criteria which involve certain methodological generalizations and scientific hypotheses. This must be done, since the whole empirical concreteness cannot be introduced into science, cannot be described or explained. We have to limit ourselves to certain theoretically important data, but we must know how to distinguish the data which are important. And every further step of the investigation will bring with it new methodological problems—analysis of the complete concrete data into elements, systematization of these elements, definition of social facts, establishing of social laws. All these stages of scientific procedure must be exactly and carefully defined if social theory is to become a science conscious of its own methods and able to apply them with precision, as is the case with the more mature and advanced physical and biological sciences. And it is always the question of an ultimate practical applicability which, according to our previous discussion, will constitute the criterion—the only secure and intrinsic criterion—of a science.

# II. Social Organization: Institutional Analysis

# 4

# THE PRIMARY GROUP

THE PRIMARY-GROUP is found not only in savage societies and among European peasants; it is not a survival of the past, but a spontaneous institution, found in all societies, in all classes, on all stages of cultural development, sometimes more, sometimes less isolated from the more complex and rational social systems, seldom, if ever, completely absorbing the interests of its members, but still constituting the most important form of social life for the immense majority of mankind. We must realize that only in a few large cities scattered over the world the primary-group has lost its importance, and even there this loss begins to be felt as a rather dangerous effect of social evolution, as is shown by the recent attempts to reconstruct the community in American cities. Of course, the relative influence of the primary-group as compared with the higher forms of social organization is stronger in the case of the savage than in that of the peasant, stronger in the case of the peasant than in that of a half intellectual inhabitant of a provincial town, and is reduced to a minimum in the life of a business man in a large city, of a politician, a scientist, an artist; but it is still only a matter of degree. Innumerable human interests all through the world are still on a stage where their pursuit is chiefly dependent on the direct social response and recognition of the

---

Reprinted from *The Polish Peasant in Europe and America* (New York: Alfred A. Knopf, 1927; New York: Dover Publications, 1958), II, 1118–21.

primary-group which constitutes the individual's immediate environment. It is therefore most important, both for theoretic and for practical purposes, to study the social process by which these interests become independent, economic, political, moral, intellectual, religious, aesthetic aims, pursued for their own sake, and social groups become rationally organized for the purpose of an efficient common pursuit of these aims. Our civilization, when taken not only in its highest manifestations but in its totality, is still in the midst of the same process of change which began half a century ago among the Polish peasants; it is on the average much more advanced, much more distant from the exclusive predominance of the primary-group type, but it is still very far from a thoroughgoing teleological systematization of values and a rational control of attitudes.

The evolution of the Polish peasant has with reference to this problem the specific importance of a social experiment in which certain essential processes are given in a relatively simple and isolated form—not merged in such a complexity of interfering phenomena as similar processes occurring in culturally more productive classes or in cultural centers with a more heterogeneous population, a richer stock of traditions, a more intense economic, political, intellectual life. We have even found that a further limitation of our subject in time and space was indispensable for methodical purposes. We are actually taking into account only a period of twenty to twenty-five years—the end of the nineteenth and the beginning of the twentieth centuries—and, except for certain important points where we use for comparison data collected in Posen under German domination, our materials are territorially limited to what was before the War Russian Poland, and in particular to that part of it which formed a separate administrative unit since the Congress of Vienna and was known as the Congress Kingdom.

During the period and in the territories which we are taking into account, the social evolution of the peasants went on, of course, in continual interaction with the wider social milieu with which the peasant community was getting more closely in touch. The gradual disappearance of the old isolation of these communities, the growing participation of the peasant in nation-wide and even world-wide social processes, his slow but progressive incorporation into Polish national and general human civilization, constitute the most essential features of this evolution. If we could leave out of consideration the dependence of the community on the state as manifested in tax paying, military service and criminal prosecution, and ignore the few outside elements which the country nobleman, the priest, the merchant brought into community life, we might say that some 50 to 75 years ago a large part of the peasant communities in Poland were almost entirely self-sufficient. Their social organization, their intellectual and religious life, their economic activities would have been immediately very little affected if the rest of humanity had suddenly progressed or regressed two thousand years. Of course, there had been a continual infiltration of outside influences, particularly due to the contact with the higher classes; but this infiltration was so slow that the social values, though imperceptibly changing and broadening the content of social life, were completely assimilated by the community without requiring any reflective and planful adaptation and readjustment, without calling for institutional organization of the relations between the community and its wider social environment. All organization which existed within the community was exclusively concerned with the internal life of the latter and ignored the social world outside of its limits.

Under these conditions, the first result of the growing connection between the community and the outside world is naturally a more or less far-going process of disorganization; new attitudes develop in the members of the group which cannot be adequately controlled by the old social organization because they cannot find an adequate expression in the old primary-group institutions. The group tries to defend itself against this disorganization by methods consciously tending to strengthen the influence of the traditional rules of behavior; but this endeavor, often efficient as long as the outside contacts remain limited to some particular field of interests, loses more and more of its effectiveness when these contacts continue to develop and extend gradually to all fields of social activity. The problem is then no longer how to suppress the new attitudes, but how to find for them institutional expression, how to utilize them for socially productive purposes, instead of permitting them to remain in a status where they express themselves merely in individual revolt and social revolution.

This problem is evidently common to all societies in periods of rapid change. We find it in a savage group brought in contact with western civilization, and in the most extensive and highly complicated modern national group where the rapid growth of new attitudes is no longer the effect of external influences but of the internal complexity of social activities. But in the case of the peasant community the solution of this problem is much easier than in the case of the savage group or in that of a whole complex national society. For the peasant community, however much isolated socially from its immediate environment, is territorially an integral part of a wider modern political unit, and the peasant class belongs culturally to a race whose upper strata have already produced a full national civilization.

# 5

# FAMILY AND COMMUNITY

IN THE first volume of this work we have studied the traditional primary-group organization of the Polish peasant as it has been handed down to the present generation from many past centuries. We noticed that this organization has been rapidly changing during the last fifty years, so that there is probably not a single peasant community where it could be found in a pure and unmixed form; everywhere new types are combined with it. We shall presently follow the life-history of an individual who, living amidst this process of change, finds in his environment no place for himself, for his fundamental attitudes correspond entirely to the old type of social organization whereas by his social status he no longer belongs to this organization and is thrown without any permanent guidance into various new conditions to which he can adapt himself always only partially and imperfectly.

We shall now try to determine in detail those new types of social organization which substitute themselves for the old ones, and investigate the process by which this substitution occurs. Although limited to the Polish peasant, our investigation will endeavor to reach conclusions which may serve as hypothetical general sociological laws, to be verified by a comparison with other societies. For the specific evolution leading from the pri-

---

Reprinted from *The Polish Peasant in Europe and America* (New York: Alfred A. Knopf, 1927; New York: Dover Publications, 1958), II, 1117, 1134–40, 1167–77.

mary-group to a social organization based upon rational cooperation is a very general phenomenon. . . .

## Disorganization of the Family

We have met in our first three volumes many cases of partial family disorganization. We did not attempt there to explain them completely but limited ourselves to a few general indications of their probable factors. In none of these cases did disorganization go farther than a loss of active solidarity and sometimes quarrelling. This is, of course, the usual situation; our materials represented an average picture of peasant life. Perhaps they even showed more disorganization than is found on the average among Polish peasants, since they were selected from letters written by emigrants and to emigrants, and wherever there is emigration, dissolution of the family is progressing more rapidly than in groups whose members remain territorially united and live in the same conditions as their forefathers did. In fact, even a rapid survey of the materials published in the preceding volumes shows clearly that emigration of individual family members abroad and emigration of whole families from the country to the city are the two main factors of familial disorganization. But it is evident that this generalization is too vague and superficial to be anything more than a starting-point of scientific research. Change of conditions is a factor, but not a cause of social happenings; it merely furnishes influences which will produce definite effects only when combined with definite preexisting attitudes and is a cause only together with the latter. In individual emigration and in changes from country to city life certain new attitudes are produced by new social values acting in combination with certain preexisting attitudes and these new attitudes are the ultimate social realities which underlie family disorganization and which we must determine and explain causally. But these new attitudes often fail to appear in spite of changed conditions, and other attitudes, which do not undermine family life but only modify its form, may appear instead; on the

## Family and Community 63

other hand, attitudes which are back of family disorganization appear not only in individuals and families that have moved to the city or abroad, but also in many of those who are still living in the country, in their old communities, so that influences similar to those which affect family life in the city or abroad must be also active in country communities. The fact that family disorganization is less general in the latter than among individuals and families living outside of their primary social milieu admits two different explanations—either the influences which, in connection with certain preexisting attitudes, produce disorganization are less widely spread and less continuous in old country communities than in cities or foreign milieux, or the process of disorganization is there more efficiently counteracted by efforts of social organization. As a matter of fact, the two reasons coexist in various proportions.

The cases which we shall analyze show disorganization either verging on or passing into crime. Such cases are, of course, relatively rare. We have had almost none in the preceding three volumes; it must be added that we could hardly expect to receive any such data when collecting documents directly from the authors or the relatives of the authors. A large quantity of criminological materials is contained in some popular newspapers. This is due to the social function of the popular newspaper destined particularly for the peasant class. The peasant newspaper is a concrete bond unifying all the peasant communities throughout the country and creating a nation-wide peasant social opinion partly by imitating, partly by modifying the type of social opinion found in the primary community. It has regular or occasional peasant correspondents in every community who describe whatever things and events they consider important. As everybody knows, nothing stirs a primary group so much as a crime, precisely because of its social abnormality. It is not strange, therefore, that crimes constituted, particularly during the early period of the development of the peasant press, the main content of the informing letters which an editor received from his peasant correspondents. He had to publish them, for the peasant press in the beginning was forced to adapt itself to the attitudes of its public in order to obtain an influence which would permit it gradually to modify these attitudes. Thus, in the Congress Kingdom, only after 25 years of intense development some peasant newspapers could stop publishing news about crimes; this coincided with the constitutional evolution of 1905 and the following years, which gave some freedom of political activities and, by partly removing the prohibition of writing about political matters, permitted the popular newspaper to offer a more constructive material to the curiosity of its readers.

The data contained in popular newspapers are, of course, not very detailed, but this disadvantage is partly offset by the fact that they have been furnished by peasant members of the respective communities and thus every fact is described as seen by the community itself, not by an outside observer.

When the father keeps the farm and has 8 children, then he has bread enough, and moreover beautiful horses, cattle and model farming. But this cannot last for ever, for when the children grow up, the father thinks how to give them dowry. And when the time comes, he gives some 500 roubles to one child; for another he has perhaps only 100 or 200 roubles, so he borrows money and gives the dowry to this daughter and son, and the rest of the children remain at home. And so, when death comes and orders him to go to eternity, he leaves perhaps four or five children at home. They have everything in the granary and barn; quite enough. Then they begin to farm [in a new way]. One takes some sheaves from the barn secretly, before the second; the second snatches a bushel or two of corn from the brother, the brother snatches anything else before the sister and so the farming goes on in a way that is painful to see. One brother keeps a hog, the other brother keeps a second hog, the third brother keeps a foal, the sister keeps some chickens and geese for herself and so: "This is mine, and that is yours." And then they sell this "their own" and give the money away to Jews for German clothes, hats, watches. But when it becomes necessary to repair anything in the farm outfit, a cart, a plow, a harrow, then [everybody says]: "I am not the farm-owner." When the village-elder comes for taxes, Bartek sends him to Maciek, Maciek to Paweł or Gaweł, etc. At last the elder sees that he will not come to the end, and he levies on the farmstock, takes a horse or a cow. Then the farm-owner must show himself and pay...[1]

[1] Letter from the archives of the newspaper *Gazeta Świąteczna;* unpublished.

In the foregoing the writer is evidently describing a typical situation, not a particular case. Such cases occur almost regularly now when the parents die and the children are left together. If the mother is alive, her presence acts as a check on the process of disorganization; even if she is not the real manager of the farm, she is at least a bond keeping the group unified and solidary. When mother or even father is alive, there may be incipient or partial disorganization; only the latter is counterbalanced in its manifestations by other attitudes.

The situation here is very clear and very instructive. Disorganization is limited to the economic field alone. It consists in a decay of the institution of economic family solidarity which consisted in an actual (though never abstractly formulated) common ownership of property and common use of income. Here property is still common though individual members do not show as much interest in it as each would if it were his personal property, which is a sure sign of the decay of the spirit of communism that in its original unreflective form implies no conscious separation of individual and social interest. In the matter of income we find a complete individualization; every member tries to set aside as "his own" as large a part of the common income as possible. Under the old family system the normal tendency of the peasant was to have as many goods as possible pass from a lower to a higher economic category, to turn all property into land and as much as possible of income into property, whereas here the tendency is just the opposite: goods which would normally be classed as property (farm-stock) are treated as income, *i.e.*, are sold and the money used for personal expenses.

The fundamental attitudes back of this social disorganization are *new personal needs*. The personal character of these needs is due to the fact that they either are *hedonistic*—the individual wants pleasures which he cannot share directly with others without diminishing his own part, such as new and more varied kinds of food, alcoholic drinks, tobacco, etc., or consist in a demand for social recognition based no longer on the importance of the family, but on the individual's "showing off" by fashionable clothes, jewelry, etc. These are then the attitudes whose origin must be explained in order to understand causally this type of family disorganization.

We remember that the process of disorganization of the old peasant social system has come as a result of the breakdown of the isolation of the peasant community. New needs are thus produced by the mere acquaintance with previously unknown values which appeal to certain preexisting attitudes. Thus, the new kinds of food, drinks, tobaccos which are obtained in the neighboring industrial center or during season emigration in Germany, by rousing previously unknown hedonistic reactions, develop a hedonistic tendency, a search for sensual pleasure for its own sake, which in matters of consumption makes the individual disassociate his own interests from those of his family, whereas these interests remained united as long as food was merely to satisfy hunger and restore strength. Perhaps also the mere fact of eating and drinking alone, away from the family group, contributed to the individualization of these needs. In the other type of needs—those developed on the ground of the desire for recognition—the break of community isolation acts in two ways. First, the individual who brings with him from the city or from abroad new clothes, jewels, etc., experiences recognition within the community (mixed in the beginning usually with unfavorable attention) which goes to himself alone, since it is known that his family had no share in obtaining these goods, as they had before wage work developed. The recognition which the individual gets is aesthetic rather than economic and makes his appearance a purely personal matter and not an expression of family wealth. Secondly, the broader the field of the individual's social relations, the less can the family standing be relied upon as means of social recognition; outside of the community, where the individual's family is not known, he has to use ostentatious, external marks of distinction as means of obtaining recognition from strangers. Thus, interest in personal appearance takes more and more the place of the interest in the social rating of the family. . . .

We can now draw certain general conclusions from our data which we shall hypothetically propose as sociological laws, to be verified by the observation of other societies.

1) The real cause of all phenomena of family disorganization is to be sought in the influence of certain new values—new for the subject—such as: new sources of hedonistic satisfaction, new vanity values, new (individualistic) types of economic organization, new forms of sexual appeal. This influence presupposes, of course, not only a contact between the individual and the outside world but also the existence in the individual's personality of certain attitudes which make him respond to these new values—hedonistic aspirations, desire for social recognition, desire for economic security and advance, sexual instinct. The specific phenomenon of family disorganization consists in a definite modification of those preexisting attitudes under the influence of the new values, resulting in the appearance of new, more or less different attitudes. The nature of this modification can be generally characterized in such a way that, while the attitudes which existed under the family system were essentially "we"-attitudes (the individual did not dissociate his hedonistic tendencies, his desires for recognition or economic security, his sexual needs from the tendencies and aspirations of his family group), the new attitudes, produced by the new values acting upon those old attitudes, are essentially "I"-attitudes—the individual's wishes are separated in his consciousness from those of other members of his family. Such an evolution implies that the new values with which the individual gets in touch are individualistic in their meaning, appeal to the individual, not to the group as a whole; and this is precisely the character of most modern hedonistic, sexual, economic, vanity-values. Disorganization of the family as primary group is thus an unavoidable consequence of modern civilization.

2) The appearance of the new individualistic attitudes may be counteracted, like every effect of a given cause, by the effects of other causes; the result is a combination of effects which takes the form of a suppression of the new attitude; the latter is not allowed to remain in full consciousness or to manifest itself in action, but is pushed back into the subconscious. Causes that counteract individualization within the family are chiefly influences of the primary community of which the family is a part. If social opinion favors family solidarity and reacts against any individu-

alistic tendencies, and if the individual keeps in touch with the community, his desire for recognition compels him to accept the standards of the group and to look upon his individualistic tendencies as wrong. But if the community has lost its coherence, if the individual is isolated from it, or if his touch with the outside world make him more or less independent of the opinion of his immediate milieu, there are no social checks important enough to counterbalance disorganization.

3) The *manifestations* of family disorganization in individual behavior are the effects of the subject's attitudes and of the social conditions; these social conditions must be taken, of course, with the meaning which they have for the acting individual himself, not for the outside observer. If the individual finds no obstacles in his family to his new individualistic tendencies, he will express the latter in a normal way; disorganization will consist merely in a loss of family interests, in a social, not anti-social action. If there are obstacles, but disorganization of the primary-group attitudes has gone far enough in the individual to make him feel independent of his family and community, the effect will probably be a break of relations through isolation or emigration. If, however, the individual meets strong opposition and is not sufficiently free from the traditional system to ignore it, hostility and anti-social behavior are bound to follow. In the measure that the struggle progresses, the new attitude of revolt becomes a center around which the entire personality of the individual becomes reorganized, and this includes those of his traditional values which are not dropped, but reinterpreted to fit the new tendency and to give a certain measure of justification to his behavior. In the relatively rare cases where both the new attitude is very strong and the obstacles from the old system are powerfully resented and seem insuperable because the individual is still too much dependent on this system to find some new way out of the situation, the struggle leads to an internal conflict which may find its solution in an attempt to remove the persons by whom the old system is represented in this situation rather than in a complete rejection of the system itself.

4) It is evidently impossible to revive the original family psychology after it has been disintegrated, for the individual who has learned consciously to distinguish and to oppose to one another his own wishes and those of other members of his family group and to consider these wishes as merely personal cannot unlearn it and return to the primary "we"-attitudes. Reorganization of the family is then possible, but on an entirely new basis—that of a moral, reflective co-ordination and harmonization of individual attitudes for the pursuit of common purposes.

## *Disorganization of the Community*

It is difficult to draw an exact dividing line between facts illustrating the disorganization of the community and those showing family decadence, since, as we have seen, the community keeps control over family life and overstepping the principles of the latter means also offending against social opinion. The community is the bearer of all traditions and in view of this the break of tradition in any line by its members may be interpreted as showing a decay of its influence. On the other hand, however, the standards of the community as a whole may evolve and the latter may drop certain traditions while remaining strong and consistent. It is not therefore the preservation or dissolution of any particular rule of behavior which is indicative of the status of a given community, but the question whether there are common rules and how well they are observed. The community is vital when social opinion concerns itself with all matters, outside happenings or individual acts, which possess a public interest, when its attitudes toward these matters are consistent and able to reach approximate unanimity, and when any common action considered necessary to solve the situation as defined by social opinion is carried on in harmonious cooperation. When the community is decaying social opinion degenerates into gossip, that is, instead of being interested in matters of a public character, it becomes absorbed in details of private life. Of course, the criteria of privacy change from epoch to epoch and from group to group, but for any time and for any community it is easy to draw the distinction, for the interest in private happenings as shown in gossip is of an aesthetic rather than practical character, and is not accompanied by the feeling that the community should interfere. Further, the decay of the community shows itself in inconsistency and disharmony of its attitudes; if social opinion hesitates between opposites from moment to moment or if it remains divided on important problems without being able to come to an agreement, much of its vitality is gone. Finally, an equally certain sign of disorganization is the inability to pass from appreciation to action, from common definition to common solution of the situation.

All those phenomena show that the attitudes underlying community life have been modified. In primary-group psychology all interests are fundamentally social and only secondarily economic, intellectual, religious, etc. When the community is in full power, it is more important to have the approval of others in defining and solving any particular situation than to define and solve this situation in a way which may be more successful, more adequate if judged exclusively from the economic, intellectual, religious, even hedonistic point of view. It is not that the individual consciously chooses between social recognition and practical efficiency, between group standards and objective economic, intellectual, religious, hedonistic standards; it is that, dominated by the desire for recognition, he unreflectively considers the way of defining and solving situations by which recognition is obtained the only right way and uncritically refuses to believe that other ways, not sanctioned by social opinion, can be more efficient practically in the long run—refuses to see the validity of any standards than those of his group.

Disorganization of the community starts in fact as soon as its members begin to define situations exclusively as economic, intellectual, religious, hedonistic, not as social, when their need for success—success, of course, as they see it themselves—in any specific line becomes more important subjectively than the need for social recognition—when they dissociate social opinion about a case from the merit of the case.

Thus some disorganization of the community is unavoidable

as soon as the latter gets in touch with the outside world and becomes acquainted with other standards than its own. This incipient disorganization can, however, be in a large measure counteracted if the members of the group have a special interest in maintaining its unity. Up to a certain degree the new tendencies may be simply suppressed. This happens mostly when they are radically opposed to the traditions of the group and, if left free to develop, would be socially destructive. When not distinctly antisocial but merely different from the set of attitudes sanctioned by tradition, the new tendencies are very often, after a period of struggle, simply left outside of the sphere controlled by public opinion, are treated as being of private concern. Thus the more intense and extensive the contact between a community and the outside world, the wider usually becomes the sphere of privacy which its members are allowed to have.

The interest by which members of a primary group are moved to keep the group together in spite of disorganizing external influences is the same general interest which underlies family life, that is, the desire for response, manifesting itself in unreflective social solidarity. Family life is, as we know, the chief means of satisfying the desire for response, whereas the community is the main milieu in which the desire for recognition is satisfied; but the difference is only a difference of degree, and a primary group member wants response from other members of his community, even not belonging to his family, just as he claims from his family recognition in addition to response. Accordingly, social solidarity, *i.e.*, reciprocity of those emotions and acts through which social response is obtained, is expected to bind members of one community in the same way, though not to the same degree, as members of one family. Whatever may be the disorganizing factors which tend to destroy the unanimity of a social group, the latter can struggle victoriously against them and, even while changing the content of its opinion, preserve its coherence as long as it remains socially solidary and its members need each other for emotional response and practical help. Its decadence is definitive only when this unreflective, primary solidarity is broken, and then the only remedy is to reconstruct the community not as a primary group, but as a cooperative organization on the ground of some special egotistic purposes which each individual can better attain for himself if all of them act together.

In short, disorganization of the community includes both 1) decay of social opinion and 2) decay of communal solidarity, and the problem of causal explanation of the respective phenomena implies a) the causal explanation of the attitudes which make the individual neglect the recognition of his community for the sake of other personal aims; b) the causal explanation of the attitudes which make the individual act in antagonism to other members of the community and thus break the communal solidarity; c) the study of the relation between these two types of causal processes.

[From the village Ozarowice in reply to request for a comparison with description of the village published forty years before.]

There is no music and revelry on Sundays as there was none then, forty years ago, but if it happens somewhere occasionally, one cannot notice mothers watching their daughters as carefully as it was written in that paper *Kmiotek* 40 years ago. There is no tavern, thanks to God, but there is sometimes even too much strong drink which kills the body and the soul. It happens that people do not begrudge it to themselves, treat themselves with it up to their ears, particularly the youth who go to hired work. There reigns also card-playing for money. In summer, when you pass through the village, you see sometimes a crowd of people upon the lawn.... Perhaps they read some book or newspaper? Far from it. They play cards so that they whiz in the air, and so they waste the vesper-time till night. I do not except myself; from the example of others I have been accustomed to these stupid cards, but I do not play for money.

And so, alas! things seem to have turned worse here as compared with what was forty years ago. The girls here mostly go under Prussian domination for work. How much they earn there I do not know, nor what is their life there; but everybody will guess what a girl can commit without parental care. Therefore German women laugh that a Polish girl earns more in Prussia than a Polish man. To tell the truth we have here already two such German acquisitions, which girls brought from Prussia to Poland as seeds [as if for propagation purposes].

Forty years ago there were fewer farmers and thus everybody had a more liberal quantity of land than now. Therefore their daughters did not go to Germany to work and were under better supervision of their mothers. And yet even among strangers one can have self-respect, keep one's self from ignominy and not bring shame upon the whole family.[2]

The old folks dress modestly in this locality but the same can not be said of the youth. It is pitiful to see so many girls who as soon as they see a stylish skirt or jacket or bobbed hair worn, by one of the worst kind perhaps, want to dress accordingly, but do not realize that it is shameful and disgraceful for the village youth. There are, I dare say, some good-for-nothing boys who, having donned a pretty, nice looking overcoat or a stylish suit of clothes and shoes, not only would not salute reverently one who wears a peasant's coat, but would not even stop to converse with him. Every one of these profligate boys reflects thus: "I dress better than that one does, I may possess a bigger fortune; then why should I speak to him." Should you visit his home, however, you would never suppose that such a dressy young man lives there, for the house is filled thick with dirt and filth. Such was not the state of affairs in Ostrów years ago. Therefore it is not to be wondered at that Roch Soczewka, during his stay here several years ago, did not find any elegance and reported to the Gazeta that all the inhabitants of Ostrów dress modestly. Today nearly one-half of the girls dress above their means and there are also several who are not worthy of mention.[3]

The common folk in our community are quite discreet and well developed. The youth might be termed a promising one, except that great opportunities for corruption are afforded across the German boundary line. As soon as spring comes every boy, girl and even married women, go across the boundary to seek work and stay there throughout the summer without any protection from evil. They do as they please; consequently the girls return home ruined and corrupted and the boys addicted to drinking.

Their parents are aware of the corruption but they do not mind it as long as their children give them their earnings. Decent girls refuse to go to work the next season because they cannot attend to their religious duties properly, must eat meat on Friday and Saturday, are coaxed into an immoral and indecent life and compelled to work

[2]   *Gazeta Świąteczna*, 1903, 13.
[3]   *Gazeta Świąteczna*, 1893, 5.

until noon on Sunday, etc., etc. Priests plead and beg from the pulpit at every opportunity that parents see to it that their children are morally and religiously reared, but their words have no effect whatever.[4]

Our girls don't know how to dress. When one of them enters the church, the dress rattles upon her. She does not kneel suitably before the holiest Sacrament, only knocks once with her knee, as a mere matter of custom, and does not even think what she is doing, for she is interested in something else: she pushes her companion with her elbow, showing how some other girl is dressed. But I don't speak of all of them; on the contrary, there are in Samorządki modest and good girls and women who can be an example for others.[5]

Some young men, sons of the best known parishioners [in Osiek] came to the Pastoral Mass [on Christmas], stood in the middle of the church, put their hands in their pockets and looked around, and whenever they saw a bald-headed old man or a girl in a hat, they took a handful of peas from their pockets and threw it upon them. ... It was difficult to believe that Christians, Catholics, dared to amuse themselves in such a way in the church....[6]

Among these documents which we have selected to illustrate the disorganization of the peasant community those give us the easiest access to the problem in which the new attitudes of the young generation are described; and at the same time these are perhaps the most typical and have the greatest importance for sociology, since it is everywhere the young generation through which new attitudes mainly penetrate a community and the struggle between social tradition and social novelty always becomes, in some measure at least, identified with the opposition between the old and the young.

If we had to find the most general difference of attitudes underlying this opposition, we should perhaps search for it in the standpoints taken by the individuals toward their personal and social future. Among the members of primary groups the desire for new experience seems to die out much earlier than among

[4]  *Gazeta Świąteczna*, 1892, 11.
[5]  *Gazeta Świąteczna*, 1910, 41.
[6]  *Gazeta Świąteczna*, 1909, 3.

those who lead a more complete, more changing and higher intellectualized life; because of the early developing desire for security and because of the relative stability of external conditions the field of new possibilities which the individual sees in the future narrows rapidly. If the individual is transported to new conditions, this field becomes indefinite, for he does not know how to control the future; but, conscious of this inability, he faces the possible new experience with fear rather than with hopeful expectation. And in view of the great dependence of the primary-group member on his social milieu, it is quite natural that his desire for security should extend to his community and he is as much or more concerned about the stability of the community organization as about that of his economic or family situation, and as much afraid of new possibilities appearing there.

In the new generation, on the contrary, the desire for new experience is always stronger originally than the desire for security and becomes checked only by a social training which limits the field of possible novelties. Even in the most conservative primary-group, where the methods of social control are particularly efficient in producing an early stabilization, the period when new experiences outside of the social routine still have a strong appeal for the individual certainly extends beyond the age of twenty. This means that there is a period of five to ten years during which almost every individual is both open to socially prohibited or unforeseen suggestions and able to act in accordance with these suggestions.

When, therefore, the community enters in contact with the outside world, the youth are naturally the first to develop new attitudes and to import new values. It is evident that under these conditions the movement, if not directed by educated and mature leaders, is not likely to be constructive, since only those attitudes tend to develop and only those values appeal to the individual which he is prepared to accept. The undirected attention of the peasant youth is thus most easily captivated by superficial aesthetic and hedonistic objects—clothes, trinkets, smoking, fancy foods and drinks. Our documents show that the disorganization of the old social system starts in this way. We have also confirmed this while personally investigating the effects of season emigration. Only a small percentage of youth remains uninfluenced by the attraction exercised by foreign dress and foreign pleasures, so that any locality in which this emigration is intense loses after a time all the superficial social traditions. Usually, however, the effects of foreign influences do not go much deeper. At first, indeed, the changes of dress, of manners, of leisure activities, which the young emigrants introduce after their return, arouse a violent reaction of the older generation, and this sometimes has disastrous effects in the fact that the youth, once revolted against tradition and its bearers, may reject not only the superficial and external mores but even those social rules of behavior without which the community cannot exist. After a time, however, we see a gradual reciprocal adaptation between the old and the young generation, mediated by those older members of the group who participate in season work abroad and by those young emigrants who settle and become regular landed members of the community. The young comply with those traditional mores for which they find no substitute in their life abroad and which therefore appear to them as essential as long as they feel dependent on the primary-group—in particular, with the principles of social solidarity as expressed in mutual help and response. The old accept, not for themselves but for their children, the new aesthetic, hedonistic and ceremonial standards imported from abroad and, as some of our documents note, show a remarkable leniency toward the young generation and a sympathetic interest in ambitions and pleasures which they do not share personally—an interest which is explained by that conversion of personal into familial aspirations which, as we know, usually follows the social maturity of the peasant. The most important permanent effect of this periodical absence of young people is a marked decrease of the seriousness with which the community and family systems are treated by their members when the place of those whose life was completely absorbed in these systems is taken by individuals who have learned to live for certain periods away from a regulated social milieu.

Emigration to America plays a relatively unimportant part in the progress of disorganization of the community. Our documents contain almost nothing bearing directly on this problem, and we know from personal investigation how small is the influence which returning emigrants exercise over community life. This influence limits itself almost entirely to the economic field—a certain improvement of the standards of living—and we may add perhaps a slight democratization of social relations. But emigration to America is much lower numerically (its highest tide, in 1912–1913, reached 130,000 as against 800,000 of season-emigrants), and this number includes a certain percentage of town population, whereas the season-emigration recruits itself exclusively from the country population. Further, no more than 40 per cent of transoceanic emigrants return. Finally, many of these leave Poland at an age when social attitudes are in a large measure fixed, and find in this country a community organization which to some degree at least is a substitute for that of their home communities. Thus, an emigrant returning from America may for a short time attempt to play the rôle of an innovator, but soon becomes absorbed in the life of the group and of his innovations only those have a social influence which bear the tests applied by social opinion. He may contribute to the evolution of the community positively in certain special matters, but can hardly be a serious factor of social disorganization. Transoceanic emigration has indeed a disorganizing effect on the life of the primary group, but in an indirect way, by acting on the imagination of those who remain. The community is no longer the only possible social milieu, in which the individual has to stay forever, and to which he *must* adapt himself; there are unlimited possibilities outside of it, and he feels much less dependent on it than in the past.

Much deeper, because more permanent, is the disorganization of the young generation in the community when it is produced by strangers who settle among the local inhabitants, bringing with them different mores, and either fail to become assimilated through racial reasons or are numerous enough to be independent of the social opinion of the community. The Jewish shopkeeper represents the first class; city workers near industrial centers, and released criminals sent to settle in a small town represent the second. The Jewish shopkeeper in a peasant village is usually also a liquor-dealer without license, a banker lending money at usury, often also a receiver of stolen goods and (near the border) a contrabandist. The peasant needs and fears him, but at the same time despises him always and hates him often. The activity of these country shopkeepers is the source of whatever anti-Semitism there is in the peasant masses. We have seen in the documents the methods by which the shopkeeper teaches the peasant boy smoking, drinking, and finally stealing; the connection established in youth lasts sometimes into maturity, and almost every gang of peasant thieves or robbers centers around some Jewish receiver's place, where the spoils are brought and new campaigns planned. Gangs composed exclusively of Jews are frequent in towns, rare in the country; usually Jews manage only the commercial side of the questions, leaving robbing or transporting of contraband to peasants.

Evidently the connection between such a shopkeeper-receiver and the youth demoralized by him remains a purely business proposition; race difference prevents even that solidarity which unifies the members of a gang of professional criminals. On the contrary, the influence exercised upon peasant youth by incomers of Polish origin, particularly by city workers, or by members of the lower middle class, is of a purely personal character and works by imitation. It is interesting to note in this connection that the peasant seldom directly imitates any of the members of the country nobility or of the city middle class; the social difference of degree seems to him too wide so that imitation appears as absurd or meaningless, whereas it is quite normal when the imitated person is only slightly higher in the social hierarchy. The disorganizing effect of this influence of incoming strangers depends, of course, on their character, their number and the closeness of their connection with the autochthonic group; in the most radical cases, in villages situated near large centers and whose population includes more strangers than original inhabitants, nothing is left of the old community except the official organization of village and commune autonomy from which the incomers are excluded unless they own real estate within the limits of the village or commune. But this invasion and dissolution of the community does not go on without struggle on the part of the old generation, and the point where the resistance of the old community is the strongest is precisely in admitting strangers to land-ownership. Here, in connection with the land problem, the solidarity of the group reasserts itself, leading sometimes even to violent group-action. Nevertheless, in the long run the struggle is always unsuccessful; a community which has a continual influx of strangers cannot preserve its integrity and sooner or later dissolves itself into a vague and incoherent social body within which organizations of a completely different type are formed.

Still more radical and rapid is the process of disorganization when the community becomes connected with some industrial or commercial center where the young generation goes to work. This has been a very frequent occurrence during the last fifty years, when in consequence of economic development of many old cities and of the appearance of new ones, innumerable peasant communities became practically nothing but suburbs whose population has a character intermediary between peasants and industrial workers. In such cases the social contacts between members of the young generation working in the city and various city groups become as close or even closer than those which they maintain with the rest of their community; the latter is reduced to a rôle similar to that of a "neighborhood" in an American city. City mores penetrate rapidly into the community; but as they offer little or nothing which could take the place of the old country mores in organizing individual life, social disorganization is often accompanied by personal demoralization. Those suburban localities usually stand in rather bad repute. Of course this is also due in a large measure to an influx of many undesirable elements from the city. We must also notice that there are interesting exceptions. And perhaps, generally speaking, demoralization is not as far-reaching as might be expected. Even as a mere permanent neighborhood, the community preserves some influence upon the individual and its opinion, divided on secondary matters, remains unanimous whenever the fundamental standards of social solidarity are concerned. There is not only a common human, but a common national stock of morals, and while an individual or a small group may act against it, he can do it only by concealing his doings from his wider social milieu; he may try to fool the opinion of the community, but he seldom dares to defy it. In general, therefore, personal demoralization is much easier among those who have immigrated into the city from more distant villages and find themselves outside of any social control, than among those who still live in their old milieu. What sometimes happens, indeed, is that in certain respects the morality of the whole group is lowered. This concerns in particular honesty in economic matters, and we have tried to explain how this happens. Economic dealings between members of a primary group have the character of social relations subordinated to the principle of solidarity, not that of plain business relations subordinated to quantitative impersonal economic valuations. When the peasant begins to deal with outsiders, he usually extends to them at first the principle of solidarity and is more than fair. Later, however, if the relations multiply and he finds that the principle of solidarity is not applied by the outsiders, he goes to the other extreme and implicitly, or even explicitly, assumes that economic exchange is not regulated by any principles whatever, that the only policy is to give as little as possible and get as much as possible by any means; it takes some time to learn and appreciate business honesty as a method of economic success. And one of the most marked signs of community disorganization is when he begins to apply to the members of his own group the dishonest methods used with regard to outsiders. But this is a problem which concerns rather the old than the young generation which we are discussing now.

A very interesting feature of the disorganization which starts with the youth is that it seldom, if ever, is purely individual but assumes a group character. This is perfectly natural when it is the effect of season emigration, for season emigrants from the same village or the same neighborhood usually go and work together, and thus common interests and memories unify them with each other and separate them in some measure from the rest of the community. But even when the source of disorganization is infiltration of strangers or work in a neighboring city, there is a general tendency of the young people with new and socially non-sanctioned attitudes to form more or less close associations, ranging from a vague group united by mere frequency of intercourse to an organized gang. Moreover, we usually notice efforts to proselyte the rest of the youth of the community and a very marked ill-will toward those who fail to respond. The individual seems to be able to emancipate himself from the dependence upon the large community only by relying for social response and recognition on a smaller community with congenial interests. This tendency seems stronger among young than among older people, probably because the former are less able to escape the censorship of public opinion by way of concealment, and also because the larger community does not satisfy sufficiently their desire for recognition, whereas in a group of the same age they can aspire for prominence. From the latter standpoint the formation of groups of young people seems almost a social necessity. It was limited until recently by the powerful cohesion of family groups, which prevented any solidarity of the young generation against the old from appearing, so that the youth of a village came together only for amusement, but the decadence of family life going on parallelly with the breakdown of the isolation of communities made the formation of solidary groups of young people for any purposes possible. Of course, these groups, as some of our documents show, are far from possessing the same degree of cohesion and solidarity as the original community. Nevertheless, their importance can hardly be overestimated. As factors of social disorganization they not only help the individual to free himself from the control of social opinion but serve as centers of attraction for those in whom the socially non-sanctioned attitudes have not yet developed. Moreover, through them the field of disorganization is apt to widen; it often happens that the group is formed under the influence of some relatively innocent interest—dress, smoking, games—and gradually its activities begin to extend to more dangerous matters. On the other hand, under proper leadership such groups have been often utilized for purposes of social reconstruction.

This type of disorganization of the community in which the

process starts with the young generation is essentially and primarily a dissolution of social opinion. The community begins by losing the uniformity of social attitudes which made common appreciation and common action possible; the introduction of new values breaks it into two or more camps with different centers of interest, different standards of appreciation and divergent tendencies of action. If the process continues, social opinion degenerates into gossip; public interest centers on matters of curiosity instead of those of social importance, and except in the condemnation of the most radical crimes, no unanimity can be reached on any point. As a consequence of this dissolution of social opinion, unless a new basis of unity is reached, there comes a more or less marked decay of social solidarity, both because divergence of appreciation and action breeds hostility and because most of the forms in which solidarity used to manifest itself are no longer adequately enforced by social opinion and rely only on individual moral feeling or desire for response.

It must be understood, of course, that the process of disorganization which starts with the young generation is a complicated matter. As a certain group of young people grow older and take the place of their parents, they have to moderate their new attitudes in adaptation to traditional problems and to old responsibilities which they are forced to face; they bring indeed a new and discordant element into the community, but not as radically new and discordant as might have been expected, judging by their earlier attitudes. At the same time, however, a new group of young people has taken their place as the revolutionary factor; the attitudes of these are different from those of the old generation, but may be also different from those of the preceding young group. And so on, with increasing complexity.

A very different type of disorganization of the community manifests itself not in a divergent evolution of the young generation but in a social disharmony within the old generation. Here the unity of social opinion is not originally affected; we find no revolt against tradition, no attempts to contest the validity of old standards. The individual who behaves in a socially prohibited way either has the consciousness of being wrong and tries to conceal his actions from the community, or else interprets the traditional standards in his favor and tries to justify his behavior from their standpoint. There is disorganization of the community only because, and in so far as, the individual members act against the principle of solidarity.

Now, this form of disorganization is not a new phenomenon, does not need external contacts to be produced; it has always existed even within isolated communities. For its origin lies in the original, temperamental attitudes of the individual. Although communal solidarity is psychologically founded on the desire for response which is, for the sociologist, one of the original individual attitudes, this attitude frequently conflicts with other equally original ones, and these conflicts can be harmonized only by an adequate social education. We shall see that the temperamental attitudes of an individual are not spontaneously regulated in their social manifestations but express themselves from moment to moment, independently of each other, under the pressure of actual personal needs. The aim of social education is precisely to organize their manifestations by subordinating them to rules. Every case of anti-social behavior which is not due to the explicit rejection of social rules but is a lack of compliance in practice with rules which the individual implicitly or explicitly acknowledges in theory, marks a failure of social education, an imperfect organization of temperamental attitudes into a character demanded by the given social environment. And since individual temperaments differ, while the educational methods used by a primary group are rather uniformly applied to all its members, some educational failures are bound to happen in every community, however strong and coherent, and breaks of communal solidarity, more or less far reaching and frequent, have occurred always and everywhere.

Nevertheless, there is no doubt that the number and importance of these breaks have greatly increased in peasant communities since the isolation of the latter disappeared. The explanation of this seems to be that the new values introduced from outside into the community life open the way for many new situations which the traditional rules of behavior did not foresee. The social education which the old generation received did not prepare them sufficiently for the difficult task of maintaining their social character in its integrity in the face of all the new suggestions which their more or less changed environment offers. Under these conditions, every individual's life-organization becomes more or less disturbed and his instincts, inadequately controlled, may easily express themselves in anti-social activities. Thus, the economic evolution of the last fifty years brought before the peasant, even the most conservative one, problems which put to a serious test his principles of social solidarity, made him find or accept new definitions of economic situations to which the traditional rules could not possibly apply and which often, directly or indirectly, led to an antagonism to other members of the community. Similarly the growing acquaintance with law made the peasant aware of the existence of standards of human relations somewhat different from his own, and at the same time put into his hand weapons of social struggle which he is more and more frequently tempted to use and abuse, particularly if somebody else has already used them against him.

We have seen that the first type of disorganization, beginning with a disintegration of public opinion due to the new values accepted and new attitudes developed in the young generation, brings with it usually a decay of social solidarity. The second type of disorganization, manifesting itself in the beginning as a decay of solidarity between the members of the old generation, cannot fail to affect in turn the unity and consistency of social opinion. As long as anti-social behavior is limited to a few isolated members of the group, the latter continues to treat it as abnormal and has no doubts as to the validity of the standards on which public opinion bases its judgments. But when breaks of social solidarity become frequent and when in view of the changed conditions every individual sees the possibility of situations to which the traditional rules can not be applied, the faith in the validity of the accepted standards is gradually shaken. The standards are not explicitly rejected, but begin to be treated as mere pious wishes which it would be desirable but which it is impossible fully to realize in practice. Public opinion is not divided at once into opposite camps, as it is when the young generation revolts against the old, but is weak and hesitant in its approvals and condemnations and loses all interest in facts which it does not know how to control, however vital these facts may be for the existence of the community. And, by a curious contrast, while in the first type of disorganization it is usually the superficial traditions—dress, ceremonial, leisure time organization—which begin to decay before all the others, and the fundamental principles of social morality remain often unshaken, in this second type the very foundation of social cohesion is weakened while the formal observances sanctioned by tradition may be kept as rigidly as ever.

This decay of the active moral control which the community exercises over its members results in turn in the growth of a specific form of social disharmony—the tendency to individual self-redress. As long as the community is efficient and its standards generally believed and applied, the individual who is or imagines himself wronged can obtain redress through his group, and either voluntarily accepts or is forced to accept whatever redress the group thinks justified. But when the community is inactive or its standards are no longer seriously and unhesitatingly acknowledged by its members, its judiciary and executive authority can no longer have any influence. According to modern ideas, of course, the individual should seek redress through the state, and in most cases the peasant does this. But we must remember that during the period of Russian domination the state was run by an inefficient, corrupt and nationally foreign, even hostile, bureaucracy. Naturally therefore, there were many cases in which the peasant, not trusting in the ability or the justice of the state authorities, took redress into his own hands. Then, of course, he measured his revenge by his wrong and his wrong by his subjective grievance. Moreover, he had little choice generally as to means and forms of redress and often took the first opportunity to avenge himself, however disproportionate the vengeance might have been as compared with the wrong. This explains the numerous cases of arson and murder through vengeance which we find in popular press and of which we have quoted a few. We may also add that a primary-group member, when passing from the community control under the state jurisdiction, is never satisfied with the standards of justice and the forms of redress which he can obtain, and there are always cases in which he will be inclined to resort to self-redress; compare, for instance, the long survival of duels.

It must be realized, of course, that the two types of disorganization of the community which we have tried to analyze and to explain separately, *viz.*, the disorganization which affects the young generation and begins by a disintegration of public opinion, and the disorganization which bears directly on the old generation and begins by a decay of social solidarity, usually go on simultaneously, though either may prevail in a given community during a given period. There are communities, indeed, particularly along the Western border of the Congress Kingdom and in Western Galicia, where as a consequence of season emigration the first type is pushed very far, whereas the old generation seems to remain solidary, perhaps precisely because it feels the need of it to defend its prestige and position in the community. In some other communities, where the contact with the outside world is maintained chiefly by the old generation, communal solidarity is breaking up, whereas the young generation does not think of revolting against the old. But, since the new influences do not fail to penetrate the whole community sooner or later situations such as described are usually only temporary.

We must say, however, that the entire process of disorganization is only temporary. For social disintegration in whatever form never goes as far as to destroy entirely in the group the demand for a regulated, organized and harmonious social life. Thus, social disintegration is bound to rouse not only reflective attention of the group, but also, among some of its members at least, conscious efforts to remedy it.

6

# LEADERSHIP, EDUCATION, AND THE PRESS

## Leadership

THE PROBLEM of leadership in Poland was particularly complicated because of the combination of two factors—class differences (more persistent among the country population than in cities) and the national situation. The peasant class left to itself would have been unable to produce for many years to come constructive leaders in numbers sufficient for its own reorganization, whereas the national situation urgently required a rapid transformation of the peasant class into a nationally conscious and culturally constructive body. Thus, members of other classes had to assume leadership, at least in the beginning; and, indeed, in no other country has the nobility and the intellectual city class shown as much active interest in organizing the peasants as in Poland during the last 50 years. But this advantage of having more than enough educated and nationally conscious men ready to fulfil the functions of leaders as soon as the need of leadership became obvious was offset by serious disadvantages resulting from the fact that these men were separated from the masses whom they in-

---

Reprinted from *The Polish Peasant in Europe and America* (New York: Alfred A. Knopf, 1927; New York: Dover Publications, 1958), II, 1307–13, 1330–39, 1360–66, 1367–70, 1389–96.

tended to lead by all those attitudes and traditions which were the source and the product of the division of classes.

As far as the nobility was concerned, there is no doubt that, if we except a small number of magnates belonging to the international aristocratic *coterie* and spending most of their time abroad, the average country squire had a wide "universe of discourse" in common with his peasant neighbor or even his manor-servant, in the professional, religious, social fields, so that he could understand him well enough for the purposes of leadership. But on both sides there were deeply rooted traditional prejudices to overcome before real collaboration became possible. The nobleman was too much inclined to treat the peasant as a permanent minor destined to be always the passive object of a more or less benevolent care of the upper classes, and to claim obedience and one-sided respect as due to his social rank or at least to his superior culture. In matters of organization he naturally tended, often quite unreflectively, to preserve more than was possible of the old system and looked with mistrust or even indignation on many of the new tendencies which began to develop among the peasants and whose first manifestations, sometimes irrational or seemingly anti-social, prevented him from seeing the constructive possibilities implied in their further development. On the other hand, the peasant mistrusted the "lords," particularly when their activity was personally disinterested, for he did not understand its motives; he had to be first educated and organized before he could grasp the full significance and appreciate the motive power of the national ideal. Further, his continually growing desire for economic advance, in connection with the remnants of the old attitude toward the wealthy estate owner (who was treated as somehow outside of and above communal solidarity, to whom neither response nor justice was due because he did not need them), often led the peasant to abuse the good-will of the nobleman-leader, and thus discouraged disinterested initiative. Finally, the fact that between the country squire and his peasant neighbors and servants there were many business relations which gave many opportunities for trouble, constituted an additional obstacle to successful leadership.

With city intellectuals, the difficulty lay elsewhere. While there were no traditional antagonisms, no inveterate class prejudices to overcome, positive bonds between these two classes were very weak and reciprocal understanding difficult, owing to the lack of contact. Only those among the city men understood the peasant more or less who had either spent their youth in the country as sons of nobles or peasants and preserved their early connections, or who were in an exceptional position to keep continual contact with the peasant class. The great majority of city-bred leaders were idealistic young doctrinaires, poorly acquainted with the practical situations of peasant life and inclined to overrate the pace of possible progress. The peasant mistrusted them less than he mistrusted the "lord," but his mistrust of the latter was connected with fear and often respect whereas with reference to the former there was an unmistakable shade of contempt.

In spite of these obstacles, we find a continually growing number of successful leaders and organizers of peasants both among the city intellectuals and the nobility; but this growth has been relatively slow. This accounts for the fact that a third social group —the clergy—has succeeded in playing a rôle perhaps even more important than that of either of the groups mentioned above, although it began quite late to participate in social reconstruction. It is evident that a country priest has the best possible conditions for becoming a social leader of his parish, particularly in the beginning of the process of reconstruction, when the great mass of his parishioners are passive, and willing to follow a leader who is otherwise acceptable to them instead of trying to be independent and to organize by their own initiative. There is no inveterate class antagonism preventing collaboration, for the priest, as long as he is considered as an essentially religious personality, is in a sense outside of the class system; only when the worldly attributes of the priest begin to predominate in the eyes of the peasant over his sacral character, reflections are made concerning his class connections. There is a certain mistrust resulting from the often exaggerated economic demands of priests; but with good-will on the part of the latter this mistrust can be easily overcome. And nobody is in a position to know the peasant better than the priest, in most cases himself a peasant or small townsman by birth and in continuous contact with his parishioners. He is, besides, already a leader in all matters connected with religion, and it needs only some effort on his part to extend this leadership to the economic and political fields. Thus it is exclusively the fault of the clergy or, more exactly, of the church as an institution, that we find relatively few priests among peasant leaders up to about twenty-five years ago. The Catholic Church as an international institution with wide political plans never, since the Congress of Vienna, favored the Polish national movement, and it did not explicitly sanction the participation of the clergy in lay social activities until 1893 and the encyclical *Rerum novarum* of Leo XIII. But when finally the Polish clergy awoke to the realization of the fact that unless they took an active part in the nationwide movement of social reconstruction they would lose almost all social influence, they were able rapidly to take an important place among the leaders. Their great rôle, however, seems to be only temporary; the spirit of independence developing among the peasants deprives the clergy of their exceptional prestige which, in less independent communities, makes the leadership of the priest appear as the most "natural" and obvious, while on the other hand the church system imposes limits on their progress, does not permit them to go as far in the new direction as is necessary to achieve the work of reconstruction.

The last in time and as yet the least important, but probably the most promising for the future is that group of leaders which grows up within the peasant class itself—not men of peasant origin who receive professional education, become incorporated into other social bodies and participate in the reconstructive movement as city intellectuals or clergymen, but those who, having achieved an intellectual and social superiority over the average peasant mass, yet remain members of their class and continue to share all the interests of this class. There have been many such leaders during the period we are studying, but the sphere of their influence in most cases has not exceeded the limits of one community or even one village. But the number of those who, through the press, through political or economic institutions had begun to influence wider circles has been growing, and their rôle seems to have enormously increased lately, during the formation of the Polish state.

In order to avoid misunderstanding we must emphasize the fact that the documents which we are quoting are not meant to characterize types of *leaders,* but to illustrate the psychology of *leadership.* There are rich biographical materials concerning prominent leaders published in Polish—few societies show as strong an interest and appreciation of individual achievements— but we cannot use them here, for the problems which they raise are entirely beyond the scope of this work. It must be added that the documents included in other chapters of this volume contain much which has a direct bearing on the problem of leadership.

[Typical example of the old-time attitude of the nobility toward the lower classes; willing to help *individuals* to advance but entirely unconscious of matters relating to social organization and the progress of the masses. The reactions of the favored individual are also typical.]

On January 1st, 1883, being 20 years old, I came with my father to serve in the manor Pawlówki. . . . On New Year, 1884, I went with my lord to church instead of his coachman. I must mention that during the year my lord had given me many proofs of his grace and favor. On returning from the church, my lord asked me whether I would like to learn to read and to write. I kissed his hand and said that I would like it very much; so he ordered me to come every evening to his office to learn. On the same day he asked me whether I wanted to be a coachman or to become gradually a farm-steward. I answered, a farm-steward. Therefore with the New Year 1884 I moved to the manor; I received there board, a separate small room; my lord gave me a bed, bed-furnishings and clothes and in the evenings taught me to read and to write, when he was at home. On the one hand I got on well, because I had good board, clothes and the protection of the lord, but on the other hand, I had many griefs and troubles because everybody envied me the lord's favor and teased me terribly. My lord required of me also not to deal with anybody, not to drink liquor at all, not to loaf around in the evening, but to spend all the moments free from work in learning. I had been accustomed to all those things from my childhood, and it was very difficult for me to renounce them all. At that time there was a sister-in-law of one of the manor-servants whom they had for a long time intended me to marry. But I knew that if I married her I would lose the favor of the lord and the career which he promised me. So I tried to guard myself against this marriage, and I succeeded.

Sometimes I was guilty, for I did secretly something which was forbidden me because, as people say, "nature draws the wolf back into the forest." The lord then scolded me in a fatherly way and explained to me that I ought not to do it. . . . I learned to read and to write, I won the confidence of the lord. I assisted him in all the farm-functions, and thanks to his favor I had for my work good clothes and 100 roubles put aside. From March 1st, 1888, I was already a land-steward on a separate farm . . . of the same lord. My lord had long subscribed to the *Gazeta Świąteczna* for me and in free moments I read it and instructed myself. I got so accustomed to the *Gazeta* that the need to read it became second nature. . . . Through reading the *Gazeta* and the books which I got to read I gained instruction and knowledge—how man is obliged to work, how he ought to act and to repay his employer with honest labor and gratitude for lifting him up from the darkness and giving him the occasion to become a useful man. . . .

In 1883 I began my service there as a driver. In 1895 I am manager of an estate of 1100 morgs, with 200 roubles wages and corresponding *ordynarya*. And I owe all this to the protection of a good lord, to instruction and to abstaining from all those bad habits to which I got accustomed in childhood and which all but drew me aside from the way in which my lord put me and on which he led me. Today I have two children and I am trying to educate them. . . . May this my record . . . be an example for others. . . .[1]

The general conclusion which our particular data seem to suggest is that leadership, viewed from the socio-psychological standpoint, is not a uniform phenomenon. The apparently simple fact of an individual's influencing the behavior of others in accordance with his will can be the result of several entirely different processes. We distinguish at least three types of leadership which may be called respectively leadership by *fear or hope*, leadership by *prestige*, leadership by *efficiency*.

The first type is the best known and the most general, since it underlies all political and most of economic control. It presup-

[1] Letter to *Gazeta Świąteczna*; unpublished.

poses that the leader has at his disposal positive or negative values which are the object of the desire or fear of others and which he can at will grant or withdraw, impose or take off. Except in the relatively rare and sociologically unimportant cases of direct physical control among isolated individuals, all such power of distributing values—whatever may be the way in which a particular individual has attained it—rests upon the existing political or economic order; it is institutional, not personal. From this results that this type of leadership has but little significance for the purpose of social reconstruction in so far as the latter implies the substitution of a new social system for the old one; a leader can use vested institutional power to overcome obstacles which other leaders by virtue of their institutional power put in the way of social reconstruction, but he cannot construct a new system with instruments whose efficiency depends on the preservation of the old system. In our particular case this form of leadership has even less importance than usual, for the Polish leaders at the period we are studying had little power of political control and political parties did not exercise any appreciable positive influence upon the movement of social reconstruction.

The mechanism of leadership by prestige is characterized by the fact that it is the personality of the leader which constitutes in the eyes of those who follow him the sanction for the ideas which he promulgates and for the behavior which he suggests by word or by example. His suggestions are put into action not because any reward or punishment is expected from him, but because they are considered practically or morally right; and they are considered right without being analyzed in reflection or tested in practice, simply because they emanate from him.

Prestige can, as we know, be attached to an individual because he is a representative of a certain class, profession, etc. Thus, the personality of a priest is endowed in the eyes of a believing peasant with a sacral character which is supposed to predominate over his individual imperfections and to impart to him, if not an absolute value, at least a value superior to that which an individual without this sacral character can possess. Superiority of social position is a source of prestige even independently of any actual power which the superior class may or may not possess. However, it is evident that this kind of prestige is not very secure in periods of rapid social evolution, since it is apt to be impaired by any mistakes which other individual members of the given profession or class can make and which are easily generalized as characterizing the whole group. Thus, we find that with the development of social consciousness among the peasants the prestige which the individual acquires personally as his own particular self is more and more clearly distinguished from and even opposed to the old group prestige; the profession or class is disparaged by contrast with its particular member and the latter exalted by contrast with his class.

Moreover, when the leader relies on the prestige of his profession or class he is forced to keep the traditions and to uphold the *esprit de corps* by which this profession or class tries to maintain its prestige, and this evidently limits his initiative. Finally, purely individual prestige has a much greater influence on the masses because of the particular and well known attraction which everything personal has for the popular mind. For all these reasons, we see that the expansion of the sphere of influence of a popular leader in social reconstruction goes along with a gradual decrease of those sides of his public personality in which his profession, class, etc., are manifested, so that the most important leaders— like Jackowski or Wawrzyniak—can hardly be characterized as priests or noblemen, but simply as individuals, each as a unique personality.

But for this very reason it is impossible to make any generalizations concerning the nature and sources of this purely individual prestige; the characteristic features which make a leader popular may be entirely different in each particular case. Of course, the leader must be judged efficient in his line and must be supposed to be well-intentioned with regard to his followers. But it is precisely the baffling point about leadership by prestige that the judgment of the mass as to the efficiency and good intentions of their leader depend upon the prestige which he already possesses, and that no proofs of real efficiency, sincerity and honesty can give a man prestige unless, for reasons which vary from case to case, his personality happens to become the center of benevolent public attention. For prestige is not the result of a rational judgment of each member of the group individually about the leader *as he is*, but the complex product of a half-intellectual, half-emotional attitude of each member of the group toward the leader *as seen by other members;* the subject of prestige is not the individual as an active personality but the picture of this individual drawn by public opinion.

It is clear that the peasant class constitutes a very favorable ground for the development of leadership by prestige as long as peasant communities preserve their character of primary groups whose members are used to think in social terms and are dependent on public opinion for their ideas and appreciations. This is a very propitious circumstance for social reconstruction, for it permits the leaders to put into effect, by virtue of their prestige, constructive plans whose objective significance is only imperfectly understood by their unprepared followers. In fact, since the very preparation for a new social organization requires social organization and the masses learn fully to understand new social ideals and institutions only in the course of their gradual realization, the process of social reconstruction could not start if the suggestions of the leaders had to be fully understood and appreciated on their own merits by their followers before being realized in action; the prestige of the leaders, at a certain stage of social evolution, gives to the new and undeveloped social forms that motive power without which the inertia of the masses could not be overcome.

But with the progressing individualization, intellectual development, and critical ability of the peasants, leadership by prestige gradually gives place to leadership by efficiency, in which an individual assumes the leading rôle because and in so far as he is considered more efficient than others—because his ideas and suggestions are judged morally or practically right and are accepted by others on their own merits after reflection or practical test. This evolution naturally occurs sooner in those fields in which the peasant's judgment is less dependent on tradition and public opinion, in which he is better able to define situations rationally from the standpoint of a proper adaptation of the means to the end, instead of defining them from the standpoint of their accordance with traditional rules. Thus, we see leadership by efficiency developing much faster in economic cooperation than in education or politics. It is also evident that the less prestige a leader possesses, the more easily the criteria of efficiency are applied to the activities which he suggests. This explains the fact that sometimes the work of great leaders decays after their retirement; they have carried social reconstruction beyond the point where it should be taken up by minor leaders growing up from the masses. On the contrary, social reconstruction which is carried on by many leaders with relatively little prestige is slower but has an uninterrupted progress.

## Education

The movement for the education of the peasants began in Poland in the middle of the eighteenth century, in connection with the general movement for national reorganization and under the partial influence of French rationalism and the "enlightenment" ideal. The peasant had to be gradually prepared for freedom and active participation in political life, and public education was to be the all-powerful method of preparation. The wide system of public schools established by the Educational Commission between 1773 and 1791 gave free access to peasant children, and many nobles, in order to encourage education, granted freedom to every serf who learned to read and write. This development was interrupted by the partitions. Under Russian domination in particular the conditions of public education grew from bad to worse, so that in the beginning of the nineteenth century the proportion of children in public schools relative to the number of the population was smaller by half than a hundred years before. The schools were not only few but poorly equipped; the teachers, mostly sent from Russia, were ignorant and inefficient. Besides, the school was used as an instrument of Russification. Similarly in German Poland where education was universal and obligatory, the chief aim of the public school was to Germanize the Poles.

Both under Russian and under German domination private teaching without state control was forbidden altogether (except individually at home), private schools under state control had to teach in Russian or German and even so were continually hampered. Polish society had thus to find some other methods to supplement state education in Russia and to counterbalance both in Russia and in Germany the anti-Polish tendency of state schools. After the revolution of 1863 had failed to give Poland political freedom, "popular enlightenment" began to be considered one of the most vital national problems. The ideas of the eighteenth century were revived, modified and developed. The peasant was to be made not only a "thinking man" and a politically conscious member of the Polish nation, but also taught how to improve his economic condition and prepared for social cooperation. Owing to the abnormal conditions of national life which had hampered the cultural development of Poland, popular education assumed a rôle which it hardly ever possessed elsewhere; it became a universal instrument of social reconstruction.

The only method of spreading education which could be always safely used was that of individual teaching or individual encouragement to self-education. Formal social organization for the purpose of public instruction was possible only in Galicia. In the Congress Kingdom each particular commune could establish primary schools under governmental control, but no educational societies were permitted; one was founded in 1905 but dissolved by the government after a year. Thus the problem was to create an informal social organization by enlisting in each community a few individuals who were willing to be educated and to help educate others, and who thus constituted a local center from which education spread through the community. The success of this enterprise depended upon the development among the peasants of such social attitudes as would make each individual wish to learn and to teach—not always an easy matter in view of the strong conservatism of the peasant.

I am sending a brief remembrance of my youth. There is no interesting adventure in question, but I think it will interest the readers as a proof that if one urgently and perseveringly desires something he attains it in the end, at least in part. I am the son of a peasant farmer. Until 10 years of age I did not know the alphabet, or, exactly speaking, I knew only the letter B. Father did not send me to school. He always used to repeat: "We have grown old and we cannot read nor write, yet we live. So you, my children, will also live without knowledge." Nothing could have suited me better. In the winter I went sledging with the boys and in summer I pastured geese.

Once my mother took me to church. I looked to the right; a boy smaller than myself was praying from a book. I looked to the left; another one just like the first held a book, and I stood between them like a ninny. I went home and told my father that I would learn from a book. My father scolded me: "And who will peel potatoes in the winter and pasture the geese in summer?" I cried then because I felt ashamed that I should grow up and not know how to read.

Once while peeling potatoes, I escaped from my father and went to an old man who knew not only how to read, but how to write well. I asked him to show me [letters] in the primer, and he did not refuse. I went home thinking: "It's too bad! Father will probably give me a licking." And it came true. Father showered a few strokes on me and said: "Snotty fellow, don't you know that, as the old people say, whoever learns written stuff casts himself into hell?" But I stole out to learn more and more frequently. The following winter father did not forbid it and slowly I learned how to read and write.

When I was twelve years old I had already read various books, but only fables, for at that time one could most frequently find in the village books like *Ali Baba, Sobotnia Góra*, etc. Once I found an old almanac on the road. I looked at it and on the last page read that there was in Warsaw a *Gazeta Świąteczna* which people order and receive by mail every Sunday. After that I said to one of the neighbors—not a young man: "Do you know, in Warsaw there is a *Gazeta* which every one, even if not educated, can read!" And that man said to me: "Look at him, the snotty fellow! He wants a newspaper!" He said to my father: "Do you know, *kum*, your son will become a real lord, for he says that he will order a newspaper."—"Ho, ho!" said my father, "but where will he get the money?"

After some time father turned me from pasturing geese to tending cattle. Once another herdsman told me that there was in Suchedniów, not far from our village, a railroad watchman whose name was Korzec, and that he had the *Gazeta*. I immediately gave my cattle to some one else to tend and rushed to Korzec. When I came in he asked me: "What do you want, boy?"—"I came to see what the *Gazeta* to which you seem to subscribe looks like." He showed me the *Gazeta Świąteczna*. I began to read and liked it very much. All right, but where shall I get the money for it?

I began to make brooms and sell them at 3 *grosz* apiece; I plaited whips, and in this way between spring and St. John's Day I saved 2 *złoty*. But that was not enough. Where could I get some more? It was hard to get away from the cattle to earn something. Once I was pasturing the cattle near a colony in the forest. Some strangers approached and one said to me: "Boy, do you know how to read? I would give you a book with interesting stories." I answered that I could and thanked him for the book, but at the same time I asked bashfully for a little money. "You rogue," said the stranger, "what do you need money for?" I said for the *Gazeta*. But he replied: "Perhaps for cigarettes?"—"No," said I crying, "I have already 2 *złoty* and I need 15 *grosz* more to have 2½ *złoty*, and the carpenter says that he will contribute as much more and that would be just enough for a quarter. . . . I took an oath at my first confession that I would not drink whiskey nor smoke cigarettes until twenty-one years old." Then that gentleman took out and gave me not 15 *grosz*, but as much as 3 *złoty* and also the book [saying], "Here you will have enough to subscribe alone to the *Gazeta* for a whole quarter." How great was my joy would be hard to describe. I immediately asked a boy to write to the editor for the *Gazeta*, and the following Sunday I already had it in the house. As soon as they saw it in the village they began to say various things about it, that only lords ought to read the *Gazeta*, that reading takes time. But I did not listen to them and only read with great delight.

I have now subscribed to the *Gazeta* for 8 years. I no longer lack money for it, as for the last 6 years I have been a forester and live on a farm of 15 morgs. I have grown so accustomed to the *Gazeta* that when Sunday comes I have in one hand the spoon and in the other the *Gazeta*. People say that reading the *Gazeta* requires a lot of time. But on a holiday is there not time enough for both praying and reading? . . . And I say that a peasant in the country needs the *Gazeta* more than one who has already been enlightened in school. We certainly can draw knowledge from the *Gazeta*. It is true that there are some newspapers which are not written for everybody, but as if in a foreign language [using learned words]. However, I am speaking about one which every one, even an uneducated, simple man, can understand. . . . I often say: "If it should be necessary to eat only once a day, I will do it, but I will not cease subscribing to the *Gazeta* until the end of my life."

In conclusion, I send a hearty "God reward" to Priest Woźniakowski for having forbidden me to smoke cigarettes. I never learned how to let money go up in smoke. Therefore I am able to subscribe to the *Gazeta*. I also send "God reward" to Marcin Korzec for having shown me the way to the *Gazeta*.[2]

Respected Writer of the *Gazeta Świąteczna!* I write to Warsaw with my own hand to subscribe to the *Gazeta* for next year, for I want to continue talking with you through it. Great God reward you for all that you have told us up to the present through the *Gazeta*.

I am the son of a poor farmer in the village Malomierzyce. . . . My father has only 3 morgs of land and that of poor quality; so we, the children, had to leave our home because of poverty. But our father did not let us go into the world without having taught each of us to read and write some. Our father was himself 40 years old and did not yet know how to take a pen into his hand. But now he knows how to write himself and has taught me, just as you see. My father always endeavored to read the *Gazeta Świąteczna*. He could not subscribe himself but borrowed it wherever possible. In the *Gazeta* he found your advice and bought the *Illustrated Method* of Kazimierz Promyk, the first and second parts and the calligraphic models. From this he learned and taught his children. . . . I am now working hard in a factory.[3]

In the village where I live, the name of which I purposely do not mention, was a farmer about whom no person could say anything good, even if he should wish to. He was an old scoundrel and whenever he had a chance he liked to empty glasses. But it happened that he occasionally borrowed my *Gazeta*. He liked it. He began to borrow it oftener, and then he used to call for it every week and had to read it through. And before we realized it—he became a very orderly farmer. He renounced whiskey; he is working like every one of his neigh-

[2] *Gazeta Świąteczna*, 1898, 31.
[3] *Gazeta Świąteczna*, 1898, 50.

bors, he is good, obliging, he goes to church every Sunday and holiday—in a word, it is difficult to recognize the man who formerly did not think of doing any good in the world. Today the old man brought me a rouble and asked me to take it for the payment of the *Gazeta* . . . and related how the *Gazeta* had led him to the proper way in his 67th year. . . .[4]

The various attitudes of the peasants toward education have an almost unparalleled sociological interest, for each of them can be found in all societies and on all stages of cultural evolution. However wide may seem the difference of culture between the legislative body of a modern state, ignoring or taking into account the problem of endowment of scientific research, and a peasant village, refusing or agreeing to subscribe to popular papers; between a wealthy business man despising all intellectual work which does not bring immediate practical results, and a peasant woman scolding her husband for his seemingly useless reading; between a scientist working his way, in spite of material obstacles and social indifference or hostility to some great discovery, and a peasant boy struggling with poverty and the opposition of his social milieu for a minimum of instruction; between the trustees of a university who fear the destructive effect of science on public morals, and an old peasant who claims that knowledge of reading and writing leads to hell, the fundamental attitudes are exactly the same.

The general unwillingness with which a conservative peasant group usually greets the appearance of intellectual interests in any one of its members can probably be best explained by its aversion to individualization in any form. A man who reads in a non-reading community has interests which the community does not share, ideas which differ from those of others, information which others cannot obtain; he isolates himself in some measure from his environment, lives partly in a sphere which is inaccessible to others and—what is worse—strange and unknown to them; thus, he in certain respects breaks away from social control. The situation is aggravated by the fact that learning has been associated with other social classes. There may perhaps be also some rem-

[4] *Gazeta Świąteczna*, 1899, 53.

nant of the mediaeval attitude toward book-lore as having magical connections, either divine or devilish; thus praying from a book in church is highly considered even in communities which are otherwise most averse to education.

When intellectual interests cease to be an exception and begin to be shared by an appreciable part of the community, the feeling of strangeness disappears. But the conservative part of the group often continues to look askance on the spread of instruction, for the latter seems to them to imply indefinite possibilities of change, to threaten a partial or total dissolution of the traditional social system, and thus arouses opposition from the standpoint of the desire for security.

It is not strange, therefore, if an average member of a conservative peasant community, knowing what reaction to expect from his environment, is not easily induced to become a "paper-man" or "book-worm," unless he has been already made partly independent of social opinion. And even without social pressure, there is not much in learning which appeals to his traditional attitudes enough to justify in his eyes the effort necessary for its acquisition. His average curiosity is satisfied by the traditional channels of personal intercourse with news-bearers and "wise men" to whose information he can apply old and known standards and whom therefore he is often more willing to believe than papers and books, which require standards unknown to him. He does not see how he could apply knowledge to the practical questions which interest him, for this application would mean in most cases a radical change of his traditional methods which he is not prepared to face. In general, as long as he is satisfied with the old type of life there is no inducement for him in new intellectual values.

The development of intellectual interests is closely connected with the breakdown of the isolation of the peasant-community and the consequent disorganization of the old system. The growing contact with the outside world develops in individuals a desire for new experience, and the paper or the book is welcomed both as a partial substitute for real new experiences when the field of the latter is limited by circumstances, and as a means by which the individual can get at least indirectly in touch with men and with possibilities beyond the narrow circle of his primary-group life. Both motives are particularly strong in young people, where we find the tendency to education often asserting itself without any explicit encouragement or even against discouraging influences. And the same break of isolation which rouses the desire for new experience in individuals weakens also the opposition of the group to the intellectual interests of its members; we have seen in a preceding chapter how the sphere of privacy allowed to the individual increases when the group is no longer able to attain a perfect community of interests and identity of attitudes.

But this spontaneous appearance of intellectual interests in particular individuals and the decrease of the tendency to repress them in the group were not sufficient to spread popular education under such political conditions as existed in Poland. It was indispensable to develop positive appreciation of intellectual values in peasant communities so as to have social opinion encourage every individual effort in this line. This has been done in two ways—by giving to intellectual development a moral significance and by emphasizing the practical applicability of knowledge in connection with economic advance.

The old appreciative attitude toward learning when used for religious purposes gave in most cases probably the starting point for the first method. It was a good thing and a distinction to read a prayer-book in church; even more perhaps to be able to read aloud the *Lives of the Saints* or some other edifying stories at private meetings during Advent or Lent when dancing was prohibited. The passage from religious to serious secular reading was easy; and thus the latter assumed a solemnity and importance which marked its adherents as serious and decent people, its opponents as lazy or light-headed. More than this: Just as a general moral superiority was supposed connected with religious interests and the knowledge about religious matters, there is a marked tendency on the part of those who show intellectual interests to assume an attitude of moral superiority toward the "ignorant."

A part of the popular literature has encouraged this attitude of righteousness which, though it often took ridiculous forms and provoked strong reactions from the uninitiated, nevertheless helped greatly to raise the standing of intellectual values in peasant communities. The public praise or blame of which individuals or groups are the object in popular papers (on account of their positive or negative attitude toward education) is very similar in its tone to praise or blame on moral grounds and has the same effect of provoking emulation or desire to reform. Further still, in contrast with, though probably not in conscious opposition to the fears of those who see in instruction the threat of social disorganization, we find in the younger generation the popular idea that instruction of itself is the panacea for all social evils, that nothing but lack of enlightenment is the source of whatever moral deficiencies are to be found among the peasants. All this tends to spread the conviction of the meritoriousness of being interested in knowledge, quite independently of its practical utility, and to convert into prestige the originally negative discrimination of which the "paper-man" and "book-worm" are the object. Learning becomes something intermediary between a moral rule and a fashion, not as generally acknowledged as the former but more seriously treated than the latter.

The emphasis put upon the practical applications of knowledge to economic problems does not in any sense contradict its moral idealization, for economic progress, in particular the introduction of new methods of production and exchange, has been also in some measure morally idealized as contributing to the development of the country. The task of the leaders in this field was rather complex. It was indispensable, first of all, to foster the desire for economic advance and the dissatisfaction with the existing status, since, as we saw, a peasant who is satisfied with his condition does not care about any new practical suggestions. Secondly, this desire had to be partly distracted from those ways which it tends primarily to take—land-hunger and emigration—into entirely new channels; the peasant had to be shown that, even when there was no opportunity of increasing the size of his farm, he could raise its value and increase his income and that, though hired work abroad sometimes was the only way of obtaining any extra capital he needed at a given moment, in most cases more permanent welfare could be reached by using his own and his children's work to develop his farming along new lines.

We shall see later by what specific methods the peasant was induced to consider improvements of his own technique desirable in general; of course, the spreading of instruction was one of the factors of this evolution. But the latter in turn was used to foster the spreading of instruction; it was only necessary to demonstrate to the peasant that he actually could learn practically valuable things from books and papers, instead of merely imitating what he has already seen done. This demonstration was in most communities undertaken voluntarily by some exceptional individuals, more enterprising than the average and more influenced by the printed word. There were, of course, many failures; but as the experimenter in the interest of his own prestige tried to conceal them, while he boasted widely of every success, the conviction of the practical utility of book knowledge has been developing very rapidly. The method by which those individuals who have already acquired some instruction are made to cooperate in spreading it among other members of their communities, either by teaching them or by persuading them to self-education, also deserves our attention. The tendency to act as a leader and adviser is, of course, a very general one; it is a specific form of the wish for mastery which, as a combination of other social attitudes, plays an important part in social evolution. Now, this tendency is sanctioned and regulated by the real intellectual leaders who more or less explicitly treat the half-educated peasant as their associate and collaborator in the work of educating others, as a member of a new kind of peasant aristocracy on whose efficient social work depends the future of the peasant class.

## *The Wider Community and the Rôle of the Press*

In most European countries the breakdown of the isolation of peasant communities was accompanied—or even preceded—by an incorporation of the peasants individually into the existing political system, so that the main problem of reconstruction which these countries had to face was, how to change the members of primary groups into members of an existing secondary group. But this was not so in Poland, which had no political frame-work waiting to include the peasant as soon as serfdom was abolished. Of course, in Poland, as everywhere, there existed ready economic and cultural institutions of the secondary-group type in which the peasants could and did participate in an increasing measure. But it is evident that none of these institutions can anywhere pretend to control all the members of a concrete social body as does the primary-group or the state.

Furthermore in Poland they were the product of other social classes, inadequately adapted to the peasants' needs, and the necessary modifications and extensions which would make them more useful to the peasant class were in the main impossible under foreign domination. And yet the rapid breakdown of traditional social forms and the urgent need of making the peasants active members of the nation—not only without the help of, but against the efforts of the dominating states—made it even more important for Poland than for other countries that the primary-group organization should be supplemented by secondary-group system which would both control the individual when the community could not do it and control the community so as to make it coöperate in national activities.

The task which Polish peasant leaders faced was thus as interesting as it was difficult. They had to reproduce under entirely different conditions the fundamental social process by which states have been built, to create a new secondary group from a plurality of primary groups. The main instrument which has always served to realize this aim—military power—could not be used in this case. Nor was any kind of free political union of peasant communes possible, for the partitioning governments were most anxious to destroy all political cohesion of Polish society; the peasant commune was completely isolated politically from other communes and had contact only with the Russian authorities. Religion and the church organization might have been, indeed, powerful means of unifying the peasant primary groups; but they could not

## Leadership, Education, and the Press

be used, partly because of the unwillingness of the central Catholic Church authorities to let the Polish clergy commit itself in national and social struggles, partly because of the suspicion with which the Russian and Prussian governments looked upon the activities of the Polish clergy, partly also because of the undemocratic character of the church hierarchy. Thus the only instrument with the help of which a secondary-group system could be constructed above the primary-group organization was the press, and the only form which this secondary-group system could assume was that of a *wider community*, in which communication through the printed word took the place of direct personal contact, and abstract moral solidarity the place of concrete social solidarity.

The problem was thus, first, to create a nationwide social opinion, standardized by the leaders, and to subject to the control of this opinion not only individuals but primary communities; secondly, to develop in individuals the consciousness of moral obligation to contribute to the material and intellectual progress of this wider community to which they belonged, regardless of any actual or expected reciprocity of services.

[Typical description of a primary group written for the sole purpose of attracting to it the attention of the wider community; this makes it at once a part of the latter.]

Our village . . . is small and in no way peculiar; however, it is a little parcel of our country on which 16 peasant families live, and thus it deserves to have people know about it. . . . As everywhere, among us there are also good and bad, well-wishing and envious people. Mostly, however, the inhabitants of Szklana are laborious, sober and honest. In spite of this, everybody complains about misery more here than elsewhere. This is because the peasants here buy too much land, more than they can afford. . . . The inhabitants of Szklana do not waste money on dress. They wear long white "Cracovian" coats. The heart rejoices when one looks at a stately man dressed in a white shirt, black trousers and waistcoat, a black hat and a white coat.

Almost everybody here knows how to read at least printed matter, and therefore education spreads rapidly. Instead of card-playing or vain and indecent talk, which still could be often heard a few years ago, today reading the *Gazeta Świąteczna* prevails. We have 2 copies of it in our small village. In the beginning, when one of the inhabitants ordered it, it was difficult to persuade anybody to read or to listen. . . . If everything is not described exactly here, please do not wonder, for I am not a writer but merely a peasant from under a straw roof, who is more accustomed to the plow than to the pen.[5]

[Shows some of the motives leading an individual to wish to inform the wider community about his place and his narrower group.]

Although I have often written in our *Gazeta* about this village, and you know it already and are acquainted with it, I have in mind to talk again about it because here I passed my childhood years, knowing neither suffering nor trouble; here I dreamed, an innocent, quiet little boy in this remote village. . . . Oh, how lovely are these whitened cottages, these low thatches lulled into sleep by the sweet stillness of the evening, bathed in the brightness of the moon! Some like better to live in a strange country on German or other [foreign] ground, but for me nowhere shines the sun as in this my native village.

Well, brothers, today I have to pride myself upon our youth who go forward eagerly as best they can and fight already quite well with ignorance. It is true that there is still a good deal of evil but we must not grieve but work until we are at last able to throw out this poisonous plant. . . . I have only one objection to the young people, that they like evening entertainments which spoil the heart and stain the soul, diminish health and . . . repute. Many a one who danced so incessantly went down to the cold grave prematurely; many a one bitterly regretted it. . . . O young people, watch yourselves!

And now, my dear neighbors, I must complain a little about you, because you have so long been deliberating in vain how to unite your lands. Many others did it long ago, because they had the understanding and will. . . . We must not lose even a moment if we want to overcome our hard ill-fortune. But you could not come to an understanding because there was a great lack of concord and on the other hand —say what you will—a great deal of hypocrisy and jealousy. Oh, but for this cursed jealousy that rules the heart of man, before which flees the holy love of our fellow-man as before a vampire, it would be better in the world, brothers; we should love each other, everyone would be as happy as a child, the vain world would become a paradise! . . .[6]

5   *Gazeta Świąteczna*, 1899, 25.
6   *Gazeta Świąteczna*, 1911, 16 [in verse].

[This peasant meeting, organized by the National Democratic Party and attended by over 1500 peasants, illustrates the passage from the wider community to the nation.]

The next day after the meeting three participants, elderly men, told us each separately [about the educatory influence of the *Gazeta*]. Here are the words of one of them: "I have belonged for five years to the National Democratic Party. There are in our commune more like me; there are some who have belonged longer, others shorter. There are also readers of the *Gazeta* like us who, however, do not want to belong to the party, and there are others who belong to other parties. We have been called here to this meeting by the National Democratic Party. It rouses us, that is true. I have read that it has been rousing the people [nationally] for 15 years already. But if it had not been for the *Gazeta Świąteczna* none of us peasants would be here at this meeting. We would be the same as our fathers were. Neither would there be speakers like those who have talked. For although the *Gazeta* did not call us to the meeting, it has made us citizens of our country, whereas formerly we were only a dark herd of cattle. The parties would have had nothing to talk with us about. They came to a ready thing."[7]

The wider community, as we see from our documents, is essentially based on the same social attitudes as the primary community—the desire for recognition and the desire for response. The main difference lies in the higher degree of intellectualization which these attitudes must acquire in the wider community. Whereas in the primary group the individual obtains satisfaction of his social instinct by a direct reaction of concrete personalities, in the secondary group he must be satisfied with an indirect reaction of an impersonal public. Of course, he does not pass without intermediary stages from the primary-group to the secondary-group psychology. On the one hand, in primary-group life there are many situations which prepare him for the secondary-group stage; on the other hand, in secondary-group life, however great may be the prevalence of abstract and indirect over concrete and direct relations, the latter never entirely disappear, and lend to all social activities some of the vividness and human interest which they possess in primary communities.

[7]   *Gazeta Świąteczna*, 1905, 52.

Even in a primary-group the individual has often to wait for recognition or response, which may never come if others do not indorse his claims. The peasant sometimes even intentionally postpones the satisfaction of his desires and does not claim at once the recognition or response to which he feels himself entitled, if he expects to get more by waiting or if he sees the possibility of startling the group by some unexpected effect. In all these cases, until recognition or response is actually obtained the individual must supplement by imagination the deficiencies of actual reality. Now, the psychological mechanism through which satisfaction of the social instinct is obtained in the wider community also consists in a large measure in supplementing actually experienced response and recognition by imagined response and recognition. The individual who sees his name or his contribution in print imagines the attitudes of the readers, and this has on him an effect similar to that which actual experience of these attitudes would have. Of course the individual expects actually to experience the imagined response and recognition when he comes into direct contact with particular members of the wider community, and many of our documents show how much the peasant needs that this expectation shall be confirmed and how eager he is to change indirect into direct connections, to meet the people about whom he knows or who know about him through the press. But the ability to be influenced by mere possibilities of social contact as implied in the printed word grows with the intellectual development of the peasant. This growth is particularly rapid when in a primary-group village or parish the majority begins to be interested in printed matter, because then the individual who has any connection with the press obtains direct recognition from his immediate milieu on the ground of his supposed recognition by the wider community.

More difficult to explain is the influence which the opinion of the wider community, indirectly manifested through the press, has not upon individuals, but upon whole primary-groups. We have seen examples of the powerful social reaction which the mention in print of a village or parish provokes in all its members. It seems that in this case we find transferred to a wider social plane the same attitude which formerly expressed itself in the dependence of the family upon the primary community. When the social horizon of the peasant was limited to his *okolica* the individual reacted to the praise or blame of his family by the community as if it were his own personal matter; this attitude not only resulted from his family solidarity but was enforced by the social environment which refused to dissociate the individual from the narrower group to which he belonged. Now when the village or the parish is the object of the social opinion of the wider community, the same phenomenon repeats itself; each member of the narrower group is affected by the positive or negative appreciation of the latter, not as an individual but as an integral part of the whole. In the *esprit de corps* of classes and of professional organizations, in national and race pride, the same attitude is found on a still higher social level; it is one of the most general manifestations of the "we"-psychology. Each member's personal reaction is strengthened by the consciousness of a similar reaction of other members, and the blame or praise to which the group is subjected by becoming the center of outside attention acquires for all its members a significance often quite out of proportion to its real import.

On the other hand, however, the wider community gives to the individual the opportunity to dissociate himself from his primary group by publicly assuming a critical attitude toward it or adopting attitudes different from those which prevail in his immediate milieu. Examples of unjustified accusations brought by individuals against their primary-groups show how eagerly this opportunity is grasped by the rebellious elements in communities where social disorganization has been progressing. Nevertheless, even this tendency to use the press as weapon in local struggles can be utilized for constructive purposes, for it makes it possible for the wider community and its leaders to act as arbiters and to impose their standards upon primary-groups. And propaganda of new ideas among the peasants can be successful only if the individuals who first accept these ideas feel independent of the social opinion of their immediate environment. But the peasant needs some social sanction for his attitudes; he may commit an isolated act of revolt but cannot maintain a permanent line of conduct without being backed by some group. The consciousness that he is a member of the wider community gives him a feeling of security which permits him to struggle for the new ideas against his primary-group; and, of course, he must consider himself superior to his environment as bearer of superior standards, otherwise his reformatory tendencies would have no justification in his own eyes. And even then he usually is not satisfied with whatever encouragement he can get from the wider community and its leaders; he strives to gather around himself a group of friends and followers whose personal response and recognition counterbalance the indifference or antagonism of the rest of the community. Thus, the very dependence of the peasant on direct social contacts makes him, once converted, a good propagandist of new ideas.

Small groups of such "enlightened" peasants scattered through the country but concentrated by means of indirect communication around some leaders acting through the popular press have constituted a continually growing nucleus of the wider community with which, through various direct personal bonds, an increasing circle of the population was more or less closely associated. As a matter of fact, at the period which we are investigating there were in the Congress Kingdom several such nuclei separated by political differences but partly connected by the cooperation of their members in various social institutions. The most important were the moderate group of which the chief organ was the *Gazeta Świąteczna* and the radical progressive group of the *Zaranie*. Occasional personal contacts between the members and the leaders, and between members belonging to different primary communities added a character of intimacy to the informal organization of these groups. Their external structure was similar to that of political parties, but their sphere of interest was much wider, for it included practically everything in which the peasant was supposed to be interested. In this respect they resembled primary communities and differed from other types of secondary groups which are always more or less specialized.

The method by which the feeling of moral solidarity was spread among the members of the wider community was calculated to develop the idealistic elements of their nature by appealing to their feeling of personal importance, and vice versa. It was assumed as self-evident that all those who belonged to the nucleus of the wider community should be actively interested in its welfare and progress, should be the first in spreading education, in contributing to common aims, in promoting new and more efficient forms of economic activity, in establishing new social institutions, in fostering harmonious social cooperation—in short, in helping to raise the whole peasant class to a higher cultural level. And on the other hand, all those who actively participated in the work of social reconstruction were considered belonging to the select minority as real collaborators of the leaders; they were treated as the "advance guard of progress," as a kind of aristocracy whose prestige was based not on their social function in the past but on their importance for the future.

At the same time, though perhaps less successfully, attempts were made to impart a new moral vitality to the old religious idea of a wide Christian community whose members owed to one another disinterested help independent of any direct social contact between them. It is hardly surprising that this idea did not have much practical significance for the peasant in the past. His economic conditions made him much oftener the object than the subject of assistance, and even when he was able to help, his primary-group had claims on all his altruism. Moreover, the clergy by the exclusive emphasis it put on purely religious matters reduced the duties of the Christian community to praying for one another and making collections for new churches. Of course, as the few documents referring to these activities show, even this type of mutual help implies altruistic emotions which can be developed and extended to other fields, but this development in so far as it actually occurred was mostly the work of lay leaders. The most efficient way of stirring altruistic tendencies has proved to be the appeal to sympathetic emotions at public meetings when the susceptibility to emotional suggestions is higher than usual, particularly in primary-group members, and the whole matter leaves a deeper impression. Calamities which befell particular communities—fire, hunger, flood—evidently found the easiest response, and more important than the actual help offered was the attitude which was developed by such response and which could be later utilized for other constructive purposes. An interesting point is that, partly as a consequence of this method of appealing to whole primary-groups for assistance, partly because the individual peasant could do but little in the line of altruistic help outside of his village or parish, this type of solidarity assumed the form of obligation of mutual assistance between primary communities rather than between individuals, whereas the organization for cultural progress was, as we have seen, essentially individualistic. This inter-communal solidarity in which the primary-group acts as a unit has not received perhaps all the attention it deserves and is not being developed sufficiently. For the peasant primary-group is not definitely breaking up; it is only being reconstructed on new foundations. The wider community will thus always be not only an organization of individuals but also an agglomeration of primary-groups, and its unity cannot be complete unless each of these groups as a whole—not alone through its individual members—is actively interested in the common welfare.

# III. Social Personality: The Definition of the Situation

# 7

# MOTIVATION: THE WISHES

IT IS impossible to understand completely any human being or any single act of his behavior, just as it is impossible to understand completely why a particular wild rose bloomed under a particular hedge at a particular moment. A complete understanding in either case would imply an understanding of all cosmic processes, of their interrelations and sequences. But it is not harder to comprehend the behavior of the "unadjusted" or "delinquent" person, say the vagabond or the prostitute, than that of the normally adjusted person, say the business man or the housewife.

In either case we realize that certain influences have been at work throughout life and that these are partly inborn, representing the original nature of man, the so-called instincts, and partly the claims, appeals, rewards, and punishments of society,—the influences of his social environment. But if we attempt to determine why the call of the wild prevails in the one case and the call of home, regular work, and "duty" in the other, we do not have different problems but aspects of the same general problem. It is only as we understand behavior as a whole that we can appreciate the failure of certain individuals to conform to the usual standards. And similarly, the unrest and maladjustment of the girl can

---

Adapted from *The Unadjusted Girl* (Boston: Little, Brown & Co., 1928), pp. 1-40.

be treated only as specifications of the general unrest and maladjustment.

In this connection students of psychology and education have been particularly interested in determining what the inborn tendencies really are. There was however no scientifically controlled work on the point until Watson undertook his experiments on newborn babies. At the time his work was interrupted he had found only three "instincts" present in the child at birth:

We are inclined now to believe that the fundamental emotional reactions can be grouped under three general divisions: those connected with fear; those connected with rage; those connected with what, for lack of a better term, we may call joy or love.

These at least deserve the name of major emotions. Whether or not other types of emotional reactions are present we cannot yet determine. . . . The principal situations which call our fear responses are as follows: (1) To suddenly remove from the infant all means of support, as when one drops it from the hand to be caught by an assistant. . . . (2) By loud sounds. (3) Occasionally when an infant is just falling asleep the sudden pulling of the blanket upon which it is lying will produce the fear response. (4) Finally, again when the child has just fallen asleep or is just ready to awake a sudden push or a slight shake is an adequate stimulus. The responses are a sudden catching of the breath, clutching randomly with the hands (the grasping reflex invariably appearing when the child is dropped), blinking of the eyelids, puckering of the lips, then crying; in older children, flight and hiding.

Observations seem to show that the hampering of the infant's movements is the factor which apart from all training brings out the movements characterized as rage. If the face or head is held, crying results, quickly followed by screaming. The body stiffens and fairly well coördinated slashing or striking movements of the hands and arms result; the feet and legs are drawn up and down; the breath is held until the child's face is flushed. In older children the slashing movements of the arms and legs are better coördinated and appear as kicking, slapping, biting, pushing, etc. These reactions continue until the irritating situation is removed, and sometimes do not cease then. Almost any child from birth can be thrown into a rage if its arms are held tightly to its sides. . . . Even the best-natured child shows rage if its nose is held for a few seconds. . . .

*Motivation: The Wishes* 119

The original stimuli for bringing out the earliest manifestations of joy or love seem to be as follows: gentle stroking and soft tickling of the infant's body, patting, gentle rocking, turning upon the stomach across the attendant's knee, etc. The response varies: if the infant is crying, crying ceases and a smile may appear; finally a laugh, and extension of the arms. In older children and in adults this emotion, due both to instinctive and habit factors, has an extremely wide range of expression.[1]

We understand of course that these expressions of emotion mean a preparation for action which will be useful in preserving life (anger), avoiding death (fear), and in reproducing the species (love), but even if our knowledge of the nervous system of man were complete we could not read out of it all the concrete varieties of human experience. The variety of expressions of behavior is as great as the variety of situations arising in the external world, while the nervous system represents only a general mechanism for action. We can however approach the problem of behavior through the study of the forces which impel action, namely, the wishes, and we shall see that these correspond in general with the nervous mechanism.

The human wishes have a great variety of concrete forms but are capable of the following general classification:

1. The desire for new experience.
2. The desire for security.
3. The desire for response.
4. The desire for recognition.

1. *The Desire for New Experience.* Men crave excitement, and all experiences are exciting which have in them some resemblance to the pursuit, flight, capture, escape, death which characterized the earlier life of mankind. Behavior is an adaptation to environment, and the nervous system itself is a developmental adaptation. It represents, among other things, a hunting pattern of interest. "Adventure" is what the young boy wants, and stories of adventure. Hunting trips are enticing; they are the survival of

[1] John B. Watson, "Practical and Theoretic Problems in Instinct and Habits," in *Suggestions of Modern Science Concerning Education*, by H. S. Jennings, J. B. Watson, Adolf Meyer, and W. I. Thomas, p. 63.

natural life. All sports are of the hunting pattern; there is a contest of skill, daring, and cunning. It is impossible not to admire the nerve of a daring burglar or highwayman. A fight, even a dog fight, will draw a crowd. In gambling or dice throwing you have the thrill of success or the chagrin of defeat. The organism craves stimulation and seeks expansion and shock even through alcohol and drugs. "Sensations" occupy a large part of the space in newspapers. Courtship has in it an element of "pursuit." Novels, theaters, motion pictures, etc., are partly an adaptation to this desire, and their popularity is a sign of its elemental force.

When 11 years old Walter McDermott was brought to court in company with three other boys, accused of breaking a padlock on a grocery store and attempting to enter the store at four o'clock A.M., March 3, 1909, and also of breaking a padlock on the door of a meat-market and stealing thirty-six cents from the cash till. Put on probation. August 19, 1910, brought to court for entering with two other boys a store and stealing a pocket-book containing $3.00. He admitted to the officers he and his company were going to pick pockets down town. He is the leader of the gang. . . .

Sent to St. Charles. Ran away March 17, 1913. By breaking a window got into a drug store, with two other boys, and stole a quantity of cigars and $1.61. Having taken the money, he gave one boy ten cents and another five cents. He gave away the cigars—eight or nine boxes—to "a lot of men and some boys." Spent the money "on candy and stuff." Committed to John Worthy School . . . October 27. His conduct has improved greatly; released on probation. . . .

December 23, 1913, accused of having broken, with an adult boy (19), into a clothing store and filled a suit case they found in the store with clothing and jewelry. Caught in shop. The officer said, "He would like to imitate Webb. He would like to kill some boy." According to his own confession, "It was six o'clock at night. I was going to confession. I met a boy and he said, 'Come out with me.' About nine o'clock we came to a clothing store, and we walked to the back, and seen a little hole. We pulled a couple of the laths off and as soon as we got in we got caught." But the officer said that previous to this they had burglarized a butcher's store and took from there a butcher's steel, and bored a hole in the wall with it. Committed to John Worthy School. Released June 26th, 1914. . . .

## Motivation: The Wishes 121

July 19, shot in a back alley twice at a little boy and once hit him. Broke with two other boys at night into Salvation Army office, broke everything he could and "used the office as a toilet room." Next day broke into a saloon, broke the piano, took cigars. Before this, July 14th, broke a side window of a saloon, stole $4.00 and a revolver. At the hearing Walter said about shooting the boy: "That boy was passing and I asked him for a match, and I heard this boy holler. I took a revolver off (his companion) and fixed a shot and hit the boy." His mother testified that he had spent only three nights at home since the time of his release from John Worthy School. He was arrested after the first offense, but escaped from the detention home. Committed to John Worthy School. . . .

Released after March 26. Committed a burglary in a grocery store, April 7th. Shot a man with a revolver in the left arm April 4th. Held up, with three other boys, a man on April 11, and robbed him of $12.00. Caught later, while the other boys caught at once. Held to the grand jury, found "not guilty" and released June 16, 1915.[2]

Vagabondage secures a maximum of new experience by the avoidance of the routine of organized society and the irksomeness at labor to which I will refer presently. In the constitutional vagabond the desire for new experience predominates over the other wishes and is rather contemplative and sensory, while in the criminal it is motor. But the discouraged criminal is sometimes a vagabond.

I have known men on the road who were tramping purely and simply because they loved to tramp. They had no appetite for liquor or tobacco, so far as I could find, also were quite out of touch with criminals and their habits; but somehow or other they could not conquer that passion for roving. In a way this type of vagabond is the most pitiful that I have ever known; and yet is the truest type of the genuine voluntary vagrant. . . . The *Wanderlust* vagrant . . . is free from the majority of passions common among vagrants and yet he is the most earnest vagrant of all. To reform him it is necessary to kill his personality, to take away his ambition—and this is a task

[2] Records of the Juvenile Court of Cook County (Illinois).

almost superhuman. Even when he is reformed he is a most cast-down person.[3]

The following description of a scientific adventure of a creative man, which I transcribe from an earlier paper, illustrates perfectly the psychological identity of a scientific quest with the pursuit of game:

Pasteur's first scientific success was in the study of crystallization, and in this connection he became particularly interested in racemic acid. But this substance, produced first by Kestner in 1820 as an accident in the manufacture of tartaric acid, had in 1852 ceased to appear, in spite of all efforts to obtain it. Pasteur and his friend Mitscherlich suspected that the failure to get it was due to the fact that the present manufacturers of tartaric acid were using a different tartar. The problem became then to inspect all the factories producing tartaric acid and finally to visit the sources from which the tartars came. This was the quest, and the impatience which Pasteur showed to begin it reminds us of a hound tugging at the leash. He asked Biot and Dumas to obtain for him a commission from the Ministry, or the Académie, but exasperated by the delay he was on the point of writing directly to the President of the Republic. "It is," he said, "a question that France should make it a point of honor to solve through one of her children." Biot counselled patience and pointed out that it was not necessary to "set the government in motion for this." But Pasteur would not wait. "I shall go to the end of the world," he said. "I *must* discover the source of racemic acid," and started independently. I will excuse you from following this quest in detail, but in a sort of diary prepared for Mme. Pasteur he showed the greatest eagerness to have her share the joy of it. He went to Germany, to Vienna, to Prague, studied Hungarian tartars. "Finally," he said, "I shall go to Trieste, where I shall find tartars of various countries, notably those of the Levant, and those of the neighborhood of Trieste itself. . . . If I had money enough I would go to Italy; . . . I shall give ten years to it if necessary." And after eight months he sent the following telegram: "I transform tartaric acid into racemic

[3] Josiah Flynt: "How Men Become Tramps," *Century Magazine*, October, 1895, p. 944.

Motivation: The Wishes 123

acid. Please inform MM. Dumas and Senarmont." He had made his kill.[4]

The craftsman, the artist, the scientist, the professional man, and to some extent the business man make new experience the basis of organized activity, of work and produce thereby social values. The division of labor which removes the problematical from the various operations of the work makes the task totally unstimulating. The repudiation of work leads to the vagabondage just illustrated and to the antisocial attitudes described below:

We have in New York at present, and have had for some years past, an immense army of young men, boys between fifteen and twenty-six, who are absolutely determined that under no conditions will they do any honest work. They sponge on women, swindle, pick pockets, commit burglary, act as highwaymen, and, if concerned, kill, in order to get money dishonestly. How do they dispose of the vast sums they have already stolen? Gambling and women. They are inveterate gamblers.[5]

And similarly, among women we have the thief, the prostitute, the blackmailer, the vamp, and the "charity girl."

2. *The Desire for Security.* The desire for security is opposed to the desire for new experience. The desire for new experience is, as we have seen, emotionally related to anger, which tends to invite death, and expresses itself in courage, advance, attack, pursuit. The desire for new experience implies, therefore, motion, change, danger, instability, social irresponsibility. The individual dominated by it shows a tendency to disregard prevailing standards and group interests. He may be a social failure on account of his instability, or a social success if he converts his experiences into social values,—puts them into the form of a poem, makes of them a contribution to science. The desire for security, on the other hand, is based on fear, which tends to avoid death and expresses itself in timidity, avoidance, and flight. The individual

[4] "Primary-Group Norms in Present-Day Society," in *Suggestions of Modern Science Concerning Education*, p. 162.
[5] Chief City Magistrate William McAdoo, in *New York World*, December 18, 1920.

dominated by it is cautious, conservative, and apprehensive, tending also to regular habits, systematic work, and the accumulation of property.

The social types known as "bohemian" and "philistine" are determined respectively by the domination of the desire for new experience and the desire for security. The miser represents a case where the means of security has become an end in itself.

Mamie Reilly's mother viewed with increasing regret the effect of premature care and responsibility on her daughter. Mamie had been working five years since, as a child of thirteen, she first insisted on getting a job. "She's a good girl, Mame is, but y'never seen anything like her. Every pay night reg'lar she'll come in an' sit down at that table. 'Now Ma,' she'll say like that, 'what *are* you goin' to do? How ever are y' goin' t' make out in th' rent?' 'Land sakes,' I'll say, 'one w'd think this whole house was right there on your shoulders. I'll get along somehow.' But y'can't make her see into that. 'Now, what'll we do, how'll you manage, Ma?' she'll keep askin'. She's too worrisome—that's what I tell her. An' she don't care to go out. Mebbe she'll take a walk, but like 's not she'll say, 'What's th' use?' Night after night she jest comes home, eats 'er supper, sits down, mebbe reads a bit, an' then goes t' bed."[6]

The following document shows the desire for security in a person who is temperamentally inclined to new experience, but whose hardships call out the desire for security. The whole life, in fact, of this man shows a wavering between the two wishes. The desire for a "secure existence" which he expresses here finally prevails and he approaches the philistine type:

I had been ten weeks on the journey without finding any work, and I had no idea how long I should still be obliged to tramp about the world, and where was the end toward which I was going. . . . I should have been very glad of my visit to Stach had it not been for the thought of my wandering. If I had been going immediately to work from Mokrsko I should certainly have fallen in love with some girl but the thought that I must tramp again about the world destroyed my wish for anything. Moreover I wanted to leave as soon as possible, for I could not look with dry eyes on how he wallowed

[6] Ruth True, *The Neglected Girl*, p. 50.

*Motivation: The Wishes*  125

in everything and had whatever he wanted. Everybody respected and appreciated him; everywhere doors were open for him, and he prized lightly everything he had, for he had never experienced any evil or misery. For if I had only one half of what he owned, how grateful I should be to God for his goodness. And tears flowed from my eyes when I compared his lot with mine. Fortune, how unjust you are! You drive one man about the world and you have no pity on him though he is whipped with wind and snow and cold stops his breath. People treat him worse than a dog and drive him away from their doors, without asking: "Have you eaten? have you a place to sleep?" And when he asks for anything they are ready to beat him, like that peasant who struck me with the whip. And what for? Perhaps this mayor would have acted likewise if he had met me somewhere on my journey, and today he sets tables for this same tramp.

What a difference between us! Why, we have the same parents, the same name! And perhaps he is better considered because he is better instructed than I? In my opinion, not even for that. Or perhaps because he is nobler and handsomer? No, not for that. He merits consideration only because he has a secure existence, because he has bread. Let him wander into an unknown country: would he be better considered than I? No, a thousand times No. So if I want to merit consideration and respect, I ought first to win this [secure] existence. And how shall I win it and where? Shall I find it in tramping about the world? No, I must work, put money together and establish my own bakery. Then I can say boldly that I have [a secure existence] and even a better one than a teacher. . . .[7]

3. *The Desire for Response.* Up to this point I have described the types of mental impressionability connected with the pursuit of food and the avoidance of death, which are closely connected with the emotions of anger and fear. The desire for response, on the other hand, is primarily related to the instinct of love, and shows itself in the tendency to seek and to give signs of appreciation in connection with other individuals.

There is first of all the devotion of the mother to the child and the response of the child, indicated in the following passage from Thorndike.

[7] W. I. Thomas and Florian Znaniecki, *The Polish Peasant in Europe and America*, III, 246, 251.

All women possess originally, from early childhood to death, some interest in human babies, and a responsiveness to the instinctive looks, calls, gestures and cries of infancy and childhood, being satisfied by childish gurglings, smiles and affectionate gestures, and moved to instinctive comforting acts by childish signs of pain, grief and misery. Brutal habits may destroy, or competing habits overgrow, or the lack of exercise weaken, these tendencies, but they are none the less as original as any fact in human nature.[8]

This relation is of course useful and necessary since the child is helpless throughout a period of years and would not live unless the mother were impelled to give it her devotion. This attitude is present in the father of the child also but is weaker, less demonstrative, and called out more gradually.

In addition, the desire for response between the two sexes in connection with mating is very powerful. An ardent courtship is full of assurances and appeals for reassurance. Marriage and a home involve response but with more settled habits, more routine work, less of new experience. Jealousy is an expression of fear that the response is directed elsewhere. The flirt is one who seeks new experience through the provocation of response from many quarters.

In some natures this wish, both to receive and to give response, is out of proportion to the other wishes, "over-determined," so to speak, and interferes with a normal organization of life. And the fixation may be either on a child or a member of either sex. The general situation is the same in the following case.

I am the unhappy mother of a dear little son, eight years old. You ask the cause of my unhappiness? I ought to be happy with such a dear treasure? But the answer is, I love my child too much. My love to my son is so great, so immeasurably deep, that I myself am worthless. My own person has not a trace of worth for me. I am as it were dead to all and everything. My thoughts by day and by night are turned toward my child. I see nothing in the world except my beloved child. Nothing exists for me except him. Every one of my thoughts, every desire and wish that awakens in me, turns

[8] E. L. Thorndike, *The Original Nature of Man*, p. 81.

around the child of my heart. I am nothing. I do not live, I do not exist. I forget myself as I forget all and everything in the world. I go around the whole day without eating and feel no hunger. I forget that I must eat. I go around often a whole day in my nightclothes because I forget that I have to dress. With soul and body, with mind and spirit I am wrapt up in my child. I have no thought for myself at all.

If clothes come to my mind, I am thinking of a new suit for my boy. I am nothing. And if I think of shoes, I imagine a pair of little shoes on the feet of my dear little boy. I myself am the same as dead. If I go to the country in the summer, I come home on account of my child. I myself do not exist. Every enjoyment in life, every happiness to which I give a thought is connected in my mind with my little boy. I myself am as if I were never at all in the world. The child is everything—my soul and my spirit, my breath and my life. He is the air I breathe. I am nothing. I don't consider myself, I don't think of myself, just as if I had never been in the world.

And so it is when my child is not well, when he has perhaps scratched his finger. . . . Oh, how I suffer then. No pen in the world can describe the terrible despair I feel. I live then as it were in a cloud, I cannot at all understand how my soul then remains in my body. My pain is then indescribable, greater than any can understand. . . . When my child is well again and his round, rosy cheeks bloom like the flowers in May and he is joyous and full of life and leaps and dances, then I myself look as if I had just recovered from a fever sickness.

Tell me, I beg you, dear editor, what can such a mama do that her dear child shall not become a lonely orphan. For I feel that I cannot continue long as it is. My strength is not holding out and a time must come when no strength to live will remain in me. . . .[9]

The varieties of love in women are greater than in men, for we are to include here not only physical passion but parental feeling—that fund of emotion which is fixed on the child. The capacity of response to the child, mother love, is notorious and is painfully evident in the last document, where the mother has no thought left for anything but the child. The mother is one who does not refuse. She does not refuse the breast to the lusty child

[9] *Forward*, February 8, 1922.

even when she is herself ailing. And while this feeling is developed as a quality of motherhood it is present before motherhood and is capable of being transferred to any object calling for sympathy, —a doll, a man, or a cause. The women of the Malay Peninsula suckle little wild pigs when these are found motherless.

I have seen (through the kindness of Hutchins Hapgood) the life history of a woman who has had sexual relations with numbers of men. At the same time she has always fed men. She has kept a restaurant, partly I think to feed men. When one of her friends committed suicide she dreamed of him for months and always dreamed that she was feeding him. While she was sexually passionate her concern was mainly to satisfy the sexual hunger of others, as she satisfied their food-hunger. When two of her lovers were jealous, unhappy, and desperate, she ran from one to the other like a mother visiting two sick children in different hospitals. More than once she attempted suicide. When she tried to explain herself to me she said that without some human relationship she felt unbearably lonely, and that she was drawn to lonely men without regard to their social condition. Many of her friends were criminals and she would speak to any bum on a park bench. She was never a prostitute. One of her friends said, "Martha is a woman to whom everything has happened that should logically break a woman's character and spirit. She ought to be a demoralized victim of society. She has done nearly everything that is supposed to ruin and destroy a person, especially a woman, but she is not a bit destroyed. She knows the so-called lowest things in life, but she wants the best and feels it. She feels what is beautiful and fine and loves it. She does things that sometimes mean sordidness in others but not in her. She gets drunk, but is not drunken. She is loose sexually in her acts, but her spirit is as simple as the flowers."

A touching expression of response from a man, a devotion to a parent as deep as mother love, is found in a letter of the psychologist William James, written to his father from England when the death of the latter was anticipated.

My blessed old Father: I scribble this line (which may reach you, though I should come too late) just to tell you how full of the tenderest memories and feelings about you my heart has for the last few days been filled. In that mysterious gulf of the past, into which the present will soon fall and go back and back, yours is still for me the central figure. All my intellectual life I derive from you; and though we have often seemed at odds in the expression thereof, I'm sure there's a harmony somewhere and that our strivings will combine. What my debt to you is goes beyond all my power of estimating— so early, so penetrating and so constant has been the influence.

You need be in no anxiety about your literary remains. I will see them well taken care of, and that your words shall not suffer from being concealed. At Paris I heard that Milsand, whose name you may remember is in the *Revue des Deux Mondes* and elsewhere, was an admirer of the *Secret of Swedenborg,* and Hodgson told me your last book had deeply impressed him. So will it be. . . .

As for us, we shall live on, each in his way—feeling somewhat unprotected, old as we are, for the absence of the parental bosoms as a refuge, but holding fast together in that common sacred memory. We will stand by each other and by Alice, try to transmit the torch in our offspring as you did in us, and when the time comes for being gathered in, I pray we may, if not all, some at least, be as ripe as you.

As for myself, I know what trouble I've given you at various times through my peculiarities; and as my own boys grow up I shall learn more and more of the kind of trial you had to overcome in superintending the development of a creature different from yourself, for whom you felt responsible. I say this merely to show how my sympathy with you is likely to grow much livelier, rather than to fade—and not for the sake of regrets.

As for the other side, and Mother, and our all possibly meeting, I can't say anything. More than ever at this moment do I feel that if that were true all would be solved and justified. And it comes strangely over me in bidding you good-by how a life is but a day and expresses mainly but a single note. It is so much like the act of bidding an ordinary good-night.

Good-night, my sacred old Father! If I don't see you again— farewell! a blessed farewell. Your William.[10]

Usually this feeling is not so profound, as shown in these examples, and may be just sufficient to use as a tool and a play

[10] *Letters of William James* (Atlantic Monthly Press), p. 218.

interest. But even then the life may be so schematized that it plays the main rôle. The following is a single item taken from an autobiography of over three hundred closely written pages in which practically the only type of wish expressed is the desire for response from men, but this wish is never very strong.

At Wichita I went to school till I was about sixteen. Between ten and sixteen I had lots of little sweethearts. I have never been able to be happy without an atmosphere of love or at least flirtation. To such a degree is this true that I fear this story will be little else than the record of my loves and flirtations, happy and unhappy. I liked to kiss little boys from the start, but never cared to kiss the girls. I have had many women pals all through my life, but I never cared to kiss them, as many girls do. I suppose I am what my friend the newspaper man calls a man's woman. Certainly I am miserable unless there is a man around, and I generally want several. Until recently I have always been in love with two at the same time. But somehow since I met Harry it is different. My love for the other sex was always of an innocent kind. I loved men as the birds love sunshine. It is not a passion, but a necessity, like the air. I am light-hearted and buoyant by nature, and never thought of doing wrong. And yet the ugly side of this passion has always been forced upon me.[11]

In many girls the awakening of love and its fixation on an object is slow or incomplete. The girl in the following example is cold as a stone toward everything but herself. Her affection is turned inward. She is the type called narcissistic, in love with herself, like the mythical Narcissus. Probably the appearance of a child will extrovert her feeling to some extent.

I have a sister of sixteen, very beautiful and proud of herself. She is of the type who care only for themselves. She would drown her parents, brothers and sisters in a spoon of water if she could only gain something by it, and without suffering the slightest remorse. Besides, she is very obstinate and must have her own way regardless of anything.... But my father and mother and the rest of the family wished her to possess the ordinary school education, so that her ignorance might not be an impediment in her future life, so we put

[11] Hutchins Hapgood, "The Marionette" (manuscirpt).

our efforts together and sent her to business school, and thank God she managed somehow to finish the course.

Well, she is now working for the past six months. She has a very good position with a large firm and earns $20 a week. Out of this, mother does not get even a cent, though she sleeps and boards at home. Moreover, she borrows money from mother whenever she can but she never repays it. As if this were not enough trouble, she acts very improperly toward the whole family. She possesses absolutely no sense of shame nor sense of pity and behaves like a wild person in the house; she scolds and shouts and is especially cruel to our younger sisters and brothers."[12]

And in certain characters, almost invariably men, the desire for response is barely sufficient to keep them in contact with or on the fringe of humanity.

Many a man leads in London a most solitary, unsociable life, who yet would find it hard to live far away from the thronged city. Such men are like Mr. Galton's oxen, unsociable but gregarious; and they illustrate the fact that sociability, although it has the gregarious instinct at its foundation, is a more complex, more highly developed, tendency. As an element of this more complex tendency to sociability, the instinct largely determines the form of the recreations of even the cultured classes, and is the root of no small part of the pleasure we find in attendance at the theatre, at concerts, lectures, and all such entertainments.[13]

Frequently in marriage the wife provides the main fund of response and the husband is assimilated to the child. Here the wife has had a love adventure, is living with another man, but is planning to visit her husband clandestinely and look after him a bit:

My Own Dear Dean: So you would like to know if I am happy. Well, dear, that is one thing that will never be in my life again. It has gone from me forever. I don't want you to think that Clarence is not good to me, for he could not be better—I have a nice home that he has bought, and chickens and a lovely garden, and if Marjorie was his very own he could not be better to her. But he is terribly

[12] *Forward*, December 17, 1920.
[13] E. L. Thorndike: *The Original Nature of Man*, p. 87.

jealous, and it makes it very hard for me, for, God knows, I never give him cause. Oh, Dean, dear, wait until you see how I have changed. If I could only live my life over it would be so different. . . .

Now, dear, please don't feel that you have no interest in life, for you have our dear little girl, and just as soon as she is big enough to be a comfort to you—well, she is yours.

Dean, if you only knew how badly I want to see you. Now, listen—Clarence leaves here August 31 for Vancouver and will be there until September 6. . . . So, if you could send me my fare one way, why, then he could not refuse to let me go. . . . Let me know what you are planning, for I want to see you and cook you some good old meals again. . . . Yours only, Patsy.[14]

It is unnecessary to particularize as to the place of response in art. The love and sex themes are based on response, and they outweigh the other themes altogether. Religion appeals to fear, fear of death and extinction, and promises everlasting security, or threatens everlasting pain, but in the New Testament the element of response, connected with the concrete personalities of Jesus and Mary, predominates. Any hymn book will contain many versified love letters addressed to Jesus. There are on record also many alleged conversations of nuns with Jesus which are indistinguishable in form from those of human courtship.

Angela da Foligno says that Christ told her he loved her better than any woman in the vale of Spoleto. The words of this passage are fatuous almost beyond belief: "Then He began to say to me the words that follow, to provoke me to love Him: 'O my sweet daughter! O my daughter, my temple! O my daughter, my delight! Love me, because thou art much loved by me.' And often did He say to me: 'O my daughter, My sweet Spouse!' And he added in an underbreath, 'I love thee more than any other woman in the valley of Spoleto.'" To amuse and to delight Gertrude of Eisleben, He sang duets with her "in a tender and harmonious voice." The same saint writes of their "incredible intimacy"; and here, as in later passages of Angela da Foligno, the reader is revolted by their sensuality. . . . In the diary of Marie de l'Incarnation there is such an entry as

[14] *Chicago American*, May 13, 1915.

"*entretien familier avec J.-C.*"; and during such interviews she makes use of a sort of pious baby talk, like a saintly Tillie Slowboy.[15]

In general the desire for response is the most social of the wishes. It contains both a sexual and a gregarious element. It makes selfish claims, but on the other hand it is the main source of altruism. The devotion to child and family and devotion to causes, principles, and ideals may be the same attitude in different fields of application. It is true that devotion and self-sacrifice may originate from any of the other wishes also—desire for new experience, recognition, or security—or may be connected with all of them at once. Pasteur's devotion to science seems to be mainly the desire for new experience,—scientific curiosity; the campaigns of a Napoleon represent recognition (ambition) and the self-sacrifice of such characters as Maria Spiridonova, Florence Nightingale, Jane Addams is a sublimation of response. The women who demanded Juvenile Courts were stirred by the same feeling as the mother in an earlier document, whereas the usual legal procedure is based on the wish to have security for life and property.

4. *The Desire for Recognition.* This wish is expressed in the general struggle of men for position in their social group, in devices for securing a recognized, enviable, and advantageous social status. Among girls dress is now perhaps the favorite means of securing distinction and showing class. A Bohemian immigrant girl expressed her philosophy in a word: "After all, life is mostly what you wear." Veblen's volume, "Theory of the Leisure Class," points out that the status of men is established partly through the show of wealth made by their wives. Distinction is sought also in connection with skillful and hazardous activities, as in sports, war, and exploration. Playwriters and sculptors consciously strive for public favor and "fame." In the "achievement" of Pasteur and of similar scientific work there is not only the pleasure of the "pursuit" itself, but the pleasure of public recognition. Boasting, bullying, cruelty, tyranny, "the will to power" have in them a sadistic element allied to the emotion of anger

[15] Burr, *Religious Confession and Confessants*, p. 856.

and are efforts to compel a recognition of the personality. The frailty of women, their illness, and even feigned illness, is often used as a power-device, as well as a device to provoke response. On the other hand, humility, self-sacrifice, saintliness, and martyrdom may lead to distinction. The showy motives connected with the appeal for recognition we define as "vanity"; the creative activities we call "ambition."

The importance of recognition and status for the individual and for society is very great. The individual not only wants them but he needs them for the development of his personality. The lack of them and the fear of never obtaining them are probably the main source of those psychopathic disturbances which the Freudians treat as sexual in origin.

On the other hand society alone is able to confer status on the individual and in seeking to obtain it he makes himself responsible to society and is forced to regulate the expression of his wishes. His dependence on public opinion is perhaps the strongest factor impelling him to conform to the highest demands which society makes upon him.

The chief difference between the down-and-out man and the down-and-out girl is this. The d.-a.-o man sleeps on a park bench and looks like a bum. The d.-a.-o. girl sleeps in an unpaid-for furnished room and looks very respectable. The man spends what little change he has—if he has any—for food and sleeps on a bench. The girl spends what little change she has—if she has any—for a room and goes without food.

Not because she has more pride than the man has. She hasn't. But because cops haul in girls who would sleep on benches, and well-meaning organizations "rescue" girls who look down and out. A pretty face and worn-out soles are a signal for those who would save girls from the perilous path, whereas an anaemic face in a stylish coat and a pair of polished French heels can go far unmolested. . . .

You will argue that any woman with an empty stomach and a fur coat ought to sell the coat for a shabby one and spend the money for food. That is because you have never been a lady bum. A fur coat gets her places that a full stomach never would. It is her entrée into hotel washrooms when she is dirty from job hunting. It gets her into department-store rest rooms when she is sore of foot. And in the last stages it gets her help from a certain class of people who would be glad to help her if she had suddenly lost her purse, but who never would if she had never had a purse.

And then, most important of all, it helps her to hang on to her last scraps of self-repect.[16]

Alice . . . wants to be somebody, to do great things, to be superior. In her good moods, she is overwhelmed with dreams of accomplishment. She pines to use good English, to be a real lady. There is pathos in her inquiry as to what you say when a boy introduces you to his mother and how to behave in a stylish hotel dining room. Such questions have an importance that is almost greater than the problem of how to keep straight sexually. Winning of social approval is an ever-present, burning desire, but she has no patterns, no habits, no control over the daily details of the process whereby this is gained. When one tries to place her in a good environment with girls of a better class, she reacts with a deepened sense of inferiority, expressd in more open, boastful wildness. She invents adventures with men to dazzle these virtuous, superior maidens. The craving for pleasures and something to make her forget increases.[17]

In many cases, both in boys and girls, particularly at the period of adolescence, the energy takes the forms of daydreaming, that is, planning activity, and also of "pathological lying," or pretended activity. The wishes are thus realized in an artistic schematization in which the dreamer is the chief actor. The following, from the diary of a sixteen-year-old girl is in form a consistent expression of the desire for recognition, but very probably the form disguises a sexual longing, and the daydream is thus an example of the sublimation of the desire for response, as frequently in poetry and literature.

I am between heaven and earth. I float, as it were on a dream-cloud which carries me up at times into a glorious atmosphere, and again nearer the mucky earth, but always on, always on. I see not man, I see not the children of man, the big ME lies in my head, in my hand, in my heart. I place myself upon the throne of Kings, and

[16] "The Lady Bum," by One of Them. *New York Times, Book Review and Magazine*, January 1, 1922.
[17] Jessie Taft, "Mental Hygiene Problems of Normal Adolescence," *Mental Hygiene*, 5:746.

tramp the dusty road, care-free. I sing to myself and call me pretty names; I place myself upon the stage, and all mankind I call upon for applause, and applause roars to me as the thunder from the heavens. I reason that mine is not inevitable stage-madness which comes to all females of my pitiful age; mine is a predestined prophecy, mine is a holy design, my out-coming is a thing to be made way for.

I bathe myself in perfumed waters, and my body becomes white and slender. I clothe myself in loosened gowns, silks as soft as thistledown, and I am transported to scenes of glory. The even stretch of green, bedecked with flowers to match the color of my pale gold gown, is mine to dance and skip upon. A lightness and a grace comes into my limbs. What joy is mine! I leap and spring and dart in rhythm with nature, and music leaps from my steps and movements and before my eyes are men. Men and women and children with heads bent forward, with eyes aglow with wonder, and with praise and love for this essence of grace and beauty which is I. What more, what more! I hang upon this idol of a dream, but it is gone. The height of happiness is reached; alas, even in dreams there is an end to happiness, the bubble bursts, and the dust and noise of earth come back to me. I shut my eyes and ears to these and seek consolation among the poor. In dreams I go often among them. With my heaping purse of gold, I give them clothes and beds to sleep upon, I give them food to nourish them and me, to nourish and refresh my fame. But do I give my gold away, and does my purse cave inwards? Ah, no! Come to my aid, my imagination, for thou art very real to me today. An endless store of gold is mine in banks of state. My name is headed on the lists of all, my money does increase even as I hand it to these poor. The poor bless me, they kneel and kiss my hands. I bid them rise, and the hypocrisy of my godless soul bids them pray and in this find restoration.

I grow weary as I walk, and truth is even harder yet to bear than ever before. I am sad, I have nothing, I am no one. But I speak soothingly to myself, bidding me treat my hungry self to food, and I promise that the night shall be long and the dreams and journeys many.[18]

[18] Jessie Taft: "Mental Hygiene Problems of Normal Adolescence," *Mental Hygiene*, 5:750.

## Motivation: The Wishes 137

On the contrary, the following is in form a desire for response, but the details show that the girl feels keenly the lack of recognition. The response is desired not for itself alone but as a sign and assurance of comparative worth.

I am in despair, and I want to pour out my bitter heart. When I have once talked out my heart I feel better afterwards.

Dear editor, why can I not find a boy to love me? I never make a hit with young people. I never have any success with them. I associate with young people, I like them, they like me, but nobody ever runs after me. No boy is crazy about me. All my girl friends are popular with young men. Every single one has a boy or more who is in love with her and follows her steps. I alone have no luck. Do not think, dear editor, that I am burning to marry; it is not yet time for that. But the thought that I am left out makes me very wretched. It distresses me and it hurts me to my soul's marrow to know that no one desires me, that people are indifferent toward me. Oh how happy I should be if somebody would love me, if somebody would come to see me. It must be such a sweet pleasure to feel that some one is interested in you, that some one comes to see you, comes to you especially, on account of yourself. Oh, why can I not have this happiness!

When I go to a party and when I come back I feel so low and so fallen. Young men crowded around my companions like flies around honey. I alone was an exception. I have not a jealous nature, but no other girl in my place would feel otherwise. Can you show me a way to win a boy's heart? What sort of quality must a girl possess in order to attract a young man?

It is true I am no beauty. But what do all the girls do? They fix themselves up. You can buy powder and paint in the drug stores. My companions are not more beautiful than I. I am not sleepy. When I am in the company of young people I am joyous, I make myself attractive, I try my best to attract attention to myself. But that is all thrown to the dogs.

Dear editor, if you only knew with how much care I make my clothes. I go through the great stores to select out the most beautiful materials. I annoy the dressmaker to death until she suits me exactly. If it happens that a hook somewhere on the dress is not in the right place, or a buttonhole has a single stitch more or less than it should have, I have the greatest distress, and sharpest heartache.

When I go somewhere to a dance I am full of hopes, my heart is beating with excitement. Before leaving the house I take a last look in the mirror. When I return home I have the blues, I feel cold. My teeth grind together. So much exertion, so much strength lost, all for nothing. A boy has talked to me, another boy has given me a smile, still another boy has made me a little compliment, but I feel that I am not near and dear to any one. I feel that my face has not been stamped on the heart of any one.[19]

From the foregoing description it will be seen that wishes of the same general class—those which tend to arise from the same emotional background—may be totally different in moral quality. The moral good or evil of a wish depends on the social meaning or value of the activity which results from it. Thus the vagabond, the adventurer, the spendthrift, the bohemian are dominated by the desire for new experience, but so are the inventor and the scientist; adventures with women and the tendency to domesticity are both expressions of the desire for response; vain ostentation and creative artistic work both are designed to provoke recognition; avarice and business enterprise are actuated by the desire for security.

Moreover, when a concrete wish of any general class arises it may be accompanied and qualified by any or all of the other classes of wishes. Thus when Pasteur undertook the quest described above we do not know what wish was uppermost. Certainly the love of the work was very strong, the ardor of pursuit, the new experience; the anticipation of the recognition of the public, the scientific fame involved in the achievement was surely present; he invited response from his wife and colleagues, and he possibly had the wish also to put his future professional and material life on a secure basis. The immigrant who comes to America may wish to see the new world (new experience), make a fortune (security), have a higher standing on his return (recognition), and induce a certain person to marry him (response).

[19] *Forward*, September 30, 1921.

## Motivation: The Wishes

The general pattern of behavior which a given individual tends to follow is the basis of our judgment of his character. Our appreciation (positive or negative) of the character of the individual is based on his display of certain wishes as against others and on his modes of seeking their realization. Whether given wishes tend to predominate in this or that person is dependent primarily on what is called temperament, and apparently this is a chemical matter, dependent on the secretions of the glandular systems. Individuals are certainly temperamentally predisposed toward certain classes of the wishes. But we know also that the expression of the wishes is profoundly influenced by the approval of the man's immediate circle and of the general public. The conversions of wild young men to stable ways, from new experience to security, through marriage, religion, and business responsibility, are examples of this. We may therefore define character as an expression of the organization of the wishes resulting from temperament and experience, understanding by "organization" the general pattern which the wishes as a whole tend to assume among themselves.

The significant point about the wishes as related to the study of behavior is that they are the motor element, the starting point of activity. Any influences which may be brought to bear must be exercised on the wishes.

We may assume also that an individual life cannot be called normal in which all the four types of wishes are not satisfied in some measure and in some form.

# 8

# THE UNCONSCIOUS: CONFIGURATIONS OF PERSONALITY

I

THE CLASSIFICATION of personalities by psychological types on the basis of extravert and introvert tendencies has a certain value. I have great respect for the work of Kretschmer, for example, and the identification of manic-depressive states with the pyknic type and the schizophrenias with the asthenic type of physique, this being the application in the field of psychopathology of the extravert-introvert concept of Jung, without the theories of Jung. It is plain, however, that persons are usually extravert at one moment and introvert at another, and the same person may be disposed in one direction at one age level and stage of maturation and in the other direction at another, and we further have no data as to the rôle played by conditioning factors, which is certainly a very great one.

At any rate, instead of taking this line of approach, I am assuming, at least for the initial standpoint for the study of the formation of the personality, that there are certain satisfactions, objects of desire, which men always and everywhere want to seek

---

Reprinted from *The Unconscious: A Symposium* (New York: Alfred A. Knopf, 1927), pp. 143–63.

## The Unconscious 141

to secure, and we may speak of these satisfactions as values. These values will be found also to fall into classes or fields, corresponding partly with instinctive or unlearned action tendencies and partly with learned or conditioned tendencies. We may speak of the action tendencies as attitudes and of the values as stimuli.

From this standpoint a personality would be regarded as an organization of attitudes, and personalities would be distinguished among themselves by their greater or less tendency to seek their satisfactions, play their rôles, in this or that field of the values. But we have to make the same remark here as with reference to extravert and introvert types—a few will be found characterized by a preponderance of this or that attitude and value, while the many will represent a mingling of all of them. Moreover, it will appear that in connection with stages of physical and mental and emotional maturation the personality will be weighted differently with the different attitudes and values, and questions will always arise with reference to constitutional traits as against habit formation.

Viewed, then, as a configuration, a personality would be a background of attitudes and values common to everybody, upon which certain attitudes and values, or constellations of attitudes and values, assume a prominent or perhaps a dominant position.

What these fields of the values are I will not elaborate here because I have done this elsewhere and more than once, but I will state my formulation of the matter in outline as point of departure.

There is, first, the field of new experience—the desire for heightened states of stimulation, physiological expansion, change, adventure, thrill, shock. Drink and drugs are an expression of it, and interest in "sensations," reports of scandal, crime and disaster in the press, and these accounts are the artistic aspect of the drink habit. Games and play are more organized expressions. Hunting and scientific pursuits contain the pattern, and it is interesting that language has applied the name "pursuit" in both connections. They are the same interest in different fields of application. Köhler's ape, within his powers, was as scientific as Millikan in his research into the electron. He divorced his interest from practical utility. After the invention of joining the two sticks he went on with his manipulations, not pausing to eat the bananas he had collected, but pulling in useless objects. My interpretation is that in defeating others in games, or being defeated, in witnessing the knockout of the prize ring or the stage tragedy, in reading of the ruin of others, we are witnessing and participating in situations of fight, flight, pursuit, adventures of life and death. The manipulatory interest is preparatory, having the relation of the trap or the arrow to the killing. Dice throwing and drink get the effect without the activity.

The second field of the values is derived from one of the original forms of response which Watson found in the new-born and which he called "love." It represents the desire for intimate relationships and contacts. It is seen in the relation of mother and child, it blossoms and proliferates in the adolescent period, expresses itself in various types of love—romantic love, adventurous love, domestic love, divine love, love of humanity. It represents the seeking and giving of affection and appreciation, whether between the sexes, in friendships, in gangs, kinship groups or intimate circles. It has its pathological expressions in homosexuality, suicide pacts, and "flight into disease," or resort to illness or disability, as in hysteria, in order to secure sympathy. We may call this interest the desire for response.

A third class of values is the object of what may be called the desire for recognition. It has to do with standing, reputation, status in the world, the appreciation of the public, not of the intimate group. It is connected with the individual's conception of his rôle, and of the public's conception of this rôle. Vanity is an aspect of it, and ambition, and fame and infamy. The actor who stops the show gets a full measure of it, and those who seek "careers" are motivated by it. Families seek to maintain status by solidarity and individuals disregard families to seek it alone— "Down to Gehenna or up to the throne."

It will appear, however, that when different claimants for recognition manifest apparently identical behavior they may be, from the constitutional standpoint, quite different personalities. The dominant, masterful, managerial, oppressive or sadistic person may have, let us assume, a glandular drive, derived apparently from the instinct of anger, while the most persistent and painful claims for recognition may come from those who are striving to compensate for feelings of inferiority, inadequacy or social neglect, and this is close to fear.

Finally, security as attitude and value is opposed to new experience, or regulative of it. It represents work as against play, utility as against pleasure, saving as against spending. The spendthrift and the miser represent the two extremes. The older generations work upon the young and the group upon the individual to suppress certain forms of new experience in favor of settled ways of life. Marriage, family responsibilities, economic aims notoriously revolutionize the personality configuration of the heedless youth.

But assuming that these attitudes and values are represented in every person in some proportions and that the type of personality depends on the character of their organization among themselves, we still have only a description, a possible classification or schedule, while we are here interested in the selection and arrangement of preferences as represented in a concrete personality. This must be understood, if at all, in connection with the experience of the individual, the kind of materials he has in consciousness, and the organization of these materials into his unique habit system and stimulus system will have to be related also to the habit systems and stimulus system of the groups with which he has more or less intimacy.

With reference to the unconscious in this connection, it is not my intention to speak of this psychologically but sociologically. And from the standpoint of the problems with which I have to deal, I seem to meet with not one but several manifestations of the unconscious. For my purpose here also, the conscious and the unconscious represent simply more and less awareness of what is going on.

## II

There is a phase of habit formation and the unconscious which could be compared rather extensively with Professor Child's data on the structuralization of the organism by the operation of the stimuli of the environment.

An observer in California, for example, visited a family of fruit-pickers and noticed a boy of twelve tossing in his sleep and picking at the coverlet and in the air. The mother explained that he was going through the movement of picking prunes. This reminds us of the Venus fly-trap which does not close its leaves with one or two strokes of the hand but with three it does. The repetition of the activity had tended to structuralize the organism of the boy.[1] Professor Whitman reports that "if a bird of one species is hatched and reared by a wholly different species, it is very apt when fully grown to prefer to mate with the species under which it has been reared. For example, a male passenger pigeon that was reared with ring-doves and had remained with that species was ever ready, when fully grown, to mate with any ring-dove, but could never be induced to mate with one of his own species. I kept him away from ring-doves a whole season, in order to see what could be accomplished in the way of getting him mated finally with his own species, but he would never make any advances to the females, and whenever a ring-dove was seen or heard in the yard he was at once attentive."[2]

Something of this kind appears in connection with the attempts of Stefansson to break the dogs of his arctic teams of their food habits. He found that his dogs would not eat anything they were not accustomed to eating. Dogs brought up on a diet of seal, caribou meat and fish were taken to a region where nothing was obtainable except geese and "for several days all the dogs in the team refused to eat, and one dog persisted for more than a week before eating at all, although he had to work part of the time." On another occasion Stefansson's party happened to kill a wolf, and as the dogs of this team had never tasted wolf meat, he took occasion to break the dogs of this food prejudice, thinking he might later be in a situation where only wolf meat was available.

[1] Arthur Gleason, "Little Gypsies of the Fruit," *Hearst's International*, February, 1924.
[2] W. S. Hunter, "Modification of Instinct," *Psychological Review*, 27:259.

"We did not," he says, "know exactly the ages of our dogs, but could judge them roughly by the teeth. One of the dogs was presumably two or three years older than any other member of the team. There were six dogs altogether. We offered them the meat for three or four days before any of them ate any of it. Then they began to eat it . . . in the order of their age, the youngest being the first to give in. The oldest dog went for two weeks without swallowing any of the wolf meat, although he occasionally took a piece of it in his mouth and dropped it again." This particular dog never gave in. He became skin and bones and it was necessary to feed him with caribou meat to save his life. On the other hand, Stefansson mentions that dogs accustomed to foraging about ships on the coast had no food prejudices whatever. The same writer had a similar experience with a tribe of Eskimo in Coronation Gulf who had never eaten a berry known as the "salmon berry," and appreciated by all other tribes whom he had met. The children tried this food readily, the men without much resistance, but the women not at all.[3] In the same connection it is notorious that the European peasant will not readily taste food to which he is not accustomed. "Was der Bauer nicht kennt, isst er nicht."

Up to this point we have a determination of preferences and the assumption of rôles, so to speak, without awareness, without conscious choice, without reference to persons, an environmental imposition, dependent on the consistent repetition of stimulus.

On the other hand, we have in much the same situations the possibility of quite the contrary. The dogs who foraged about ships became cosmopolitan in taste, the gourmet, as over against the peasant, makes the selection of foods a leading rôle. The repetition of stimulus leads also to aversion. Pairs of men get on each other's nerves. Madame de Maintenon said: "I have always observed that our great aversions have their birth in the repetition of trivialities." There are situations where married people grow alike and the more frequent ones where they acquire quick aversions. Recently an old woman said, "What can I do now?" when she lost her husband after seventy-seven years.

[3] V. Stefansson, "Food Tastes and Food Prejudices of Men and Dogs," *Scientific Monthly*, 11:540–43.

The repetition of stimulus hampers movements and limits new experience on the one hand and gives heightened stimulation on the other. This is seen in those situations called ambivalent and represented in the relation of mother and child. Bleuler reports of one of his patients who had poisoned her child that she was later in great despair, but he noticed that during her moaning and crying she smiled quite perceptibly. And in one of his sketches Anatole France represents a little boy who when his mother came to kiss him good-night put his arm around her neck and gave her a hug, but wished that he could strangle her. I have been told of a boy who could weep over the song, "Where is my wandering boy tonight?" and then go home and beat up his mother.

This region I am in the habit of calling the "visceral unconscious." I give one more example involving a conflict between this unconscious and the region of the conscious. A white woman loves poetry, reads the poems of Dunbar and seeks an occasion to meet him. She knows he is black, but she is conditioned by such phrases as "equality," "fraternity," and prepared to be very cordial to a black poet. During the interview she holds up very well, but afterwards, on her return home, she is nauseated.[4]

### III

This is the region of the formation of aversions and preferences and evidently furnishes some of the basic factors in the structuralization of persons and societies. There is another region of the unconscious which may be described as the "lapsed conscious." It occupies a large and useful place in every life but simple and primitive societies are more heavily weighted with it. There the action systems tend to become stable, universal and invariable. There is harmony between the habit system and the stimulus system. This statement is an oversimplification, but it holds in principle. Dr. Krauss, the folklorist, stated to me in Vienna that he had seen a Serbian boy take his breakfast from his mother's breast on the doorstep before driving geese to pasture,

[4] Communicated to me by Professor R. E. Park.

and this may be taken as a symbol of the primitive early and complete induction of the individual member into the habit system of a group.

In this situation, the verbalization of behavior, the voices of the living and the voices of the dead, the laws and the prophets, result in a body of collective habit—the "collective representations" of Durkheim and Lévy-Bruhl and the "collective unconscious" of Jung. But for the individual it is a "lapsed consciousness," structuralized, shall we say, in the habit system, but not structuralized in the sense of organically inheritable, merely as a body of habit traditionally perpetuated.

What we call individuation means that the habit system of the group is not changing as fast as the stimulus system of the individual. The nature of the change of a stimulus system may be seen by comparing the varieties of new experience presented to the young today in connection with commercialized pleasure, newspaper stories, going into the city to work, etc., with the attitudes and values, the norms of the older generations. These norms were once formed by words and gestures, often by bitter processes of consciousness, and then lapsed into habit, into the unconscious. Habit is a definition of a situation. And new stimuli, rival stimuli suggest new definitions of situations. Consciousness seems to appear in just this connection.

In our present society, where the evolution of the stimuli systems is more rapid than the evolution of the habit systems, I have noticed from the reading of cases a number of types of the behavior reactions to the habit system, and I will mention three of these. In one the behavior corresponds to the habit system, in another the habit system is largely ignored, which amounts to antisocial behavior, and in the third a new organization of the personality is effected by the repudiation of the old habit system and the personal selection of stimuli.

In Philadelphia (a case recorded by the White-Williams Foundation) there are two girls, the father dead or removed, the mother very poor. They were given a dime at school to buy milk, but they returned a nickel, explaining that one of them did not drink her milk. Attractive enough, they were followed in the street, but never picked up. The extensive record shows all the features which we usually think of as producing delinquency, but no delinquency.

On the other hand, in Chicago there is a very admirably kept record, in the Institute for Juvenile Research, of a girl who for about nine years has been doing almost everything that is good and bad, but nothing vicious. I call her the "polymorphous normal" girl, with apologies to Freud. She gets up in the night to give the younger children a drink, scrubs the floors and cleans the house. She runs away, steals from home, kicks up a pile of refuse in the street, cries, and tells a pedestrian she has lost a bill and her mother will punish her. She gets the money, buys sweets, goes to the movies, but always shares with the children of the neighborhood. Beaten, she stays out all night, and sleeps under the steps. She has been sent here and there, I am told, on vacations and into homes as many as twenty-seven times. She follows all pleasing stimuli.

A Boston girl (one of Dr. Healy's cases) was brought to the court by her mother who complained that there "must be something wrong with her head." She detested her father who was petulant, unclean, locked up the music box when he was not at home, read the Polish paper aloud evenings and would have no comments. Now it appeared that the girl, when she was about eight, had lied about her age in order to get a library card. She read a great many fairy tales and day-dreamed a good deal, imagining she was a princess. At about twelve she became interested in love stories, and read them so much she became sick of them and went over to mystery stories. Later she left home, went into a publishing house, sent part of her wages home, associated with a nice set of girls, and joined them in dramatic performances, dances and debates. She had no sex experiences, but married well. After leaving home she went up, and the family went down. A visitor reported: "The house itself was dirty, the floors strewn with papers and bits of cloth, the bathroom so neglected it seemed impossible to use, and the beds were covered with dirty linen. The mother said that since Stasia had left no one had cared whether the place was orderly or not." The reading was the critical experience through which she had selected the behavior patterns not in the family system. But what had put her up to the reading?

It is precisely because children, with about the same family situations, organize their interests in so diverse ways that students of the child are making their records as minute and complete as possible. Sometimes a critical experience, as in the case of Stasia, comes to the front and dominates the configuration.

The degrees of intimacy and distance in connection with various types of relationship to groups, and the effect of this on personality patterns is something I cannot dwell on. It would be best illustrated by cases. But I will single out one example to illustrate what I mean. It has to do with what I regard as a gross exaggeration of intimacy in modern family life. The modern small family of three or four or more is something that has never before existed, as a general thing. Formerly the family was a kinship group of forty, sixty, a hundred or more persons. When Dr. Znaniecki was translating Polish materials he found it impossible to use the term "family" as we use it. He called the kinship group the "family," and our conception of family he called the "marriage-group." That meant that formerly the parents and children were themselves incorporated in a larger regulating group. Now (without pausing to describe how this has come about) with the dissolution of the large group the small family has become introverted, turned upon itself, and has taken a pathological trend in the direction of demanding and conferring response. Love in the family is the only pleasure seeking to which no limits are set by the moral code, short of incest. I will point out one of the effects of this situation on the configuration of personalities.

Both mother love and child love are built originally on a rather slender instinctive basis. I was reading in a paper by Dr. L. Pierce Clark that the newborn child does not grasp the mother's breast because he is hungry but in the last struggle not to be removed from the womb he holds on with his teeth, so to speak—that the milk is not appreciated as nourishment but as a libido stream. Now this is pure mythology, autistic thinking. Probably the first attitude of the child toward the mother, the tendency to grasp the breast, is not different from the attitude of the newly hatched chick toward the grain of wheat—it is something in each case to peck at and secure, a nutritive value. The newborn child does not prefer his mother's face or footstep. Experiments show that the tearing of a piece of paper is a greater stimulus than the mother's voice. But if the mother feeds and warms and cuddles him he will within a few weeks recognize her, prefer her, select out her voice and footstep. He is conditioned to her. This intimacy is then cultivated by language and gestures and more love response provoked. At any rate, these intimacies become most dangerous for the personality configuration of the child. You know what happens—the spoiled child, tantrums, negativism, exactions going so far that in one case the child would sleep only on the body of his mother in a certain position. And the intimacy, the exactions and the response of so intimate and perverse a relation cannot be carried over into the world at large where the man has to play his rôle and seek his recognition.

Response and recognition are the same thing in different fields of application. They both seek appreciation. But response operates in relations of intimacy and where you are permitted to have, in the main, what you want when young. The family, and friendship groups and marriage and the gang all represent response. The gang is an organization which will help you get what you want. There has been discussion as to what is the Sicilian mafia. Mafia, as I understand it, means that if Paolo wants to kill a man he goes to a café and sits in plain view all evening and his friend Luigi kills the man. The public, on the other hand, is an enmity group. Not even a profession, as Professor Park has pointed out to me, is an intimate group. It wishes you to honor the profession but does not wish you honored. The public makes heroes but it is even more pleased to unmake them. Corbett relates that when he entered the ring at New Orleans to fight Sullivan he realized that everybody wanted to see him killed. When he drew blood from Sullivan he realized that everybody wanted to see Sullivan killed. The cries of "Kill him" when a fighter is groggy are one of the most appalling expressions of mass psychology. To overcome the public, force recognition is very sweet to some. The actor has a full measure when he "stops the show."

In this general situation I have seen, and no doubt you have seen, young persons and old, who bring to everybody an urgent expectation of that pattern of response from the public which they got from an indulgent mother. The feeling of inadequacy arising in the transition from the intimacy situation to the enmity situation, the inability to get the reaction to which they have been conditioned, the consequent feeling of inferiority, play a large rôle in the psychoneuroses. The regressions of psychopathology seem, from the cases, to some extent a resignation of recognition and a retreat to response.

## IV

We may now turn to that manifestation of the unconscious which I take to be one of the main interests of this meeting—the synthetizing force, *force créatrice*, which participates in, or perhaps we may say, does the work of the creative imagination. For the sake of completeness we may call this the "cortical unconscious," though it is in fact cortical + visceral + lapsed. And, of course, I can only describe what it does, not determine what it is. The region of phantasy, of the elaboration of the materials of memory, psychic intimacy with self, detachment from persons and groups and time and place, give the most favorable situation for the development of unique personalities and products. And in this respect the day-dreamer, the lunatic, the mathematician and the creative artist are alike. The social values are different but the process is the same. Gauss, the mathematician, expressed this when he answered an inquiry as to how he was getting along on a problem. "I have long had my results," he said, "but I do not yet know the steps by which I shall reach them." Helmholtz said his best ideas came to him after breakfast, on fine mornings, walking up a hill.[5] Bleuler was, I believe, the first to point out that the

---

[5] P. G. Nutting, "Factors in Achievement," *Scientific Monthly*, 7:333.

schizophrene is far from being in a stupor. He is so absorbed in his own reflections that he will bite you if you interrupt him. Any one who can dream profusely seems to me talented. What I most admire in William McDougall is that he went to Zürich and dreamed some dreams for Jung. Not the least of the expressions of the genius of Freud is his volume on Leonardo da Vinci, if we regard this as a piece of artistic phantasying.

If we attempt to analyze this process, to see what is its mechanism, we may note, first, that the material for elaboration may be furnished by an incident, a critical experience. In the dream the initiation of the theme may be some intra-organic stimulation, some posture on the bed. The neck twisted on the pillow may initiate a dream of strangulation by a burglar and the elaboration may result in a drama of money, women, life and death. A physiologist has recently produced elaborate dreams by changing the tension of the skin through the application of adhesive tape.[6] Or the experience may be social. Bakst, the scenic artist, declared that his style was determined by an experience at the opera when he was four years of age. Patti, the prima donna in *La Sonnambula*, according to the exigencies of the drama, drank poison and fell dead. The child made an outcry, and after the performance was taken to the dressing-room of the singer to be reassured. She took him on her lap and with her make-up material drew red and black lines on his cheeks and over his eyes. At home the nurse planned to wash his face, but he would have none of it. He slept in the make-up, and psychologically it was never washed out. Oliver Caswell, deaf, dumb and blind, was under the care of Dr. Howe, who developed Laura Bridgman. Oliver was a murderous little beast. In his fights with boys he drew his finger across his throat, making horrible sounds. It developed that before he lost his senses, at the age of three, he had witnessed the slaughter of a hog. Circumstances then shut him off from experience, and he had evidently greatly elaborated this simple theme. Miss Mateer has some materials illustrating the early fixation on materials. A

[6] A. J. Cubberley, "Bodily Tension Effects upon the Normal Dream," *British Journal of Psychology*, January, 1923, 243–65.

child of three and a half centered all his energies for months on the fear that the world's supply of paper would give out before he grew up, and another of five spent his time in such chants as,

> Life is a dark hole,
> Life is a dark hole,

where we seem to have a tendency toward schizophrenic autism.[7]

Bleuler, illustrating the imaginings of his schizophrenic patients, gives the case of an escaped inmate, who enters an inn, goes to bed and announces that he is waiting for the queen of Holland, who wants to marry him. Commenting on the case Bleuler points out that the man's life is not disturbed in other respects. He works and behaves regularly, but here he is *living* a fairy tale, not *reading* a fairy tale, not *telling* a fairy tale, but *living* one.[8] This particular retreat from reality gives opportunity to play any rôle you wish with none of the checks encountered either in the intimate group or in the enmity group. You can have response, recognition, new experience in whatever proportion you want, with security. Bleuler claims that his patients always choose a rôle endowing them with the qualities in which they are most hopelessly lacking.

The difference between the schizophrene or the day-dreamer and the artist is that the artist selects his materials and elaborates them with regard to social patterns and social values. We are not concerned here with what the values are, or what is the importance of art, merely with the process of the artist. The artist seeks materials appropriate for elaboration. He may have them in his own experience, he may go out to get new experience, atmosphere, or he may explore the experiences of others in this connection.

[7] Florence Mateer, *The Unstable Child*, p. 50.
[8] E. Bleuler, "Austistic Thinking," *American Journal of Insanity*, 69:873–78.

# 9

# SITUATIONAL ANALYSIS: THE BEHAVIOR PATTERN AND THE SITUATION

THE LINES of social research have largely converged on the question of behavior reactions and the processes involved in their formation and modification. It appears that the particular behavior patterns and the total personality are overwhelmingly conditioned by the types of situations and trains of experience encountered by the individual in the course of his life. The question of heredity remains a factor, but this is also being studied in terms of behavior; it is, in fact, defined as the phylogenetic memory of experience—memory organically incorporated.

In approaching problems of behavior it is possible to emphasize—to have in the focus of attention for working purposes—either the attitude, the value, or the situation. The attitude is the tendency to act, representing the drive, the affective states, the wishes. The value represents the object or goal desired, and the situation represents the configuration of the factors conditioning the behavior reaction. It is also possible to work from the standpoint of adaptation—that is, how are attitudes and values modified according to the demands of given situations.

---

Reprinted from *Publications of the American Sociological Society: Papers and Proceedings, Twenty-second Annual,* 1927, pp. 1–13.

Any one of these standpoints will involve all the others, since they together constitute a process. But I wish to speak at present of the situational procedure as having certain experimental, objective, and comparative possibilities and as deserving of further attention and elaboration. As I have said, the emphasis of this standpoint by no means obscures the other factors; on the contrary, it reveals them. The situations which the individual encounters, into which he is forced, or which he creates, disclose the character of his adaptive strivings, positive or negative, progressive or regressive, his claims, attainments, renunciations, and compromises. For the human personality also the most important content of situations is the attitudes and values of other persons with which his own come into conflict and co-operation, and I have thus in mind the study of types of situation which reveal the rôle of attitudes and values in the process of behavior adaptation.

The situational method is the one in use by the experimental physiologist and psychologist who prepare situations, introduce the subject into the situation, observe the behavior reactions, change the situation, and observe the changes in the reactions. Child rendered one point in the situation more stimulating than others by applying an electric needle or other stimulus and made heads grow where tails would otherwise have grown. The situational character of the animal experimentation of the psychologists is well known. The rat, for example, in order to open a door, must not only stand on a platform placed in a certain position, but at the same time pull a string. A complete study of situations would give a complete account of the rat's attitudes, values, and intelligence.

The study of behavior with reference to situations which was begun by Vervorn, Pfeffer, Loeb, Jennings, and other physiologists and was concerned with the so-called "tropisms" or the reaction of the small organism to light, electricity, heat, gravity, hard substances, etc., was continued, or paralleled, by the experiments of Thorndike, Yerkes, Pavlov, Watson, Köhler, and others with rats, dogs, monkeys, and babies as subjects, but until quite recently no systematic work from this standpoint has involved the reactions of the individual to other persons or groups of persons.

That is to say, the work has not been sociological, but physiological or psychological.

Recently, however, there have developed certain directly sociological studies of behavior based on the situation. These are either experimental in the sense that the situations are planned and the behavior reactions observed, or advantage is taken of existing situations to study the reactions of individuals comparatively.

We may notice first the significant work of Bühler, Hetzer, and Tudor-Hart[1] upon the earliest social reactions of the child. Working in the Vienna clinics they divided 126 children into 9 groups of 14 each, the first group containing children 3 days old and under, and the last group containing those 4–5 months old, and experimenting with sound-stimuli they observed the rate at which the child learns to separate out and give attention to the human voice among other sounds. All the children noticed all the sounds (striking a porcelain plate with a spoon, rattling a piece of paper, and the human voice) sometimes, but the reaction of the newborn to noises in the first weeks is far more positive than the reaction to the voice, even to loud and noisy conversation: 92 per cent of frequency to the noises and 25 per cent to the voice. But in the third week the proportion is about the same, and in the fourth week the reaction is more frequent to the voice. The first positive reaction to the voice, other than listening, is a puckering of the lips, a sucking movement. The quality of the voice or the person speaking is at first of no significance. A child of three months when scolded angrily laughed gleefully. As yet angry tones had not been associated with punishment. A voice of any kind meant feeding.

Working with another group of 114 children, not newborn but borrowed from nursing mothers at a milk depot, placing them together in groups of two or more, and giving them toys, the most various reactions were disclosed in the unfamiliar situation. Some were embarrassed and inactive; others were openly delighted;

[1] Charlotte Bühler, Hildegard Hetzer, and Beatrix Tudor-Hart, *Soziologische und psychologische Studien über das erste Lebensjahr* (Quellen und Studien zur Jugendkunde), Jena, 1927.

some pounced upon the toys and paid no attention to the children; others explored the general environment; some robbed their companions of all the toys; others proffered, exchanged, or exhibited them; some were furious in the new situation, already, in the first year, positively negativistic. It is impossible to say to what degree these children had been conditioned by association with their mothers and how far the reactions were dispositional. But it is plain that by the end of the first year the most positive personality trends had been established. At this early age the experimenters think they distinguish three main personality types: the dominant, the amiable or humanitarian, and the exhibitionist, or producer.

Situational work of this type is now being carried on in several child-study institutes in the United States, and is foundational for the work in which we are more directly interested. Anderson and Goodenough, for example, and their associates, working in Minneapolis and observing the reactions of children among themselves in spontaneous play, found that a given child participating in play actively with all the other members of the group successively might be found leading or dominating in 95 per cent of the situations, whereas another child, under the same conditions, was found to be in the leading position only 5 per cent of the time. That is, within a constant period one child is getting twenty times as much practice in meeting social situations in a given way as a second child. We have here a type of organization of behavior where not only the lack of practice but the habit of subordination will have the most far-reaching consequences in the development of efficiency and personality. Observations will now be undertaken by the same observers on the effect of the alteration of the composition of groups with the object of giving the less dominant children opportunity to assume more important rôles.[2]

Another item in the program of this institute is the study of habit formation in connection with games of skill. It has appeared that the children develop idiosyncrasies in their technique of

[2] John E. Anderson, "The Genesis of Social Reactions in the Young Child," in *The Unconscious: A Symposium*, pp. 69–90.

throwing a ring at a peg. If an effort, however awkward, happens to be successful, the child tends to adopt and perseverate in this method, regardless of his later insuccesses.[3] Evidently the fixation of many undesirable social habits has this origin. Whimpering, crying, lying, vomiting, bed-wetting have had an initial success in dominating the mother, and may become a part of the child's behavior repertory. It is to be remembered also that the initiation of one mode of reaction to a situation tends to block the emergence of other types of reaction. Moreover, it appears from other sources that children are capable of developing dual and contrasting behavior reactions in different types of situations. Miss Caldwell, in Boston, working mainly with Italian children, has astonishing records showing consistently defiant, destructive, negativistic behavior in the home and relatively orderly behavior in the nursery school. And this duality of behavior is carried on for years—bad in one situation, good in another.

Freeman and his associates in Chicago are now publishing a situational study of the greatest importance based on the placing of about six hundred children in foster homes, in response, apparently, to the following challenge by Terman: "A crucial experiment," Terman says, "would be to take a large number of very young children from the lower classes and after placing them in the most favorable environment obtainable compare their later mental development with that of the children born into the best homes." In this experiment comparisons were made between results on intelligence tests which had been given before adoption, in the case of one group, and the results after they had been in the foster home a number of years. Another comparison was made between children of the same family who had been placed in different homes, the home being rated on a scheme which took into consideration the material environment, evidence of culture, occupation of foster father, education and social activity of foster parents. Both of these comparisons had held heredity constant, letting the situation vary. A third comparison held environment constant, letting heredity vary, that is, concerning itself with a comparison of the intelligence of the own children of the foster parents and of

[3]   *Ibid.*

the foster children. The results, stated in a word, show that when two unrelated children are reared in the same home, differences in their intelligences tend to decrease, and that residence in different homes tends to make siblings differ from one another in intelligence. This study is limited to the question of intelligence, but it is obvious that a fundamental study of behavior could be made by the same method.

Esther Richards, of the Phipps Psychiatric Clinic in Baltimore, has been experimenting with psychopathic children by placing them in homes and on farms and moving them about until a place is found in which they are adjusted. She discovered that there were whole families of hypochondriacs showing no symptoms of organic deficiency. To be "ailing, and never so well" had become a sort of fashion in families, owing, perhaps, to the hysterical manifestations of the mother. These attempts are rather uniformly successful as long as the parents remain away from the child. One boy had been manifesting perfect health and robust activity on a farm, but conceived a stomach ache on the appearance of his mother, which disappeared with her departure. And it is the prevailing psychiatric standpoint that the psychoneuroses —the hysterias, hypochondrias, schizophrenias, war neuroses, etc., are forms of adaptions to situations.

Dr. Harry Stack Sullivan and his associates, working at the Sheppard and Enoch Pratt Hospital, Baltimore, are experimenting with a small group of persons now or recently actively disordered, from the situational standpoint, and among other results this study reveals the fact that these persons tend to make successful adjustments in groupwise association between themselves.

The sociologist has found the behavior document, the life-record, a very useful aid in exploring the situation and determining the sources of maladjustment. It is true that this introspective method has the disadvantages encountered in the taking of legal testimony. It has been shown by students of testimony that in case of false testimony the witness frequently brings a preconception, a behavior schema, to the situation, that he testifies egocentrically, overweighting certain aspects and adding perceptual elements and interpretations as a result of his own memories and experiences; his perceptions of the events of which he testifies are thus anticipatory and reminiscent. And he has also excluded from perception factors which he did not anticipate. The same holds in varying degrees of the human document. Shaw, working with the Institute of Juvenile Research in Chicago, has pointed out that some of his subjects prepare dry and objective chronicles while others are mainly self-justificatory and exculpatory. A document prepared by one compensating for a feeling of inferiority or elaborating a delusion of persecution is certainly as far as possible from objective reality. On the other hand, this definition of the situation is from one standpoint quite as good as if it were true. It is a representation of the situation as appreciated by the subject, "as if" it were so, and this is for behavior study a most important phase of reality.

The psychologists and social workers connected with the juvenile courts and child clinics, the visiting teachers, and other organizations are now preparing extensive records tending to take the behavior of the child in connection with all the contacts and experiences which may have influenced the particular delinquency or maladjustment. And finally the regional and ecological behavior surveys with which Park, Burgess, Thrasher, Shaw, Zorbaugh, and others are identified attempt to measure the totality of influence in a community, the configuration and disposition of social stimuli, as represented by institutions, localities, social groups, and individual personalities, as these contribute to the formation of behavior patterns.

The merit of all these exploratory approaches is that they tend to bring out causative factors previously neglected and to change the character of the problem. Thrasher's study of 1,313 gangs in Chicago changes the character of the crime problem, and this study merely opens up a new situation. Other researchers, not yet published, will show that, recruited from the gangs, criminal life is as definitely organized in Chicago as the public school system or any other department of life, the criminals working behind an organization of "irreproachable" citizens. Shaw has studied the cases of boys brought before the juvenile court in Chicago for stealing with reference to the number of boys participating, and finds that in 90 per cent of the cases two or more boys were involved. It is certain that many of the boys concerned were not caught, and that the percentage of groupwise stealing is therefore greater than 90 per cent. This again throws a new light on the nature of the problem of crime. Again, Burgess and Shaw have studied the incidence of delinquency for different neighborhoods and find that in the so-called "interstitial zones," lying along the railroad tracks and between the better neighborhoods, the boys are almost 100 per cent delinquent, while in other neighborhoods there is almost no delinquency. Burgess found one ward in a city of 12,000 population with about eight times as many cases of juvenile delinquency as in any of the other wards.[4]

These are examples of factors of delinquency which turn up or come to the front in the course of the exploration of situations. But with reference to the relationship of the factors, their distribution in the ratio of delinquency, or even the certitude that we are aware of all the factors, we are in one respect in the position of the person who gives false testimony in court. We overweight the standpoint acquired by our particular experience and our preconceived line of approach. In the literature of delinquency we find under the heading "causative factors" such items as the following: Early sex experience, 18 per cent for boys and 25 per cent for girls; bad companionship, 62 per cent for both sexes; school dissatisfaction, 9 per cent for boys and 2 per cent for girls; mental defect, 14 per cent; premature puberty, 3 per cent; psychopathic personality, 14 per cent; mental conflict, 6.5 per cent; motion pictures, 1 per cent, etc. Now it is evident that many young persons have had some of these experiences without becoming delinquent, and that many mentally defective persons and psychopathic personalities are living at large somewhat successfully without any record of delinquency; some of them are keeping small shops; others are producing literature and art. How can we call certain experiences "causative factors" in a delinquent group when we do not know the frequency of the same factors in a non-

[4] E. W. Burgess, "Juvenile Delinquency in a Small City," *Journal of Criminal Law and Criminology*, 6:726–28.

delinquent group? In order to determine the relation of a given experience to delinquency it would be necessary to compare the frequency of the same experience in the delinquent group and in a group representing the general non-delinquent population. It is now well known that the findings of Lombroso in his search for a criminal type went completely to pieces when Goring and others compared a series of criminals with a series taken from otherwise comparable non-delinquents. Lombroso's "criminal stigmata" are simply physical marks of the human species distributed pretty uniformly through the general population. Similarly, it is obviously absurd to claim that feeblemindedness or psychopathic disposition is the *cause* of crime so long as we have no idea of the prevalence of these traits in the general population. No subject is perhaps in so naïve and grotesque a position in this respect as psychoanalysis. The "Oedipus complex" and the "Electra complex"—the "fixation" of son on mother and daughter on father—are discovered and weighted by Freudians and made prominent sources of the psychoneuroses and of delinquency, whereas the clinical records show a multitude of cases where children with behavior disturbances are either indifferent to the parents or directly hate them. Again, with regard to economic factors as cause of crime, we find, for example, in the records of the White-Williams Foundation of Philadelphia (an organization dealing primarily with non-delinquent children) the same unfavorable economic conditions, broken homes, etc., which are usually assigned as "causative factors" in the studies of delinquency, but in this case without delinquency.

The psychiatrist Kempf, speaking of the diagnosis and classification of nervous diseases, has given the opinion that if twenty cases were given to twenty psychiatrists separately for diagnosis and their findings were sealed and given to a committee for a comparison of the results the whole system of diagnosis would blow up. And something of this kind would happen if students of delinquency, under the same conditions, attempted to name the causative factors in a crime wave or in the heavy incidence of delinquency in a given locality. The answers would certainly be weighted on the side of bad heredity, gang life, poverty, commercialized pleasure, decline of the church, post-encephalitic behavior disturbances, etc., according to the different standpoints represented.

Since the establishment of the first juvenile court in 1899 there has been a very careful elaboration of procedure with reference to the treatment of the young delinquent—systematic study of the case, oversight in the home or in a detention home, placing in good families, psychiatric social workers, visiting teachers, attempts to improve the attitudes of parents toward children, recreation facilities, children's villages and farm schools—and there is, I think, a general impression that there is a steady improvement, an evolution of method, and a gradual approach to a solution of the problem of delinquency. But there is no evidence that juvenile-court procedure or any procedure tends to reduce the large volume of juvenile delinquency. This is not surprising in view of the present rapid unstabilization of society connected with the urbanization of the population, the breakdown of kinship groups, the circulation of news, the commercialization of pleasure, etc. But it is more significant that the methods of the juvenile courts, when applied by their best representatives and in the most painstaking way, cannot be called successful in arresting the career of children who once appear in court, that so many first offenders become recidivists and eventually criminals. Healy and Bronner, who were the first court psychologists, and whose work commands the highest respect in the world, have recently reviewed this point on the basis of the records of their cases during the past twenty years in Chicago and Boston. They say:

Tracing the lives of several hundred youthful repeated offenders studied long ago by us and treated by ordinary so-called correctional methods reveals much repetition of offense. This is represented by the astonishing figures of 61 per cent failure for males (15 per cent being professional criminals and 5 per cent having committed homicide), and 46 per cent failure for girls (19 per cent being prostitutes). Thus in over one-half the cases in this particular series juvenile delinquency has continued into careers of vice and crime. . . . This is an immense proportion to be coming from any series of consecutive cases studied merely because they were repeated offenders in a juvenile court. It represents a most disconcerting measure of failure.[5]

They mention that no less than 209 of the 420 boys whom they knew when they appeared in the Chicago juvenile court had later appeared in adult courts, and of these 157 had received commitment to adult correctional institutions 272 times. The first court appearance is thus not to be regarded as the initiation of a reform, but in many youthful offenders it appears as a sort of confirmation or commencement ceremony initiating a criminal way of life. There are, indeed, many records of positive successes under juvenile court treatment, especially among the cases of Healy and Bronner, but the most successful workers confess that they do not know how they obtained their successes, whether through their own efforts or through spontaneous changes in the child.

Now there is reason to believe that we are deluded or not properly informed as to the efficiency of other behavior-forming situations and agencies on which we are confidently relying for the control of behavior and the development of normal personality. We assume that good families produce good children, but certain of the experimental nursery schools, selecting their children carefully in order to avoid material already spoiled, find nevertheless that they have drawn from the best families a large percentage of problem children. Our school curricula, based on reading ability and lesson-transfer, drive many children gifted along perceptual-motor lines into truancy and delinquency. It would be possible to show by cases that the home and the school are hardly less unsuccessful behavior-forming situations than the juvenile court.

Naturally the greatest amount of attention, up to the present, has been given to the study of abnormal behavior in the forms which come to public attention, become a nuisance; but behavior difficulties are widespread in the whole population, and it is certain that we can understand the abnormal only in connection with

[5] Healy and Bronner, *Delinquents and Criminals: Their Making and Unmaking*, pp. 201–2.

the normal, in relation to the whole social process to which they are both reactions. The same situation or experience in the case of one person may lead this person to another type of adjustment; in another it may lead to crime; in another, to insanity, the result depending on whether previous experiences have formed this or that constellation of attitudes.

The answer is, we must have more thoroughgoing explorations of situations. In our planning we should include studies and surveys of behavior-forming situations, measurements of social influences which will enable us to observe the operation of these situations in the formation of delinquent, emotionally maladjusted, and stable personalities and determine the ratios. A plan of this kind, which has been discussed by some of the sociologists present, proposes to take selected localities or neighborhoods in given cities, including, for example, the interstitial zones where delinquency is highest and the good neighborhoods where delinquency is lowest, and study all the factors containing social influence.

A survey of this kind would involve a study of all the institutions—family, gang, social agencies, recreations, juvenile courts, the daily press, commercialized pleasure, etc.—by all the available techniques, including life-records of all the delinquent children and an equal number of non-delinquent children, for the purpose of tracing the effects of the behavior-forming situations on the particular personalities.

It is known also that cities and other localities differ greatly as total behavior-forming situations. Healy and Bronner estimated, for example, that their failures in Chicago were 50 per cent and in Boston only 21 per cent. The difference is certainly not due in the main to differences in juvenile-court procedure, but to differences in the attitudes of the population, and this in turn to differences in the configurations of social influence. The juvenile court of Cincinnati has excited interest by the fact that it institutionalizes very few children, uses foster homes rarely, has only a nominal probation system, and is thought nevertheless to have greater success than other cities. The court procedure in Cincinnati is not elaborate; the co-operative agencies are not well organized. Nearly all the youthful offenders are simply turned back into the community. Is the relative success in this situation due to lack of too much zeal, to a refusal to treat and classify the child too promptly as delinquent? Is the large and stable element of German and German-Jewish population a factor in the situation? Rochester, New York, is the only city in the country where the visiting-teacher organization is incorporated in the public school system. What is the efficiency of this effort to treat the child in the pre-delinquent stages of his behavior difficulties? An inventory and measure of the social influences of selected cultural centers taken comparatively is thus very desirable.

There is a type of behavior reaction going on every day before our eyes which has to do with the participation of masses of the population, often whole populations, in common sentiments and actions. It is represented by fashions of dress, mob action, war hysteria, the gang spirit, mafia, omertà, fascism, popularity of this or that cigarette or tooth paste, the quick fame and quick infamy of political personalities. It uses language—spoken, written, and gesture. It is emotional, imitative, largely irrational and unconscious, weighted with symbols, and sometimes violent. It is capable of manipulation and propagation by leading personalities and the public print. Its result is commonly and publicly accepted definitions of situations. Its historical residuum constitutes the distinctive character of races, nationalities, and communities. This is the psychology of the evolution of public opinion and of social norms. As long as the definitions of situations remain constant and common we may anticipate orderly behavior reactions. When rival definitions arise (as between the wets and drys at the present moment) we may anticipate social disorganization and personal demoralization. There are always constitutional inferiors and divergent personalities in any society who do not adjust, but the mass of delinquency, crime, and emotional instability is the result of conflicting definitions. When, as Justice McAdoo says, a large number of young men in New York City have made up their minds that they will live without working, this is a new definition of the situation and the formation of a criminal policy.

Now these expressions of public opinion, the rise of common attitudes, the establishment of a group morale, the culmination of emotional outbursts, and the formulation of more deliberate policies have also a situational origin—one in which the situation is weighted with pre-established attitudes, with conflicts arising over definitions of situations and influenced by the propaganda of word, print, and gesture, and it is desirable that selected types of behavior-forming situations should be studied along these lines.

And, finally, I will not here emphasize the point which I have attempted to exemplify in a particular study, that it is desirable to extend our studies of this situational character to the large cultural areas, to the races and nationalities, in order to understand the formation of behavior patterns comparatively, in their most general and particular expressions.

# 10

# ANALYTICAL TYPES:

# PHILISTINE, BOHEMIAN,

# AND CREATIVE MAN

WE ARE in the habit of calling "primary groups" those societies which through kinship, isolation, voluntary adhesion to certain systems of definitions, secure an emotional unanimity among their members. By virtue of their unanimity the mob and the jury are also momentary primary groups.

Clear examples of the primary group are the South Slavonian *zadruga* and the Russian *mir*. When there arises in these communities the necessity of defining a new situation, it is not even sufficient to reach a unanimous decision; each member must voice his opinion and agreement, make it explicit. Cases are recorded wherein a conflict between the traditional communal definition (say of poverty) and that of the great state, a member has appeared before the communal assembly, sustained by the confidence in a new and authoritative definition, only to wither and collapse before the white scorn of a solidary group. If a member is stubborn his family members and close friends weep, embrace, implore— beg him not to disgrace them and his community by showing the

---

Reprinted from "The Persistence of Primary Group Norms in Present Day Society" in *Suggestions of Modern Science Concerning Education* (New York: Macmillan Co., 1917), pp. 171-97.

## Philistine, Bohemian, Creative Man 169

neighbors that they cannot agree. It has been remarked by students of the *mir* that boys six or eight years of age speak and act like grown men. They repeat the standard definitions of "our community," "our people."

The savage tribe is another example of the primary group. It was once imagined and is still popularly believed that the savage is the freest person in the world, but ethnologists know that savage life is regulated by an almost incredibly minute and rigoristic code. The native Australian boy is permitted to speak to certain persons (mother-in-law, older sister, younger sister, etc.) only at certain specified distances—a hundred yards, thirty yards, ten yards. During a period lasting from ten to twenty or even thirty years, he is taken by the old men through a series of intermittent ceremonies, some single periods lasting as long as four months, with dramatic ceremonies—as many as five or six in a single day and night—and oral drill, defining all possible situations of tribal life, and with a result which I can only indicate by saying that, as to marriage, he is related to a girl (among the Arunta) by a ceremony called *tualcha mura* for which we have no parallel, but which means not that he marries the girl but that he eventually marries the daughter of the girl when the latter has married another man and has a marriageable daughter, and that, as to food, he will not only not eat certain foods but believes that if he does this he will die, and in some cases actually does die.

The Polish peasant uses a word, *okolica*, "the neighborhood round about," "as far as the report of a man reaches," and this may be taken as the natural external limit of the size of the primary group—as far as the report of a member reaches—so long as men have only primary means of communication. But with militancy, conquest and the formation of the great state we have a systematic attempt to preserve in the whole population the solidarity of feeling characterizing the primary group. The great state cannot preserve this solidarity in all respects—there is the formation of series of primary groups within the state—but it develops authoritative definitions of "patriotism," "treason," etc., and the appropriate emotional attitudes in this respect, so that in time of crisis, of war, where there is a fight of the whole nation against death, we witness, as at this moment, the temporary reconstitution of the attitudes of the primary group.

Similarly, in the great religious systems such as Christianity and Mohammedanism, we have a systematic attempt to make the whole world a primary group, to win men away from the merely communal, human and worldly definitions (or to reaffirm these) by a system of definitions having a higher value through their divine derivation. God is the best definer of situations because he possesses more knowledge and more prestige than any man or any set of men and his definitions tend to have finality, absoluteness and arbitrariness and to convey the maximum of prepossession.

How rigid and particularistic these definitions became at one time in the western world it would be superfluous to point out, especially if you are acquainted with the Westminster Catechism, but perhaps you did not know that Dr. Lightfoot, vice-chancellor of Cambridge University, announced at one time that "man was created by the Trinity on the 23rd of October, 4004 B.C., at 9 o'clock in the morning," stating that the height of Adam was 123 feet 9 inches, that of Eve 118 feet and 9 inches.

In the Mohammedan world, as in the Puritan world, there was an effort to define *every* present situation in terms of the past. "There are," says Lane, "some Muslims who will not do anything that the Prophet is not recorded to have done, and who particularly abstain from eating anything he did not eat, though its lawfulness is undoubted. The Imam Ahmad Ibn-Hambal would not even eat watermelons, because, although he knew that the Prophet ate them, he could not learn whether he ate them with or without the rind, or whether he broke, bit, or cut them. And he forbade a woman, who questioned him as to the propriety of the act, to spin by the light of the torches passing in the street by night, which were not her own property, because the Prophet had not mentioned whether it was lawful to do so, and was not known ever to have availed himself of a light belonging to another person without that person's leave."

But I do not wish to leave the impression that definitions are dependent for their validity on their authoritative source. All usual and habitual practices are emotionalized, become behavior norms, and tend to resist change. The iron plow-share, invented late in the 18th century, was strongly condemned on the ground that it was an insult to God, therefore poisoned the ground and caused the weeds to grow; and until recently the old farmer laughed at the soil-analysis of the city chemist. The man who first built a water-driven saw-mill in England was mobbed; the English war department informed the inventor of the first practical telegraphic device that it had no use for that contrivance; in the last generation there was a persistent opposition to the introduction of stoves and organs into churches, and if we omit recent years, and in recent years only the scientific and practical fields, it would be difficult to find a single innovation that has not encountered opposition and ridicule.

The whole problem of culture hinges on the relation of the individual to society. Each is an indispensable value to the other. The whole fund of instrumental values through which the individual realizes his desires and achieves his creative activities is provided by society, while the type of social organization, the variety of the cultural content, the rapidity of social change, the creation of particular values, depend on the individual. But the nature of the individual, demanding a maximum of new experience, is in fundamental conflict with the nature of society, demanding a maximum of stability, and it would be interesting to analyze the various particular effects of the repressive action of society on the individual—the psychic wounds which confront the psychiatrist; the complete and masochistic resignation expressed in the hymn-books ("Lead, kindly Light, amid the encircling gloom"); the sullen repression of rage during a whole lifetime, represented by Jean Meslier, curate of Epigny, who left at his death in 1733 a testament in which he declared that he had never believed a word of his teachings and that his ardent wish was that the "last king might be hung with the entrails of the last priest"; the meticulous manipulation of scientific data, represented by the Egyptologist Wilkinson who falsified the dates from the monuments to fit the accepted date of the flood; the alternating violation of the definition and confession of error, represented by Galileo and the army of recanters; the straining of the definition to include the desire for new experience, represented by those geologists who at one time reconciled geological time with the Biblical account of creation by assuming six days, indeed, but extremely long ones; or by the plea which I read some years ago (1910) in the Vienna *Neue Freie Presse* for the legal toleration of incineration of the dead, based not upon sanitary grounds or those of individual liberty, but upon the claim that "burial" as used by the church authorities did not mean "depositing the body in the ground," but any disposition of it, etc.

But as general result of this conflict we have the development of three types of individual, dependent on the different temperamental dispositions and on the degree and steadiness of the pressure exercised by the given social organization. These we may call the philistine, the bohemian and the creative man. The philistine is the individual who adapts his activities completely to the prevailing definitions and norms; he chooses security at the cost of new experience and individuality. The bohemian is unable to fit into any frame, social or personal, because his life is spent in trying to escape definitions and avoid suppressions instead of building up a positive organization of ends and attitudes; he has avoided philistinism at the cost of character and success, because he had a strong personal tendency to revolt against social pressures or because the pressures were not strong or consistent enough. The philistine and the bohemian are produced by the social effort to impose upon the individual a life-organization and to mold his character without regard to his personal tendencies and the line of his spontaneous development, and both are relative failures.

In contrast with these two types, the philistine tending to accept all the definitions and the bohemian tending to reject all of them, the creative man reconciles his desire for new experience with the desire of society for stability by redefining situations and creating new norms of a superior social value. He disorganizes the old system momentarily, but provides the elements for a more efficient organization. The creative man and the criminal are equally violators of the norms, disorderly individuals from the standpoint of the primary group, but in the creative man this disorderliness is expressed in the setting and solution of problems, in the creation of new values, while in the criminal it is merely negative—destructive of the existing system. All of these types except the philistine represent individualization in the fact that they reject existing norms, but the individualism of the creative man is an intermediary stage between one system of values and another; his function is to produce changes in the social order corresponding to favorable variations in biology.

Professor Watson emphasized the meaning of higher levels of efficiency, and higher levels of social efficiency are reached through the individualization of function represented best by the scientific specialization of our time. Individualization is a relative term—the individual always remains incorporated in some world of ideas—but practically the creative man secures sufficient individualization to do his work, retains enough recognition to keep him sane, by escaping from the censure of one group into the appreciation of another group. And this escape seems to go on at a rate corresponding with the increased facility of communication. The world has become greatly diversified, containing not only races and nationalities with differing norms and cultural systems, but various worlds of ideas represented by various scientific, religious, artistic circles; and by the fact of reading alone the individual can associate himself with those persons or circles preadapted to his ideas, and form with them a solidary group.

It does not follow, therefore, that the creative man is a temperamental rebel. He may even be a philistine at heart. Charles Darwin was not a rebellious person; he was simply engrossed in a pursuit, and was very timorous about it. In common with his naturalist friends he had long realized that something terrible was about to happen to the Old Testament, but when he finally had the proofs that species were not immutable he wrote to his friends that it was "like confessing murder," and in spite of the appreciation of the scientific world he felt deeply to the end of his life the censure of the religious-primary group which accused him of a determination to "hunt God out of the world."

Dr. Meyer pointed out in his lecture that we must learn to appreciate the varying standards of normality. We recognized already that there are varying standards of abnormality, and I assume that if individualization were so complete as to remove its subject from participation in any world of common ideas whatever, this would be a form of insanity. The case of Julius Robert Mayer, discoverer of the law of the conservation of energy, is almost a case of this kind, for he did not succeed in associating himself sympathetically with the set of men pre-adapted to his idea —Joule indeed tried to plunder him and Helmholtz ridiculed him as a "lucky guesser"—and at the same time he remained in his narrowly provincial Heilbronn, where he was treated as the town fool, accused of the delusion of grandeur, forcibly handled in two insane asylums. Even toward the end of his life, after he had received generous recognition from Tyndall and also from Helmholtz, he regarded himself as insane in his home town. When Düring wished to visit him he refused to receive him in Heilbronn, but arranged to meet him in the neighboring Wildbad, saying that a visit to his home would excite unfavorable comment. "Since everyone here," he wrote, "regards me as a fool, everyone considers himself justified in exercising a spiritual guardianship over me."

But we are not to regard creative activity and changes in the norms as associated solely with creative individuals or even with design. The work of the Chicago Vice Commission illustrates the contrary fact. This was not a radical body, its "representative" character precluded this. Indeed it explicitly stated its policy of including its activities within the existing norms. We read in the introduction to its report: "[The Commission] has kept constantly in mind that to offer a contribution of any value such an offering must be, first, moral; second, reasonable and practical; third, possible under the constitutional powers of our courts; fourth, that which will square with the public conscience of the American people."

Nevertheless the work of this commission unwittingly resulted in the modification of two norms, namely, "circulation of information about sexual matters illegal," and "research into sexual matters taboo." The post office declared the report obscene literature, and the members of the commission were technically liable to penitentiary sentence. The Postmaster General revoked this decision, thus modifying one norm, and the participation of a large body of respectable citizens in a research into sexual questions tended to bring such research under a new norm. But I have speculated on the fate of the individual who might have perpetrated this report single-handed.

But why, we may ask, if a society is orderly and doing very well, is it desirable to disturb the existing norms at all. "Little man, why so hot!" And this question reduces itself ultimately to a basis of idealism. It becomes a question of happiness, of the degree of fulfillment of wishes within the society, and on the other hand of levels of efficiency as between societies in the ultimate struggle against death—as in the present war. The Arunta society is surpassed in orderliness only by the ants and other animal societies, where every act is predefined once and forever in terms of organic structure and external situation. The Chinese society represents a high degree of stability on a relatively high level of culture. "Amuse them, tire them not, let them not know," is one of the oldest Chinese political maxims.

Now, the superior level of culture reached by the western world is due to a tendency to disturb norms—introduced first into the material world by the physicists and gradually extending itself in connection with the theory of evolution to the biological world, and just now beginning to touch the human world. And this tendency to disturb norms becomes an end in itself in the form of scientific pursuits whose aim is the redefinition of all possible situations and the establishment eventually of the most general and universal norms, namely scientific laws. And the success of this method from the standpoint of efficiency is shown in the wonderful advance in material technique resulting from research for law in the fields of physics and chemistry, exemplified, for example, in mechanical inventions and modern medicine.

But up to the present we are working in the social world with norms developed either by the method of "ordering-and-forbidding," or by that of empirical, communal "common-sense," and our level of efficiency in this field remains relatively low. The main purpose of what I have said up to this point was to show that "human behavior norms" are not only very arbitrary, but, precisely because behavior norms, so highly emotionalized that they claim to be absolutely right and final and subject to no change and no investigation. Moreover, every norm claims to be *the* norm, the normal, and any departure from it is abnormal. And eventually every practical custom or habit, every moral, political, religious view claims to be *the* norm—not to recognize, in Dr. Meyer's phrase, the varying standards of normality—and to treat as abnormal whatever does not agree with it. In practice, as I have shown by examples, a social technique based upon a rigid system of norms tends to suppress all the social energies which seem to act in a way contrary to the norm, and to ignore all the social energies not included in the norm. Furthermore, the norms do change, in spite of the emotional prepossessions; traditions and customs, morality, religion, and education undergo an increasingly rapid evolution, and it is evident that a system proceeding on the assumption that a certain norm is valid finds itself absolutely helpless when it suddenly realizes that the norm has lost all social significance and some other norm has appeared in its place.

The classical example of the decay of old norms in an evolving society and their persistence in doctrine and practice after they are dead is that of "classical studies as learning norm." Granting that these studies placed us at one time in the possession of cultural values superior to those contributed by the stream of Semitic influence, granting, if you please, with Sir Henry Maine that "nothing moves in the modern world that is not Greek in its origin," recognizing also that in a hierarchized society they retained for a time an adventitious meaning in the prestige they gave to their devotees—and prestige has a real value as a tool for the control of the minds of men—these studies did eventually lose their value as universal "learning norms" in an industrial world, but they persist in our curricula, and their retention is justified by a mental process which we may call the rationalization of an emotion. Their advocates wish their survival, and they rationalize the wish in the claim that these studies have an indispensable disciplinary value—a mental process resembling the law of magical causation whereby the appearance of the desirable and the disappearance of the undesirable effect is decreed, or virtue is transferred from an object of superior value to one of inferior value by contagion.

Similarly in the religious world, while the church has practically if not doctrinally abandoned the norm, "history of the world, unfolding of the will of God," and is doing all kinds of work under the Kantian norm, "history of the world, fulfilling of the will of man," yet a minister was able to say, and recently, that a well-known settlement worker "had done more harm than all the ministers of Chicago could make good" because she was not working under his norms.

As an example from another field I can only refer, without prophecy, to the retreat of "freedom as political norm," and of the whole individualistic system of norms developed in this country during the past two centuries, in the face of the present world crisis.

All that I have said up to this point impresses me, and I hope it will impress you, with the urgency of a more exact and systematic study of human behavior on a scale and with a method comparable with those already provided for the physical and biological sciences. We have a failure of the "common-sense" method, not only in education and the relation of races and nationalities, but in connection with crime, prostitution, slums, insanity, abnormality, labor problems and all kinds of unhappiness. It is only by following the example of the physical sciences and accumulating the largest possible amount of secure and varied information and establishing general and particular laws which we can draw on to meet any crisis as it arises that we shall be able to secure a control in the social world comparable to that obtained in the natural world, and to determine eventually the kind of world we want to live in. I take it that the only reason we have not followed the path of the natural sciences long ago is the partially unrealized fear of disturbing our behavior norms. For evidently there were laws and consequently practices in the physical world that would never have been discovered by the "common-sense" method, and obviously the same is true of the social world. . . .

A social science must be upon the basis of the physical sciences—it must go on endlessly and without reference to immediate practical applicability. The men who were instrumental in the constitution of the physical sciences pursued their problems as ends in themselves, without any reference to practical applicability. Their work was, to begin with, illegitimate anyway, hedonistic and disorderly, and the society which opposed it had no expectation of practical applicability, but anticipated only harmful disturbance of norms. But it happened that these men adopted the course which in the end yielded the largest number of results of practical applicability precisely because they had unlimited liberty in the setting and solution of problems, and thereby established the greatest variety of laws.

The sciences do reach a point where they are consciously turned in the direction of practical applicability, that is, they anticipate that by following certain directions certain practical results will appear (and the life of Pasteur is perhaps the best example of this); but the history of the sciences shows that only a *method* quite free from dependence on practice can become practically useful in its applications. We do not know what the future of science will be before it is constituted and what may be the applications of its discoveries before they are applied.

As to education, I have no special competence to speak in this field, but from being associated with educational methods I have some impressions; and if I venture to name some of them, I ask you to receive them as a friendly communication from one universe of discourse to another.

I have the conviction that the prepossessions of all of us are at a given moment deeper than we suspect, that society is in a hypnoidal state with lucid intervals, that these prepossessions are the emotional result of behavior norms of the primary-group type, that educators unconsciously conform the schools to primary-group ideals, that in conformity with primary-group ideals of solidarity our curricula strive for uniformity instead of diversity, that there is a consequent disharmony between education and life, because the individual no longer organizes his life on the basis of primary group relations, but the educational system prepares him to do so.

## Philistine, Bohemian, Creative Man  179

I suspect that we should increase human happiness, efficiency and productivity if we should provide the young person with an adequate technique in connection with a limited body of informational definitions and place him face to face with problems. I was impressed with a casual remark of Mr. Dewey, that if it were necessary he would be willing to have the student forget all the informational data imparted to him during the four years of college life, if he could substitute for this a consuming interest in something.

I have concluded that we are so prepossessed with the idea of giving the child the maximum of informational data that this becomes an end in itself, that the mass of learning norms is so great that the youth actually passes the physiological and psychological age where he is due to erupt along creative lines. I am aware that in our universities we create and find already created an attitude of expectancy with reference to definitions and systems of definitions, that the student is extremely reluctant to undertake any but approved and supervised lines of interest, that he brings to all problems a too great docility, that he grows old and cautious among the multiplicity of definitions, and that we have in our doctor's dissertation what we deserve.

I am impressed with the fact that great men so frequently did their great work very young. Newton had discovered the law of gravitation, integral calculus, had made discoveries in light, had developed the binomial theory, at the age of 24; Linnaeus had his sexual system of plants ready at the same age. Ludwig, Brücke, Helmholtz, du Bois Reymond, were reforming physiology at the average age of 25. Mayer, Joule, Colding, Helmholtz, were all under 28 years of age when they did their work on the conservation of energy. Goethe, Schiller, Byron, Keats, Shelley, Liebig, Sadi-Carnot, are striking examples of creative work at an early age. I have reflected upon how much it seemed to help Shakespeare and O. Henry to be compelled to be in a hurry and abandon the conventional norms and break all the rules.

I think it is significant that so many creative men were poor in school, and I cannot escape the conclusion that being poor in school was an unconscious protective device for escaping from a multiplicity of learning with no relevance to their aptitude, and that, in view of what was going to happen, they had to be the worst pupils. The chemist Ostwald, in his interesting book, *Grosse Männer*, has pointed out that the precocity of such men as Leibnitz and Sir William Thomson would have done them no good if the schools had been "better" in their time.

A learned man has been at some pains to determine how many men became later productive in literature who did not learn to read in childhood. I believe he did not find any, but it would be of interest to know how many became productive in literary lines who barely learned to read and no more—did not parse or diagram or etymologize or make comparative and historical studies in paragraphing.

I recognize the importance of what we call general culture, of contact with various worlds of ideas, but I am convinced that great blocks of our curricula, both those representing norms outworn but persisting through their emotional rationalization, and those representing real but not universal values, or values disproportionately emphasized in the curriculum, should be transferred to the region of amateur work or sport, and that this can be so arranged as to minister to the emotional needs and contribute at the same time to the efficiency of the individual.

Now, whether these opinions are entirely justified or not, the whole of what I have said makes it impossible for me to wish to disparage our educational system or our educators in comparison with our other social practices. Indeed, if stones are to be thrown, the sociologist is the last man to throw them. It does not solve the problem to attack this or that weak point in our system. If I wanted to run amuck, I think I should not select the educational but the legal field for this purpose; and if the legislator wanted to do the same thing, I think he would select the sociological.

I hesitated to make those remarks about education because I feared you would think I thought they were of fundamental importance. That would be to miss the whole point. The point is that we have not got a method in the social world. The primary group norms are breaking down, mainly owing to the facilitated communication gained through discoveries in the natural sciences and their practical application. The very disharmony of the social world is largely due to the disproportionate rate of advance in the mechanical world. We live in an entirely new world, unique, without parallel in history. History has not helped us. It cannot help us because we do not understand it: we do not even understand an election. We must first understand the past from the present. We must view the present as behavior. We must establish by scientific procedure the laws of behavior, and then the past will have its meaning and make its contribution. If we learn the laws of human behavior as we have learned the laws of mathematics, physics, and chemistry, if we establish what are the fundamental human attitudes, how they can be converted into other and more socially desirable attitudes, how the world of values is created and modified by the operation of these attitudes, then we can establish any attitudes and values whatever.

And we are not to speak of "ultimate" or "supreme" values. The ultimate value is the value you desire at the given moment. But if your "ultimate" values mean the abolition of war, of crime, of drink, of abnormality, of slums, of this or that kind of unhappiness, then you can secure these values, and you can secure whatever seem to you "ultimate" values afterwards, but they cannot be secured without a science of behavior, and more than an "ultimate" mechanics or an "ultimate" medicine could or can be secured without the preceding sciences of mathematics, physics, and chemistry.

And, finally, if we recognize that social control is to be reached through the student of behavior, and that its technique is to consist in the creation of attitudes appropriate to desired values, then I suggest that the most essential attitude at the present moment is a public attitude of hospitality toward all forms of research in the social world, such as it has gained toward all forms of research in the physical world. The Chicago Vice Commission could not be called on to do more than face a penitentiary sentence.

# 11

# SOCIAL TYPES:

# IMMIGRANT ROLES

EACH IMMIGRANT brings to America an individual correlation of the wishes which rule human conduct. In one the desire for recognition predominates; in another the desire for security; and so on in many variations. This individual organization of wishes is what we call character. Likewise each immigrant group as a whole brings a more or less marked character. And while we do not ignore the fact that character is partly due to temperamental qualities—the characteristics of the Swedes, the Jews, the Italians, may be connected with their original, inborn, temperamental dispositions—it is nevertheless certain that character in both individuals and groups is mainly built up by the process which we have referred to above as "the definition of the situation"—by gossip, conversation, disputes, doctrines, by the whole of the experiences and social influences which modify, qualify, and organize the wishes. Thus, the Sicilian *omertà*, the Catholic church and confessional, the Lutheran faith, the doctrine of anarchy, the principle of democracy, are more or less dominant in defining the situation in certain groups and tend to characterize partially these groups and their members. We are able, therefore, to distinguish roughly various immigrant types, represent-

---

Adapted from *Old World Traits Transplanted* (New York: Harper & Bros., 1921), pp. 81–107.

ing different heritages. It is not true, however, that we can treat any given immigrant group strictly *en bloc* from the standpoint of heritages. We find a great homogeneity in this respect in certain groups (and we are inclined to assume more than exists), but in all groups certain individuals resemble individuals in other groups more than they resemble the average member of their own group. Thus a Jewish intellectual probably has more in common with an intellectual of any other group than with a ritualistic Jew. Certainly the difference between an intellectual Pole and a Polish peasant is as profound as possible. In general, where the process of defining the situation rationally instead of customarily has been introduced, a wide divergence will be found between individual members in a group.

In this study we do not attempt to characterize immigrant groups in their totality. We are able to study only the *types of attitudes* brought to America by immigration, and the following indication of types is made from this standpoint, though it will become evident, here and later, that certain attitudes are more or less peculiar to certain groups. The terms used below are more or less arbitrary and the types are usually not pure.

## *The Settler*

All emigration represents some crisis in the life of the emigrants. The decision to leave home is usually precipitated by some incident of immediate significance, probably one destroying the economic basis of life—as where the hereditary land fails to support a growing family, or the property of a Jew is destroyed by a *pogrom*. What the peasant immigrants call "securing an existence" is practically always a motive. And the whole attitude of the immigrant in America is frequently determined by the type of experience at home which has led him to come here. The settler either sets out with a resolve to break with the past permanently, to seek a home in the new country, and transfer his interests to it, or this may become his attitude, perhaps, after a series of hardships here. Extremely and permanently hard economic conditions, such as exist in Sweden and Norway, are favorable to this decision. In general, when the organization of life at home, the traditional attitudes and values resemble our own, the decision to make a home in America is more natural.

In Hungary I had a wife, two children, house, six acres of land, two horses, a cow, two pigs, and a few poultry. That was my fortune. This same land that afforded an existence to my father and grandfather could not support us any longer. Taxes and the cost of living in the last few years have advanced so greatly that the expenses cannot be covered from as much as a small farm can yield.

[Things became worse, an early spring storm killed his crop, he had to buy his bread for money.] My horses were killed from disease. I had to sell my cow to buy winter clothes for the family. There was no money to work the land and without horses and work the land will not produce. I had to mortgage my home. . . .

As a farm laborer in Hungary can earn only enough for bread and water, how is he to pay the taxes, living expenses, and clothing? There was but one hope, America, the golden land of liberty, where the rivers and mountains are full of gold. . . .

We will never go back to Hungary. It only deprived us of our home and land, while in America the soil covers our child. We have a home, money, and business, everything acquired in America. We lost everything in Hungary. We love Hungary as our native land, but never wish to live in it again. . . .[1]

## The Colonist

We may distinguish two general types of success, according to the standard in the mind of the individual. The one is associated with an extraordinary gratification of the wishes, or of some of them—for example, the "will to power"—the other with their limitation. The small shopkeeper may be as successful in his way as a Napoleon, because his wishes are limited. The typical settler has been accustomed to a severe limitation of the wishes in the home country and relative hardship here is considered success. But in the first generation of immigrants this success is never felt

[1]  Janos Kovacs of New York City (interview).

as complete. The economic success may be complete, from any standpoint, but there are sentimental losses. In a Swedish volume there are 128 short life histories of immigrants, and the most general attitude in them is: "I have been successful. I have property. My children have superior advantages. But *I have lost my life.*" This means, of course, not only that the writer has had a hard time here, suffered sentimental losses, but that he has regretful memories of home conditions, of occasional leisure and festivities, of joys and sorrows shared by an intimate group.

We define the colonist as one in whom these memories of home are, from our standpoint, "over determined" (to use the psychoanalytic phrase): one who never forgets nor wishes to forget, whose allegiance is to the home country, whose superior values are the home values. The English are historically great colonizers, and they furnish good representatives of this type in America. The German is also likely to show the colonist's attitude, and the same is true of the French, and of any people who have an eminent position among the nationalities. Their representative feels something akin to the pride in family. These are often very fine types, but the old loyalty yields stubbornly to the new, and the subject is usually careful to let you know that he is contributing more to America than America is contributing to him.

Major Ian Hay Beith, in his delightful little essay entitled "Getting Together," gives some advice to an Englishman as to what he should remember in conversing with an American, and to an American as to what he must bear in mind in talking with an Englishman. To the Englishman, he says: "Remember you are talking to a man who regards his nation as the greatest nation in the world. He will probably tell you this." To the American, he says: "Remember you are talking to a man who regards his nation as the greatest in the world. He will not tell you this, because he takes it for granted that you know already." . . .

[One contribution which an Englishman is able to make to America] is the historic memory which British birth and education give a man. He inevitably escapes the shallowness of a retrospect that is bounded by 1776 or 1619, or even by 1492. . . . [Another] contribution which every immigrant can bring to America consists in the positive good which he has derived from the civilization of his native country. It is at this point that one may seem to be setting oneself up, in a ludicrously pharisaic fashion, as an example. I must therefore beg the reader to understand that . . . I am thinking not of what I am, but of what any Englishman ought to be. . . .[2]

## The Political Idealist

Members of the "oppressed and dependent" nationalities of Europe bring to America forms of the Freudian "baffled wish" and of the "inferiority complex." They are obsessed by the idea of the inferior status of their group at home, and wish to be a nationality among other nationalities. Their organizations here seek to make America a recruiting ground for the battle in Europe. Consequently they wish first of all to save their members from Americanization, to send them home with unspoiled loyalty, or to keep them a permanent patriotic asset working here for the cause at home. They regard America as merely the instrument of their nationalistic wishes. Their leaders wish also to get recognition at home for their patriotic activities here, and superior status on their return. They speak of the penetration of America by their own culture. Thus the Poles, the most ambitious of them, call the Polish-American community the "fourth division of Poland, and refer to the whole body of Poles in America as *"Polonia Americana."* At the same time the material position of the leaders of these groups—the editors, bankers, priests—depends on keeping the group un-American. We find that the aims of these nationalists are often more explicitly and naïvely stated in communications sent to Europe than in their American publications. . . .

Another group of political idealists, embittered against the social order represented by the state and by private property, perhaps disgusted with humanity, are the propagandists of some revolutionary scheme—bolshevism, anarchy, communism—for

[2] Horace E. Bridges, *On Becoming an American*, pp. 39–40.

the redistribution of values. They continue in this country a struggle against organized society which they had been carrying on at home. They bring here and exploit grievances and psychoses acquired under totally different conditions. We are sufficiently familiar with the type:

I hated the rich because they are murderers, and the poor because they would become such if they had the opportunity.[3]

We must mercilessly destroy all the remains of governmental authority and class domination . . . all legal papers pertaining to private ownership of property, all field fences and boundaries, and burn all certificates of indebtedness—in a word, we must take care that everything is wiped from the earth that is a reminder of the right to private ownership of property. . . .[4]

The bourgeois is useless and the government is unnecessary for the development of the commercial and industrial life of the people. . . . It is better to die, and if we are going to die . . . why don't we seek those who are responsible for such disorders and iniquities and execute them?[5]

We have nothing against the blindness of the bourgeoisie and expect nothing else from them. Because the bourgeoisie, which includes lawyers, priests, physicians, writers, merchants, etc., have the same habit as a prostitute; she sells herself to the one who pays more money. . . .[6]

## *The Allrightnick*

This term is one which the Jews of the New York East Side apply to successful members of their race who have found a comfortable berth outside of the Jewish community and within the cosmopolitan group of the "Americanized" Americans. There are, however, other and deeper implications in the term. Here it is used to characterize an opportunistic type which is not peculiar

[3] Letter to *Forward*, February 4, 1918.
[4] *Novomirsky: Manifesto of Anarchists—Communists*. Reprinted in the *New York Times*, November 10, 1919.
[5] *Cultura Obrera* (Spanish Newspaper, New York), April 17, 1919.
[6] *Robotnik* (Ukrainian Newspaper, New York), April 17, 1919.

to the Jewish race—namely, the individual who realizes a very natural ambition to gain access to and some sort of recognition, or at least toleration, in the native American community, or what passes for it, but who does so at the sacrifice of the ideals of his own national and family group. In the case of the Jew, the *allrightnick* may simply be a man who has been a socialist, who has gone into business and become a bourgeois. The mental type is a familiar one, found wherever the transition is made from one cultural group to another, as in the case of the missionary convert.

The poor Jew whom I now scrutinized more closely wore an old shabby coat, an old cap, his hands were black from dust and cold. And his face—what a face! Pale, bony, wrinkled. In each wrinkle there was compassion. And this Jew who sells cookies on the street has three sons and a daughter—all fairly prosperous!

"How is it possible?" slipped off my tongue.

"You mean, of course, why am I not living with them? . . . I did not want to live with them. You understand, I cannot live among machines. I am a live man and have a soul, despite my age. They are machines. They work all day and come home at night. What do they do? Nothing. Wait for supper. During supper they talk about everything in the world—friends, clothes, money, wages, and all sorts of gossip. After supper they dress up and go out. Where to? Either the theater, banquet, or movie. Or else their friends call and they drink, eat, and play cards; or they start the machine and it plays and they dance. The next day again to work and so on for the rest of their life. . . . They have all been to school—educated people; but just try, for the fun of it, and ask them if they ever read a book. Not on your life. Books have nothing in common with them; Judaism has nothing in common with them; Jewish troubles have nothing in common with them; the whole world has nothing in common with them. They only know one thing—work, eat, and away to the theater. How can they do this? I am asking you; how can one lead a life like that?" And in his voice there was a deep anger. . . .

His voice grew louder and became very angry. "And I—I cannot live like that. I am no machine. I like to think, I like to be in good mood, I want to talk to people, I want to get an answer to my questions. When I live among shoemakers I know that the shoemaker is a blind man; but when I live among educated people, then I expect them to be *Menschen.*

"When I first came here I used to speak and argue with them. But they did not understand me. They would ask: 'Why this and that? This country is not Russia. Here everybody does as he likes.'

"Gradually I realized that they were machines. They make money and live for that purpose. When I grasped this situation a terror possessed me and I did not believe these were my children. I could not stand it to be there; I was being choked; I could not tolerate their behavior and I went away...."[7]

## *The Caffone*

The Italians in America apply the term *caffone* (literally, "simpleton") to a man of their nationality who has the least possible association with any group, has no regard for opinion, wears, for example, the same clothes during his whole stay in America, avoids all conversation, ignores his surroundings, and accumulates the sum of money he has in mind as rapidly as possible. We use the term here to designate the pure opportunist, who is unwilling to participate either in the American life or in that of his national group.

The *caffoni*, who were in Sicily mostly *villani* [serfs], are looked down upon by their own people and especially by that class of Italians who want to stay here and who feel injured whenever the Italian name is hurt. To this superior class a good name for the Italians is a requisite of their progress. The *caffoni* don't care. All they want is to make money and go back. So we often see the superior class preaching and speaking to the *caffoni* in meetings, in groups and individually, persuading them to uphold the Italian name. The *caffoni* listen, but then they shrug their shoulders and it is all over. "It does not give me any bread whether Italians have a good name in America or not. I am going back soon."[8]

7   Olgin, *Forward*, February 4, 1917.
8   Gaspare Cusumamo, *Study of the Cinisi Colony in New York City* (manuscript).

## The Intellectual

Our documents show that the "educated" immigrant is usually more misadapted to American society than the workman. He does not, unless he is a technician (chemist, engineer), bring a commodity which we want to buy (as does the laborer), and he must usually make such a place as he can among his fellow immigrants. The following document shows the situation of the *intelligentsia* of one group:

The characteristic note of the corporate life of Hungarian-American intellectuals is one of utter hopelessness, born of the consciousness of isolation, both from the main currents of American and of old-country life, and of the realization of the doom hanging over the American-Hungarian community. This is the paradox of the immigrant colony —that it is constantly losing its best element, which manifests its superiority just by being able to detach itself and to merge into the larger American life. . . . There are new "movements" every now and then to "organize" American Hungariandom [*"amerikai magyarsag,"* a collective term like *Deutschtum*]. The conscious or avowed purposes of these movements vary; their common unconscious element is to make a showing of some sort, to prove [for themselves] that there *is* such a thing as a Hungarian-American culture and a Hungarian-American future; but these movements invariably collapse or die of sheer inertia. The Hungarian-American socialist press is wont to attack these movements as mere attempts at organized graft, and undoubtedly there is an element among the "leaders" which is trying to exploit these campaigns for personal gain. Nevertheless, it is plain that there is some moral purpose behind them—factors ranging from personal vanity and craving his winnings from the rest, but nobody producing new values.[9]

There is a type of intellectual, the product of a superior and systematic training, who comes rarely but who can contribute particular values to the culture of any nationality. Now, modern progress evidently depends in part on communication in space,

[9] Eugene S. Bagger, *Hungarian Intellectuals and Leaders* (manuscript).

on the ability to assemble from all parts of the world values which happen to exist there. Economic efficiency, for example, does not reject any value because it is foreign. But it appears that of all the immigrants who come we are least prepared to receive the foreign intellectual, who is at the same time the type of immigrant best fitted to make a cultural contribution.

Very often the intellectual who comes here has been a failure at home or is a predestined failure anywhere, but will nevertheless attribute his failure here to America's inability to appreciate him.

# IV. Change: Social and Personal

# 12

# ASSIMILATION: OLD WORLD TRAITS TRANSPLANTED

IMMIGRATION IN the form it has taken in America differs from all previous movements of population. Populous countries have planted colonies, states have been conquered and occupied, slaves have been imported. But when a single country is peacefully invaded by millions of men from scores of other countries, when there are added to one American city as many Jews as there are Danes in Denmark, and to the same city more Italians than there are Italians in Rome, we have something new in history.

Naturally the mass and quality of this immigration is important to us because it cannot fail to have an influence on our whole system of life. Every country must have an organization for securing order and efficiency, not only to insure the happiness and prosperity of its citizens within its boundaries, but also to protect it from foreign attack. The various nationalities and civilizations of the world are in a state of rivalry, and a low efficiency in any country may lead to its destruction, actual or economic. Our wish to assimilate the immigrants who remain here means that we want to make them a practical part of our organization.

There is an interesting parallel between the influence which a

---

Adapted from *Old World Traits Transplanted* (New York: Harper & Bros., 1921), pp. 259–308.

country wishes to exercise over its members and the influence of what geographers and naturalists call an "area of characterization." In the natural world an area of characterization is a geographical region sufficiently marked in its physical features to put a characteristic imprint on its flora and fauna. In the same way, the human inhabitants of a country develop a body of characteristic values. A country is an area of cultural characterization.

## Required in a Democracy

Among the distinguishing features of the American "area of characterization" is the principle that no man is to be used as a tool and thus placed in the category of purely material values, and we have consequently repudiated the ancient conception of the state, in which by a system of "ordering and forbidding" great things were achieved, indeed, but only by keeping the masses permanently in the category of things.

Our state system is based on the participation of every member and assumes in all the wish and ability to participate; for in the last analysis we mean by democracy participation by all, both practically and imaginatively, in the common life of the community. Our democracy is not working perfectly at present because not even the native born are participating completely. Our old order was a territorial one. The autonomy of the political and social groups was based on size and geographical isolation. So long as the group remained small and isolated, individuals were able to act responsibly, because the situations they dealt with came easily within their understanding and capacity. But the free communication provided by the locomotive, the post, the telegraph, the press, has dissolved distances. As a result men find themselves in a system of relationships, political and economic, over which, in spite of their traditional liberties of speech and action, they no longer have control. The conditions of their daily living are vitally affected by events occurring without their knowledge, thousands of miles away.

It is similarly impossible for average citizens to grasp all the elements of the political issues on which they give decisions. The economic nexus holds them in an inevitable interdependence; they are politically disfranchised while retaining the ceremony of a vote. No longer able to act intelligently or responsibly, they act upon vagrant impulses. They are directed by suggestion and advertising. This is the meaning of social unrest. It is the sign of a baffled wish to participate. It represents energy, and the problem is to use it constructively. While we are forming a new definition of the situation, we are subject to emotional states and random movements.

The founders of America defined the future state as a democracy characterized by the largest possible amount of individual freedom, but this ideal has not been fully realized. At best we can say that we are in the process of giving this country the cultural characterization of such a democracy.

While we have on our hands this problem we are importing large numbers of aliens, representing various types, in the main below our cultural level. Some of them bring a greater and more violent unrest than we know here: psychoses acquired under conditions where violence was the only means of political participation. Others belong to the nationalistic, opportunistic, or in fewer numbers to the radical elements, who not only do not regard this country as their country, but do not regard it as a country at all— do not recognize that we have a characteristic body of values and the right to preserve these values.

The immigrant usually brings a value which is very important to us—labor—and it would be possible to regard him in a narrowly practical way as a merely material value, just as the Negro in slavery and Chinese labor in early days were regarded as material values, and as the Germans regarded the 600,000 laborers from Austria and Russia who crossed their borders annually and returned to their homes at the end of the harvest season. But we know from our experience with slavery and from the German experiences with the *Sachsengänger,* that this attitude has a bad effect both on the aliens and on the culture of the group which receives and uses them as mere things. If visitors are disorderly, unsanitary, or ignorant, the group which incorporates them, even temporarily, will not escape the bad effects of this.

Every country has a certain amount of culturally undeveloped material. We have it, for instance, in the Negroes and Indians, the Southern mountaineers, the Mexicans and Spanish-Americans, and the slums. There is a limit, however, to the amount of material of this kind that a country can incorporate without losing the character of its culture. For example, the "three R's" represent our minimum of cultural equipment, and we are able to transmit this much to practically everybody. With this equipment the individual is able to penetrate any sphere of life; without it, he cannot move upward at all. But if we should receive, say, a million Congo blacks and a million Chinese coolies annually, and if they should propagate faster than the white Americans, it is certain that our educational system would break down; we could not impart even the "three R's." We should then be in a state of chaos unless we abandoned the idea of democracy and secured efficiency by reverting to the "ordering and forbidding" type of state.

This is the general significance of immigration to our problem of democracy. We must make the immigrants a working part in our system of life, ideal and political, as well as economic, or lose the character of our culture. Self-preservation makes this necessary; the fact that they bring valuable additions to our culture makes it desirable. Now we can assimilate the immigrants only if their attitudes and values, their ideas on the conduct of life, are brought into harmony with our own. They cannot be intelligent citizens unless they "get the hang" of American ways of thinking as well as of doing. How fast and how well this is accomplished depends (1) on the degree of similarity between their attitudes and values and our own, giving them a certain preadaptation to our scheme of life and an ability to aid in their own Americanization; and (2) on how we treat them—our attitude toward their heritages. These are, roughly, the elements in our problem of assimilation.

## Similarity of Heritages

It is one of the ordinary experiences of social intercourse that words and things do not have the same meanings with different people, in different periods of time, in different parts of a country—that is, in general, in different contexts. The same "thing" has a different meaning for the naïve person and the sophisticated person, for the child and the philosopher. The new experience derives its significance from the character and interpretation of previous experiences. To the peasant a comet, a plague, an epileptic person, may mean, respectively, a divine portent, a visitation of God, a possession by the devil; to the scientist they mean something quite different. The word slavery had a connotation in the ancient world very different from the one it bears to-day. It has a different significance to-day in the Southern and Northern states. "Socialism" has a very different significance to the immigrant from the Russian pale living on the "East Side" of New York City, to the citizen on Riverside Drive, and to the native American in the hills of Georgia.

The meaning any word has for an individual depends on his past experience, not only with the things the word means, but with many other things associated with it in his mind. For example, the concept evoked in his mind by the word "food" is determined not only by the kinds of food he has eaten, but also by the normal state of his appetite and digestion, the ease or difficulty with which he secures his daily ration, whether he grows, hunts, or buys it, whether or not he prepares it, whether he has ever been near starvation, and so forth. No two people have exactly the same experience by which to define the same word, and sometimes the resulting difference in meaning is immeasurably great. This is the meaning of the saying of the logicians that persons who attach different meanings to the same words and the same things are in different "universes of discourse"—that is, do not talk in the same world.

All the meanings of past experience retained in the memory of the individual form what is called by psychologists the "apperception mass." It is the body of memories with which every new item of experience comes in contact, to which it is related, and in connection with which it gets its meaning. The difference in the interpretation of words is merely an example of the fact that persons whose apperception masses are radically different give a different interpretation to all experience. The ecclesiastic, the artist; the mystic, the scientist; the philistine, the bohemian —are examples of classes not always mutually intelligible. Similarly, different races and nationalities, as wholes, represent different apperception masses and consequently different universes of discourse, and are not mutually intelligible. Even our forefathers are with difficulty intelligible to us, though always more intelligible than the eastern European immigrant, because of the continuity of our tradition.

The set of attitudes and values, which we call the immigrant's heritage, are the expression in ideas and action of his apperception mass. "Heritages" differ because the races and nationalities concerned have developed different apperception masses; and they have developed different apperception masses because, owing to historical circumstances, they have defined the situation in different ways.

Certain prominent personalities, schools of thought, bodies of doctrine, historical events, have helped to define the situation and determine the attitudes and values of our various immigrant groups in characteristic ways in their home countries. To the Sicilian, for example, marital infidelity means conventionally the stiletto; to the American, the divorce court. These differences sometimes go so far that it is impossible for those concerned to talk to one another. The Western World, for example, appreciates learning, and we have signalized this in our schools. The Jews also show this appreciation, and even the Polish peasant appreciates learning, though not for his class. But in one of the documents cited earlier, we have a complete repudiation of learning; the situation is here defined in terms of piety, somewhat as we defined it before Darwin. We can imagine that if the Oriental who signs this document met a Western entomologist at dinner, and, interrogating him as to his interests, found that he spent his life in examining potato bugs, moving them from one temperature to another, from one degree of humidity to another, from one altitude to another, to see if their spots changed, if they changed whether the change remained permanent under all conditions, or whether new generations reverted to the previous type if removed to the old conditions—in other words, that he was trying to create a new species—the Oriental would conclude that his interlocutor was not only impious, but insane.

If the immigrant possesses already an apperception mass corresponding in some degree to our own, his participation in our life will, of course, follow more easily. While we have given examples of heritages strange to us, the body of material presented shows that he does not differ from us profoundly. We can best appreciate the immigrants' mental kinship with ourselves negatively, by comparing them with what they are not. If the immigrants practiced and defended cannibalism and incest; if they burned their widows and killed their parents and broke the necks of their wayward daughters, customarily; if (as in a North African Arab tribe) a girl were not eligible for marriage until she had given her older brother a child born out of wedlock, to be reared as a slave; if immigrant families limited their children by law to one boy and one girl, killing the others (as in the Ellice Archipelago); or (as in the Solomon Islands) if they killed all, or nearly all, their children and bought others from their neighbors, as our farmers sell young calves to butchers and buy yearlings; if immigrant army recruits declined target practice because the bullet would go straight anyway if Allah willed it—then the problem of assimilation would be immensely complicated.

In comparison with these examples immigrant heritages usually differ but slightly from ours, probably not more than ours differ from those of our more conservative grandfathers. Slavery, dueling, burning of witches, contempt of soil analysis, condemnation of the view that plants and animals have been developed slowly, not suddenly created, are comparatively recent American values and attitudes.

## Psychology of Assimilation

It is evidently necessary that the people who compose a community and participate in common enterprises shall have a body of common memories sufficient to enable them to understand one another. This is particularly true in a democracy, where it is intended that the public institution should be responsive to public opinion. There can be no public opinion unless the persons who compose the public are able to live and think in the same world. The process of assimilation involves the development in the immigrant and the native of similar apperception masses. To this end it is desirable that the immigrants should not only speak the language of the country, but also know something of the history of the people among whom they have chosen to dwell. For the same reason it is important that native Americans should know the history and social life of the countries from which the immigrants come.

It is important also that every individual should share as fully as possible a fund of knowledge, experience, sentiments, and ideals common to the whole community, and himself contribute to that fund. It is for this reason that we maintain and seek to maintain freedom of speech and free schools. The function of literature, including poetry, romance, and the newspaper, is to enable all to share vicariously the inner life of each. The function of science is to gather up, classify, digest, and preserve, in a form in which they may be available to the community as a whole, the ideas, inventions, and technical experience of the individuals composing it. Not merely the possession of a common language, but the widest extension of the opportunities for education, is a condition of Americanization.

For the immigrant to achieve an apperception mass in common with the American community, involves the development of new attitudes on his part, and his old experiences are the only possible foundation for the new structure. If a person becomes interested in anything whatever, it is because there is already in him something to which it can appeal. Visitors to the Dresden

Gallery are all affected by the Sistine Madonna in approximately the same way because they bring to it a similar body of socially created appreciations—the sanctity of motherhood, the sufferings of our Lord, the adoration of Mary, the aesthetic appreciation of female beauty, and so forth. No amount of explanation or persuasion would arouse the same feeling in an African black man. Livingstone relates that an African mother brought to him through the dust and heat a child pitiably misshapen through rupture. Two native men uncovered the basket and were moved, not to pity, but to laughter. These Africans evidently would not appreciate the painting of a Madonna because they have not developed our tenderness toward children, because white men and women impress them somewhat as cadavers and albinos impress us,[1] because they have not our tradition of chivalry and know nothing of the sufferings of our Lord.

A certain identity of experiences and memories between immigrants and Americans is of main importance for assimilation, because, in the process of learning, a new fact has a meaning and makes an appeal only if it is identified with some previous experience, something that is already known and felt. Thus, when we appealed to the patriotism of our immigrants during the war, we found a ready response, because they knew what patriotism is. The Bohemians in a Cleveland parade carried a banner with the inscription: "We are Americans through and through by the spirit of our nation," and interpreted this by another banner: "Americans, do not be discouraged. We have been fighting these tyrants for three hundred years." . . .

## *Tolerance vs. Suppression*

The apperception mass of the immigrant, expressed in the attitudes and values he brings with him from his old life, is the material from which he must build his Americanism. It is also the material we must work with, if we would aid this process. Our

---

[1] Livingstone states that after a long residence among black men, white men reminded him of celery and white mice.

tools may be in part American customs and institutions, but the substance we seek to mold into new forms is the product of other centuries in other lands. In education it is valuable to let the child, as far as possible, make his own discoveries and follow his own interests. He should have the opportunity of seeking new experiences which have a meaning for him when connected with his old experiences. A wise policy of assimilation, like a wise educational policy, does not seek to destroy the attitudes and memories that are there, but to build on them.

There is a current opinion in America, of the "ordering and forbidding" type, demanding from the immigrant a quick and complete Americanization through the suppression and repudiation of all the signs that distinguish him from us.[2] Those who have this view wish the repudiation to be what the church fathers demanded of a confession of sin—"sudden, complete, and bitter."

It is notable that this destruction of memories is the plan of both those who demand a quick and complete Americanization and those who demand a quick and complete social revolution—the extreme Americanists and the extreme radicals. In the anarchist-communist manifesto we read: "We must mercilessly destroy. . . . We must take care that everything is wiped out from the earth that is a reminder." Both positions imply that there is nothing of value for the future in the whole of past experience; whereas we have shown, in speaking of the psychology of assimilation, that "reminders" are precisely what the individual uses in making constructive changes in his life; and in the chapter on demoralization we pointed out that the absence of reminders, forgetfulness of the standards of the community, failure to live in the light of the past, reduce a man to the basis of the instincts, with which humanity first began. . . .

There is an element of pure prejudice in this theory of Americanization. It appears as intolerance of the more obvious signs

[2] "Broadly speaking, we mean [by Americanization] an appreciation of the institutions of this country, absolute forgetfulness of all obligations or connections with other countries because of descent or birth"—Superintendent of the New York Public Schools, *N.Y. Evening Post*, August 9, 1918. Quoted by I. B. Berkson. *Americanization*, chapter 2.

of unlikeness. Where color exists, it is the mark specially singled out by prejudice, but since our immigrants are mainly not colored, language becomes the most concrete sign of unlikeness and the foremost object of animosity. It is certainly true that a man cannot participate fully in our life without our language, and that its acquisition is rightly considered a sign and rough index of Americanization. But the American who does not know the details of the immigrant's life and problems cannot imagine how useful his language is here in the first stages. Take an actual case. The Danes are distinguished farmers, but here the soil, the demand, are unfamiliar and they have trouble. The American government could help them, but they do not know this. Even if they did they could not inquire in English; they would not know whether to address the President or the Senate; and they would not address either because they would not know with what honorific form to begin the letter. A certain Danish editor invites communications on specific plans and troubles of this kind. In each case (and the number is relatively large) he sends with his reply a letter in English, addressed to the Department of Agriculture, asking for the proper bulletin. The Dane is to copy the letter and send it. This much he will do, and the bulletin somehow gets read. Here again is the typical process of assimilation—the identification of the immigrant's success with America; here, too, is an example of what we mean when we say that the immigrants must assist in their own Americanization. Prejudice against language thus means bringing into disrepute one of the tools most useful in assimilation.

Again, the Yiddish language is a very useful heritage to the Jew, and this is a clear case of utility, without any obstinacy or sentimentality. The Jews associate their nationalism with Hebrew, the language of the Jews and the one that their national idealists are seeking to restore. Yiddish is a German dialect, with a mixture of Hebrew, Polish, and so forth, developed originally by the Jews as a business expedient. It is an uncouth speech, with very limited power of literary expression, and nothing with which a man would seek to identify himself. The Jews in America drop it as soon as possible, and it is really difficult to induce a Jew to speak a few words of it in order to show you what it is like. And yet the Jewish community in New York City pays annually more than $2,000,000 for Yiddish newspapers. These newspapers and other Jewish institutions do thousands of particular and very personal services for Jews which American institutions could not do and which no one could undertake without the use of Yiddish. Language is a tool which its possessor cannot afford to throw away until he has another. . . .

## *Immigrant Organizations Valuable*

Following the instinctive prejudice against strangeness, many Americans distrust immigrant organizations, as such, and consider them obstacles to assimilation. On the contrary, we have emphasized the importance of these organizations. Indeed, the amount of immigration which we can continue to tolerate or encourage depends on their character.

Organizations, beginning in the family and community, are the means by which men regulate their lives. The healthy life of a society always depends more on the spontaneous organization of its members than on formal legal and political regulations. It is only in an organized group—in the home, the neighborhood, the trade union, the co-operative society—where he is a power and an influence, in some region where he has status and represents something, that man can maintain a stable personality. There is only one kind of neighborhood having no representative citizen—the slum; a world where men cease to be persons because they represent nothing. In the slum men live in an enforced intimacy, but they do not communicate. They suspect one another and keep away from one another. They cannot maintain a personality because there are no standards; if standards of decency, morality, and sanitation exist they are imposed from without. A slum is a place, composed at first of the poor, which has become inevitably a refuge for criminals and disorderly persons—a place of missions and lost souls.

If the face-to-face organization which made the immigrant

moral at home is suddenly dissolved in this country, we have the general situation presented in the documents on demoralization. We saw there that men, removed from the restraining influence of an organized community, tend to follow their immediate impulses and behave in monstrous ways. Ethnologists have shown that when the uncivilized races come into contact with the products of our civilization they appropriate the vices and ornaments, the whisky and beads, and leave the more substantial values. The same tendency appears among immigrants, especially the children. The term "Americanization" is not used popularly among the immigrants as we use it. They call a badly demoralized boy "completely Americanized." Thomas and Znaniecki have presented a large mass of materials on the demoralization of the Poles in America, and they conclude that the "wild" behavior found in this group is to be explained by the fact that "the individual does not feel himself backed in his dealings with the outside world by any strong social group of his own, and is not conscious of being a member of a steadily organized society. . . . This does not, of course, apply to the relatively intelligent and socially responsible immigrants who take an active part in the construction of Polish institutions and have an economic ideal which gives stability to their lives. [It characterizes] that floating unorganized mass of the intellectually backward immigrant population which constitutes among the Poles from one-fourth to one third of the total number."[3]

The organization of the immigrant community is necessary as a regulative measure. Any type of organization which succeeds in regulating the lives of its members is beneficial. If you can induce a man to belong to something, to co-operate with any group whatever, where something is expected of him, where he has responsibility, dignity, recognition, economic security, you have at least regulated his life. From this standpoint even the nationalistic societies do more to promote assimilation than to retard it. There is no doubt, for example, that the nationalistic newspapers do not want their readers to become Americanized, but

[3]  W. I. Thomas and Florian Znaniecki, *The Polish Peasant*, vol. v.

they make them more intelligent, more prepared to be Americans, simply by printing the news of what is going on in America, and this they have to do in order to circulate at all. The nationalistic organizations are the means by which certain men make their living and get their distinction; they assist the home countries materially in their struggle for freedom, they stimulate some older people to return to Europe, but they have almost no effect in keeping the immigrant, especially the young generation, estranged from American life. . . .

The propaganda of hate carried on notably by the Italian press, and described by an Italian in the note below,[4] is also partly nationalistic in its aim. While not among the dependent nationalities, Italy has been particularly active in preserving the allegiance of her emigrated subjects, and her leaders have acted, so to speak, as representatives of a country that is trying to control a colony. They have used hate, because enmity is the motive through which men can be aroused and controlled most easily. But here also, if we recognize the fact that editors are playing on attitudes that are already there, not creating them, the propaganda has slight importance. Italians who returned to Sicily after the war, are now returning to America. They found that it was

[4] "I have seen a large number of articles from Italian newspapers, written by Italian professional men concerning America, which if translated and published, would open the eyes even of the blind. America is described in these articles as a ruthless, rapacious, hypocritical, puritanical country. American men are superficial, weak, ridiculous; American women are vain and prefer to have a good time rather than to be good wives and mothers; churches in America are places of business; social and philanthropic work is established to furnish fat salaries to innumerable officeholders; the political life is incurably corrupt; and everything else is termed "Americanate," meaning the quintessence of foolishness. A sensational divorce case, a scandal at the City Hall, Dowie or Billy Sunday, anything and everything is used as a pretext for a long philippic against America. I have seen Italian newspapers with laudatory articles on America written in English, which no Italian would read, and with an article in Italian in the same issue, that the American would not understand, painting America in the blackest colors."—E. C. Sartorio, *Social and Religious Life of the Italians in America*, p. 50.

"too small" over there. They had entered their own country as immigrants, and suffered again the disillusionment of the immigrant. The fault to be found with the nationalistic organizations is not that they do the damage they imagine they are doing, but that they fail to do the constructive work of which, as organizations, they are capable; that they do not help their people to identify their success with America, in such ways as we have exemplified above in the case of the Danes and Jews.

We have not developed American institutions adapted to meeting the first needs of the immigrant and preserving in him the good qualities which he brings. Usually he reaches our institutions only after he has become a failure. The immigrant organizations are doing very positive services for their members by maintaining their sense of social responsibility, of responsibility to some type of community. But more than this, our experience has shown that, while it is possible for an individual immigrant, especially if he represents a relatively cultured type, to identify himself directly with American society without an intermediate connection with a group of his own nationality, in the main the immigrants are becoming Americanized *en masse,* by whole blocks, precisely through their own organzations. The organization as a whole is influenced, modified, Americanized by its efforts to adjust itself to American conditions. This happened, for example, when the immigrant athletic organizations recently joined the American Amateur Athletic Association; for this alliance implies acceptance by the immigrant of all the American athletic standards. Similarly, the immigrant who penetrates American society as a member of an immigrant group forms a bond between this group and American society. The Letts in New York City felt pride in a young violinist who had played at their weekly entertainments. For his further development the Lettish organization sent him to the American teacher, Damrosch. The individual thus forms a link between the immigrant society and American society. He will transmit the influence of his American contacts to the immigrant organization.

We illustrated the important fact that the immigrant is not a highly individualized person. He has been accustomed to live in a small, intimate, face-to-face group, and his conduct has been determined by this group. Naturally he needs the assistance of such a group for a time in America, and naturally this group is composed of his own people. This general condition explains the perfect success of our government in its appeal to the immigrant population for subscriptions to the Liberty loans. The appeal was not made to the immigrant individually, but through his organizations.

The type of organization which the immigrants bring with them from home is one which we ought to appreciate. It represents the individual's responsibility to society which we have in a measure lost, and are consciously attempting to restore by the reorganization of the local community. It is a type of organization which can be made the basis of all kinds of co-operative enterprise —the basis, in fact, on which the local community will again function. Co-operation is an attitude already present in immigrant consciousness, and co-operative economic enterprises are arising spontaneously among immigrant groups—the Finns, the Italians, the Poles, and others. This is especially true since younger men of immigrant parentage, who have gone through our schools, who are American in feeling, are beginning to assume the leadership in the immigrant groups and to employ constructively the traditional spirit of co-operation.

If we wish to help the immigrant to get a grip on American life, to understand its conditions, and find his own rôle in it, we must seize on everything in his old life which will serve either to interpret the new or to hold him steady while he is getting adjusted; the language through which his compatriots can give him their garnered experience, the "societies" which make him feel "at home," the symbols of his home land, reminding him of the moral standards under which he grew up. Common courtesy and kindness exact tolerance for these things, and common sense indicates that they are the foundation of the readjustment we seek.

## Perpetuation of Groups Impossible

The evident value of these immigrant organizations during the period of adjustment raises another question. Is he to remain permanently in one of these racial organizations, and are they to continue as centers of cultures diverse from and competing with that of America? This question touches a larger aspect of the heritages, relating to the ideal character of our national life—whether we shall strive for a uniform or a diversified type of culture and whether the perpetuation of immigrant traits and organizations will accomplish this diversity.

We have recognized the importance of a resemblance between the members of a community which will enable them to understand and influence one another. In a peasant community, as in a herd or flock, great unanimity in following tested habits is sufficient, without any great intelligence, to enable all to live. But as communities progress the members behave more and more independently, use more freedom. Communities progress, indeed, because certain of their members insist on using more freedom.

The civilization we have is the product of an association of individuals who are widely unlike, and with the progress of civilization the divergence in individual human types has been and must continue to be constantly multiplied. Our progress in the arts and sciences and in the creation of values in general has been dependent on specialists whose distinctive worth was precisely their divergence from other individuals. It is even evident that we have been able to use productively persons who in a savage or peasant society would have been classed as insane—who were, perhaps, insane. Until recently our conception of insanity has been to some extent determined by the standards of the "primary group," which demands uniformity in its members. Many persons who had the qualities of genius have simply passed as queer in their local communities. Julius Robert Mayer, the discoverer of the law of the conservation of energy, was twice confined in insane asylums by the people of the provincial town of Heilbronn. Where else did a man belong who went about arguing that "heat was a mode of motion," that if a house burned down it was not destroyed? Indeed, he considered himself insane in his home town, and when the physicist Düring wished to visit him he declined to receive him in Heilbronn, but arranged to meet him in the neighboring village of Wildbad. "Since everybody here," he wrote, "considers me a fool, everybody considers himself justified in exercising a spiritual guardianship over me."[5] We have already pointed out that the Mohammedan could regard a modern scientist as insane. However, we have had so many profitable returns from the queer behavior of such men as Mayer, Darwin, and Langley (whose experiments with the flying machine were regarded by many as insane), that we have changed our definition of insanity and regard any man as sane the sum of whose activities is valuable to the community.[6]

The value of the principle of diversity has already been fully recognized in the scientific world and in the specialized occupations. Efficiency in these fields is based on far-going individualization of function. The astronomer or the physiological chemist awaits the result of the physicist or the chemist as condition of further steps in his own investigation. The more diversified the personalities, the more particularized the products of these personalities, the greater the likelihood that we shall find among them the elements for the realization of our own plans, the construction of our own values.

In the civilization having the highest efficiency all are not in the same "universe of discourse," but there tend to be smaller groups or circles who understand one another and co-operate. Although they are not understood by everybody, their products become useful to everybody. The physicists, for example, represent such a circle. The physicist demonstrates a law which the public cannot understand; but the engineer understands it and applies it in the invention of machines which become of general use.

[5] The details are in Ostwald's *Grosse Männer*.

[6] "When we begin to acknowledge *many standards of normality* we take away the sting of a stigma"—Adolf Meyer, *Suggestions of Modern Science Concerning Education*, p. 143.

Now representatives of the different immigrant groups claim a similar social value—that, on account of their racial peculiarities and the fact that they have developed by their past experiences different apperception masses, they are predisposed to individualized functions as groups, and that by permanently organizing along the lines of their aptitudes they will not only express their peculiar genius, but contribute unique values to America. . . .

This position would seem very secure only if the groups represented in immigration were specialized by heredity, so that some of them could do certain things that others could not do, or do them better—if some of them were poetical, some philosophical, some born physicists. But it is not apparent that even the most distinct races, the black, white, and yellow, are characterized in this way. The anthropologists think that if such differences exist they are not very great. Certainly the Japanese have shown that in general they can do anything that we can do, and have not shown that they can do anything that we cannot do. It is easier to explain why the Jew is in the needle trades, is not a farmer, and is intelligent, on the ground of circumstances—that he has had a given racial history—than on the ground of inborn aptitudes.

In any case, so far as European immigration is concerned, we do not have to do with races at all in the proper sense. The "races" of Europe are all mongrel, and are classified on the basis of language and custom. The Magyars, for example, came in from Asia only a thousand years ago, but they are so interbred with Germans, Ruthenians, Slovaks, Rumanians, Serbians, Croations, that it is difficult to find an example of the original Magyar type. The Prussians were not originally Germans at all, but a Baltic tribe, akin to the Lithuanians. Even the Jews are greatly intermixed with both Asiatics and Europeans. Twenty per cent of the Jews are blond.[7]

We have referred to the fact that the peasant does not greatly fear death for himself, but is terrified by a pest or war, where the existence of his groups is threatend. Men fear extinction, not only

[7] Details are in Franz Boas' *The Mind of Primitive Man.*

for themselves, but for their groups. We do not wish to have our families die out; we cannot think calmly of the white race as dying out; we do not wish to have even the birds and the flowers die out. We wish only our enemies to die out. The thought of a given group being swallowed up by another group leaves the apprehension of death in the minds of it members. The dread of the death of their communities is the instinctive basis of the wish of the immigrant groups to remain separate in America. The rational and practical basis of the wish is the claim that they will in that way have more security, recognition, and efficiency.

# 13

# CONFLICT:

# REVOLUTIONARY ATTITUDES

ALL THE cases of social disorganization include an active opposition to the traditional social schemes of behavior; in this respect the rejection of a fashion, a theft or murder, an attempt to overthrow the existing class organization or political order, a religious heresy, are fundamentally similar, being equally the manifestations of tendencies which can find no adequate expression under the prevailing social system and, if allowed to develop sufficiently, lead to a decay of this system. . . .

That kind of active opposition to existing rules which we term revolt is individualistic in its bearing, even if many members of a group happen to participate in it; it implies only, on the part of each individual, personal demands for some values which he could not have under the traditional system. A revolutionary tendency may also involve such personal demands and in so far be an act of revolt; but its essential feature is that it includes a demand for new values for a whole group—community, class, nation, etc.; each individual acting not only in his own name but also in the name of others.

Secondly, revolt does not intentionally and consciously aim

---

Reprinted from *The Polish Peasant in Europe and America* (New York: Alfred A. Knopf, 1927; New York: Dover Publications, 1958), pp. 1265-74, 1280-85, 1296-1300.

at the destruction of the old system in general; its purpose is in each particular case the satisfaction of some particular wish. The break of rules is only, in a sense, incidental to this satisfaction and the decay of the traditional system comes spontaneously, as a result of an increasing number and variety of cases of revolt. Whereas the immediate aim of revolution is to abolish the traditional system or at least some of the schemes of behavior which are its part, to destroy permanently their influence within the given group, and thus to open the way to a general and permanent satisfaction of those needs which cannot be freely satisfied while the system lasts.

In view of these differences between revolt and revolution, the methods which prove more or less efficient in suppressing the former often fail when applied to the latter. Thus it is clear that a peasant community which willingly and of its own accord represses individual revolt against its traditions and mores, can hardly be made to cooperate wholeheartedly with the higher social classes in suppressing those tendencies of its members which aim to modify the existing social order for the benefit of the peasant class. Such a community may, indeed, be opposed to the revolutionary activities of its individual members for fear that a repression from outside will have disastrous consequences for the whole group, or because its desire for security is stronger than the desire for any new values which revolution is expected to bring. But this opposition lacks the moral indignation that accompanies the suppression of personal revolt against those principles which keep the community together; often in this case it is the revolutionary member of the group who draws his energy from a feeling of righteousness connected with his activities.

Further, we have seen that one of the most efficient means of inducing the individual to accept against his wishes any particular traditional definition is to connect this definition with a wide, coherent and powerful system of emotions and beliefs, like the religious system in which he was brought up. It is evident that this method works only as long as the individual revolts against particular rules which hinder the satisfaction of his particular desires, but does not wish or dare to attack the system in its entirety. Thus it cannot be utilized to suppress a revolutionary tendency whose characteristic feature is precisely that it turns against the domination of a whole traditional system. Attempts to apply this method in periods of social unrest may even hasten the outbreak of revolution, for if the opposition to the traditional system as a whole has begun to develop in social consciousness, it is apt to grow with every act which tends to repress new needs in the name of this system.

The only efficient method of dealing with revolutionary attitudes is, as we shall see later, the substitution of a new and more satisfactory system for the old one—a substitution in which the revolutionary elements of society shall be made to cooperate. And it will prove that this method is successful in dealing with facts of personal revolt, at least in those cases in which revolt is not an expression of individual abnormality, of pathological misadaptation of the individual to the fundamental conditions of social life, but results from the development and growing popularization of new needs. In a word, in so far as disorganization is a social process, not a fact of individual pathology, it is an unavoidable stage of social evolution and cannot be remedied by trying to stop this evolution but by directing it. Revolution is thus the crucial test of the methods of social reconstruction; any method which, even if it succeeds in suppressing particular cases of personal revolt, cannot prevent the appearance and development of revolutionary attitudes in the sense defined above. It may be useful in periods of relative social stability but should be rejected as soon as social unrest begins to grow, for it only retards the process of reconstruction and contributes to increase the chaos of the intermediary period.

Our study of the revolutionary attitudes of the Polish peasant will be limited to two fields—class revolutionism and religious revolutionism. For several reasons, we cannot study here political revolutionism as manifested in the national uprisings of the Poles against the partitioning states, particularly against Russia. Though within the period which we are taking into account there was a national revolution (partly connected with a social revolution) in 1905–6, the latter was mostly supported by city workmen and the peasants as a class participated in it very little. There has been, indeed, during this whole period a growing national revolutionary movement among the peasants which finally led to their active participation in the last and successful struggle of 1914–19; but the documents referring to this movement were, for obvious reasons, kept secret all the time. What actually transpired and was accessible to our investigation, was an increasing national consciousness manifesting itself in social organization and cultural cooperation. . . .

This revolution of 1905–6 would be, indeed, a very interesting object of study; but it would be absolutely incomprehensible without a thorough analysis of the psychology of the Polish factory workmen and their leaders, of the economic and political conditions found in Polish industrial centers and many other problems which would lead us far beyond the limits of this work. We therefore introduce here only a few documents concerning this revolution to illustrate some of its effects on the peasants' class or religious attitudes.[1]

## Class Revolutionism

The class system in the country was, as we know, very rigid until recently, much more rigid than in cities. This holds true not only of Poland, but practically of all Europe. In particular, the distinction between the peasants and the gentry, the two oldest and most definitely fixed classes, has been maintained for so many centuries, owing to serfdom, that up to the present it often appears to the popular mind as in a sense rooted in the nature of things; the deep differences of culture help at least as much as economic inequality to maintain it. The growth of intermediary elements—ruined nobles, bourgeois settling on land,

[1] It should be understood that our subject-matter is revolutionary attitudes, not revolutionary acts. A revolutionary attitude which manifests itself in a vague dissatisfaction with existing conditions may be more significant sociologically than one which is expressed in an act of overt rebellion—if it is more general and lasting.

wealthy or educated peasants—and the contact with the new, different, more flexible social hierarchy which has developed in cities, have done much to diminish this distinction; and yet the latter until recently appeared to the average peasant as the most striking feature of that wider social order of which his community was a part.

But if the class distinction during the last fifty years remains essentially the same as before, class antagonism has certainly decreased in an incalculable measure since the abolition of serfdom. At the time which we are here taking into account, the opposition of interests between the peasant farmers and the large estate-owners reduced itself to two points. The first was the question of servitudes or the rights to pasture peasant cattle on manorial land and take dry wood from manorial forests, which was intentionally left unsettled by the Russian government in order to foment discord between the peasants and the nobility. The second was the more fundamental problem of distribution of land. The growth of the country population has resulted in a division of many peasant farms into lots below the minimum necessary for living, and in an enormous increase of the number of landless peasants, whereas there were yet many disproportionately large private estates of the nobility, and vast territories which the Russian government had either appropriated after the partitions or confiscated after the revolutions of 1830 and 1863. Now, the peasants have from immemorial times cherished the idea—found in all agricultural communities—that cultivated land should belong to those who cultivate it with their own hands while non-cultivated land is nobody's property. In connection with this, we know that the desire for economic advance which developed among the peasants very powerfully during the second half of the last century manifested itself chiefly in a general "land-hunger" which demanded to be satisfied by any means. Naturally, therefore, the tendency to take away and to divide the estates of the government and of the nobility has been continually growing; and the endowment of peasants with land after the abolition of serfdom was easily interpreted as a precedent. This tendency, sometimes formulated but usually concealed from the upper classes, was the most serious factor of whatever class antagonism was found between the manor-owner and the peasant farmer.[2]

Much deeper was the antagonism between the gentry and the landless peasants employed by them as manor-servants. The situation of the latter was hardly improved by the agrarian reforms of the nineteenth century; they had personal freedom already (since 1808 in the Congress Kingdom), and the reform of 1864, which for the landed peasant meant freedom from duties toward his lord and undisputed property of his farm, for the landless peasant meant practically nothing except a change from a patriarchal relation with more subordination but more security to a "hired work" relation with more independence but less mutual personal interest. The difficult economic condition of the country under foreign domination, particularly in Russian Poland where the government intentionally tried to ruin the Polish nobility, combined with the conservatism usually characterizing agricultural classes and with the continually increasing offer of cheap labor, contributed to maintain the wages of the manor-servant on a level barely above the starvation limit. The contrast between his situation and not only that of his employer but even that of an average peasant farmer facilitated the development of revolutionary attitudes.

The Russian paper *Warszawskij Dniewnik* gives such official descriptions of strikes[3] in the country: . . .

2   The problem has been recently (July, 1919) settled by the Polish government in accordance with the demands of the peasants. Private estates will be limited to 300 morgs (400 acres), the excess will be bought by the government and sold to landless peasants and poorer farmers on easy terms; all the forests and waters will become state property. This also solves in a large measure the problem of the manor-servants.

3   The case quoted is not really a strike as the governmental paper intentionally misrepresents it, but an attempt to obtain by force governmental property which the peasants consider as belonging to them by right, since it consists in estates of Polish nobility which the government confiscated after the revolution of 1863 without giving the peasants the shares to which they considered themselves entitled according to the law of 1864.

"The peasants of the village Żwyocin . . . tried on March 15th to pull down a building on the farm Luśniki, belonging to a majorat-estate. The head-forester of the governmental forest informed the chief of the district about it and he sent six watchmen and two country constables to guard the building. The peasants came together, about 400 people, beat the guarding watchmen, pulled the farm-buildings completely down and took the building-material home. Some years ago the peasants had claimed to have some rights to this farm, but the governmental office for peasant affairs in Piotrków and later the Senate also rejected these claims. Since August last year the peasants began to perform illegal deeds upon this farm. They did not allow the forest-guards to do any work in the field and the land of the farm remains up to the present unsowed. A few men, as main inciters, will be tried in court."[4]

[The objection of the Polish peasant to state ownership of the soil proves that bolshevism could never gain the support of the country population in Poland. The statement of this writer that the peasants do not need *equality* of land is, however, not representative of the standpoint of the average peasant and is probably due to the influence of the clergy. As we mentioned in the preface to this chapter, the majority of the peasants do want equal division of land, but under *individual ownership*.]

Now in our community . . . we do not like it at all that Russian members of Parliament tend to the nationalization of the land with the aim of satisfying the needs of those peasants who possess land or only a little. Whereas we, the peasants of the Polish Kingdom, declare that such a scheme, far from satisfying us, only irritates us more, . . . that through nationalization of the land our existence will not be improved but made even worse, since we do not need equality of land but we do need equality of rights, we need self-government, we need that the land held as government land by generals, by members of the imperial family, or taken from convents, be divided among us as property (I do not say gratuitously, but on convenient terms) . . . Otherwise we will defend our property to bloodshed because we know what farming of communal lands means,[5] and we do not wish to

4    *Gazeta Świąteczna*, 1905, 14.
5    In Russia all the land not belonging to the crown or to the manor belonged in bulk to the village (mir) and was allotted every year for

starve, to go as hired workmen to other nations, nor to become beggars for centuries. . . . [But] today we cannot limit anybody as to how much land he should own; we should conform to the proverb: If you work, you will have. . . . [Demand for limitation] only incites the ones against the others and nowadays this is completely unnecessary since we are all the sons of one mother earth and for this reason we should abstain from such statements until we have self-government and then we shall talk the whole matter over in common. This is the opinion of us peasants near Sandomierz.

[Signed] A peasant by the gift of God. Tomasz Kolembasa.[6]

In the village Wola Przybylska . . . the village-group and the manor made an agreement for the exchange of servitudes [the peasants resign their rights of pasturing and collecting dry wood on the manorial lands and receive in exchange some land and forest]. But when it came to allotting the forest, it proved that the peasants did not want the lot which the owner of the estate, Countess J., had apportioned for them, but demanded another one which precisely then began to be cut by order of the manor. Having particularly liked this piece of forest, the peasants declared that they would not suffer its destruction, and when in spite of this the cutting was not stopped they went in a crowd to the forest and drove the wood-cutters away. . . . [Interference by the commissioner for peasant affairs, by the mayor and constables came to naught.] Then the head of the country police came to the commune. Having arrested the village-elder and the three most unruly farmers, for four days he talked with every farmer in succession and persuaded them that they had no right to this piece of forest. . . . The village group calmed down and not only ceased to hinder the cutting of the forest, but many . . . hired themselves to do this work. . . .[7]

---

cultivation to the individual villagers who, of course, refused to improve it since manuring, draining, irrigating, etc., required a heavy outlay that the profits from one year's farming would not cover.

6     Letter to *Gazeta Świąteczna;* unpublished.
7     *Gazeta Świąteczna,* 1899, 51.

## Religious Revolutionism

The Polish peasant is not a mystic; religion is for him a matter of social organization on the basis of given mythical beliefs and magical practices rather than of personal mystical connection with the divinity. This is why, as we have already noticed, there have never been any popular heresies, for beliefs and practices divergent from those of the church never assumed in the eyes of individuals a sufficient mystical importance to make them break with the social system of the church. Religious revolution became possible only recently when this social system began to be felt as unsatisfactory, and it took the form of a revolt against the social control exercised by the church, not against the religious dogmas and ceremonies for which the church stands. Divergence of dogmas and ceremonies came secondarily as a rather artificial addition of theologians who participated in the movement. Two interesting examples are taken here to illustrate this new process of growing religious heterogeneity.

The first is the heresy of the *Mariawitas*. This heresy was started, indeed, in a half-mystical way by a few priests grouped around a woman visionary, Kozlowska, who seems to be vaguely identified by them and by herself with a new incarnation of a vague feminine divine principle whose first and chief personification is Mary—thence the name of the sect. But the real significance of the latter and the source of its popularity lie elsewhere— the vow of poverty which the priests of the *Mariawitas* make. In the relations which exist between a priest and his parishioners in a country parish money-matters constitute a very difficult situation. The standard of living of the priest is on the average much higher than that of a peasant-farmer. Moreover, many priests, particularly those of peasant origin, consider their profession a career made for the benefit of their families and exploit their flock rather ruthlessly. As long as the prestige of the priest remains unchallenged the peasants interpret his economic demands as necessarily resulting from his position, and the honor of the parish community seems to require that its priest be at least as well-to-do as other priests, just as it requires a church building of a certain size and aesthetic perfection. But, of course, along with this standard there always coexisted the opposite standard of simplicity and disinterestedness, which some of the clergy applied in their behavior. This standard has been lately more and more popularized by the democratic propaganda, and the *Mariawita* movement is thus in harmony with a certain evolution of popular opinion which may lead to a complete modification of the peasant's attitude toward the clergy.

Another interesting example is the case of the paper *Zaranie*. The latter, a brilliantly edited popular weekly, radically democratic, standing on the exclusive ground of the interests of the peasants as a social class and tending to develop among them class solidarity as against the higher classes, had been for several years attacking on every occasion the abuses of priests. The clergy, after vainly trying to counteract its influence by counter-propaganda, resorted to radical means and simply forbade the peasants to read *Zaranie*. In one diocese the bishop even went so far as to excommunicate the paper and its readers, who were not to receive absolution for their sins until they stopped reading it. Naturally, this action provoked the indignation not only of the radical but even of the moderate elements of Polish society, and among the peasants furnished a pretext for the expression of all those revolutionary attitudes which had for some time been growing in connection with the rôle which the church played in controlling all social life in the country for the benefit of the clergy and of the upper classes.

[One out of many like incidents during the first ten years of the development of the *Mariawitas*. Both sides were aggressive, the *Mariawitas* as a new sect, somewhat more. Description somewhat exaggerated.]

Our parish Dobra had almost 3,000 Catholics; but in 1906, on February 6th, a great misfortune befell us. On that day falls the yearly church-festival of St. Dorothy in our parish. About 6,000 persons from the neighborhood were gathered to receive the absolution of their sins and to listen to the word of God. But then the local priest,

Paweł Skolimowski, who is now a *Mankietnik* [nick-name for *Mariawita*], ascended the chancel. Instead of proclaiming the words of God ... he suddenly—O my God!—begins to throw mud upon our priests and bishops. And as their custom is, he spoke about the holy sacrament. ... And the people present, except some few, believed him and his wicked words ... and began to oppress our Catholics. Once all the farmer *Mankietniks* of the Village Imielnik met and went to the village-elder, Jan Plucinikowski, demanding of him that he give back the eagle and the seal, signs of an elder, because he was not a *Mariawita*. Plucinikowski said ... they should accuse him before the chief of the district; if the latter dismissed him, he would gladly give them the signs back. But the arrogant *Mankietniks* resolved to reach their end. Wojciech Góralczyk and Antoni Wiśniewski came forward, bound Plucinikowski with ropes and demanded the signs. Only when the son of Plucinikowski ... came in and took an ax, they all fled. ...

Then once, on August 2nd, 1906, on the day of Our Lady of the Angels, Skolimowski proclaimed that it was a holiday. But since immemorial times our parish has never kept this holiday, so our Catholics began to work as on every working-day. But they, the bigot *Kozłowskis* from different parts, whose number reached 7,000, went through the fields, together with the socialists, drove people away from work, and overthrew carts [filled] with grain. But what was worse—O my God—they went to the houses of the true Catholics, put revolvers to their heads and compelled them to submit to the control of the *Kozłowit* priests. And they went in crowds to the house of Żurek, where our orthodox priest lived. ... [He was away.] They threw his books, clothes, medals and images out of his room and tore two gowns [either because the *Mariawit* priests had abandoned black gowns for gray or because, professing poverty, they owned only one gown each]. ... It went so far that during 8 days we had to hide ourselves and not spend the nights at home, because the crowd, headed by a certain Słoma, a socialist from the city of Łódź, wished to compel us to fall away from the true Roman Catholic faith. ... But gradually all this came to an end. On November 28th, 1906, with a committee and the chief of the district, we took our church back. But it was very sad, because only the four walls were left; the *Mankietniks* robbed us of all the furniture, images, altars, banners, etc. ...

Among 3,000 inhabitants there are 1,800 *Mankietniks* and 1,200 Catholics. The *Mankietniks* are gradually coming back to their senses and returning to the bosom of the Roman Catholic Church. But in the end I must complain . . . against my brothers the Catholics; . . . they persecute them at every step and so confirm them in their false *Kozłowit* learning.[8]

[This is typical of the innumerable letters denouncing the activities of country priests which the paper *Zaranie* received after it had made its anti-clerical position clear. All the accumulated grievances of a public or private character used this opportunity to express themselves. There was also much imitation of the letters already published.]

In our dear *Zaranie* one may read correspondence from different regions, but of our country around Rawa nobody writes. One might believe milk and honey were flowing around us. But here also manifold needs exist, only the people are still sleeping the sleep of the just. . . .

The parish Łęyonice . . . contains 1,000 souls. The people are poor and ignorant to a degree that you would hardly encounter in any other part of the Polish Kingdom. With every step you discover misery. The houses are like booths, the stock is dwarf-like, and if you look at a man, pity grasps you; he looks as pale and ragged as a beggar.

In the year 1905 the curate of this parish was Father . . . Wojewódzki. And since the priest's house was, as he declared, already old and no longer habitable, the parishioners decided to build a new one. Indeed, brother readers, those paupers, under the pressure of the curate's exhortations, erected a parsonage like a little palace, larger than the local church, containing 14 rooms and 12 cellars. The old parsonage they sold to the curate . . . and he transformed this old thing where dwelling was an impossibility into an elegant house for which he received several hundred roubles. And since the workmen had still a claim of more than a hundred roubles, he promised to satisfy them out of his own pocket, but he never paid them. Would it not have been better to build for this money some schools rather than a priest's house?

Now for more than a year the curate of this parish has been Father Siedlecki and he demands payment of the rest of the contribution [pledged to Wojewówzki], whereas the parishioners, on account of

[8] Letter to *Gazeta Świąteczna;* unpublished.

the above mentioned Wojewódzki's obligation and because they can afford no more, do not pay that contribution. Father Siedlecki, wishing to induce the parishioners to pay, one Sunday some weeks ago spoke publicly from the pulpit, after the sermon, the following words: "Wishing that those who refuse to pay the contribution may lose everything but the amount which they refuse to pay, wishing that they may never succeed in making money, wishing that they may pass away miserably, let us pray: Ave Maria...." But this is not the end. Some weeks ago he saw one of his parishioners driving past the church on Sunday, and since the few pennies which the man would have offered on the plate were lost to him, he said the same day from the pulpit: "Wishing that those who avoid this our little church and drive to town instead may encounter a sudden death, let us pray with devotion: Ave Maria...."

In the parish of Łęgonice there is no school, no agricultural society, no coöperative store and the gentlemen-landowners do not care about civilizing the peasant. The benevolent pastor cares equally about it.... [There are 10 empty rooms in the parson's house where a school could be established.]...[9]

In comparing the typical documents here quoted, we notice that the revolutionary attitudes of the peasants seem usually roused by the propaganda of leaders belonging to the intellectual class. This conclusion is further corroborated by the history of the revolutionary movements in Poland during the nineteenth century; with few exceptions, the leaders of these movements have been intellectuals, most of them of noble origin. This is, of course, what should be expected in view of the nature of revolution as compared with mere revolt. To start and lead a revolutionary movement a combination of intellectual development, of familiarity with social and political problems and of social idealism was needed which could be seldom found among peasants, for until recently the great majority of those numerous but isolated individuals of peasant origin who received a higher education were too absorbed in their personal careers, too interested in making a place for themselves above the peasant class, or at least too dependent on the newly acquired cultural values and standards

[9] Letter to *Zaranie;* unpublished.

of the upper classes, to identify themselves with a peasant revolutionary movement.

On the other hand, the importance of intellectual leadership should not be exaggerated. It certainly plays a much smaller rôle in revolution than in social reconstruction. What it does is merely to formulate and to generalize attitudes which already exist and tend to active expression. It helps to change revolt into revolution by showing that some particular situation which provokes revolt is an integral art of a complex social status which hinders the satisfaction of many conscious or half-conscious wishes, and that the grievances of the revolting individual or community are not private but public grievances, that many other individuals or communities suffer similar wrongs under the same system. But intellectual agitation is powerless unless there are in the masses the attitudes necessary to pass from a dissatisfaction with particular situations to the criticism of the whole social organization, and from feelings of private wrong to feelings of public indignation.

In our case these attitudes, to which the revolutionary agitation has successfully appealed, are easy to determine. First of all, during the last 50 to 100 years a very general and deep change took place in the peasant's attitudes toward life, a change which may be best expressed by saying that, while formerly the individual's life organization had only the maintenance of his social and economic status in view, now his attitudes have become organized with reference to a general tendency to advance, of which land-hunger, social climbing, emigration to cities or abroad, are partial manifestations. This tendency is not a matter of personal, temperamental disposition, but a social current spread by imitation and fed by the popularized information about new possibilities of advance. Now the traditional social organization, particularly the class system and the church, was based on the principle of permanence of existing social and economic relations; it made a small allowance for the climbing of individuals but not for the advance of masses. Thus when the tendency to advance became a mass phenomenon the class system and the church were more and more distinctly qualified as obstacles to be overcome; and the fact that many representatives of the nobility and the clergy took *explicitly* a definite stand in favor of the immovability of the social order and against any changes helped the peasants to become conscious of the nature and the reasons of their own originally vague aspirations and contributed to turn an evolution of social forms into a struggle of social classes. And since at the same time, in view of the economic and cultural situation of the whole country, in certain fields the opportunities for advance were hardly improving at all, sometimes even deteriorating, dissatisfaction with the existing conditions often developed into a general bitterness and depression. Thus we saw what a deeply pessimistic attitude toward life could be found among the manor-servants who had no hopes of ever improving their economic situation. The particular bitterness characterizing the attacks of those interested in intellectual advance upon the clergy is explained by the fact that educational opportunities under Russian domination were exceptionally poor, and that many members of the clergy, instead of cooperating with the efforts of the progressive part of Polish society to promote popular education in spite of the Russian government, counteracted these efforts at every step.

The second general and fundamental attitude which we find back of the revolutionary movements of the peasants can be characterized as the consciousness of the social power and moral righteousness of a solidary community. This consciousness, which sometimes assumes naïvely exaggerated proportions, has evidently its source in the importance which the community originally possesses in the eyes of each of its members, who feels controlled and dominated by it and accepts its judgments as supreme standards of right. When thus a community whose members have still preserved this primary attitude enters into conflict with outside social elements—individuals of other classes, religious or political institutions, etc.—and acts as a solidary unit, it is surprising to see what an almost unlimited faith all the members individually have in the justice of their common standpoint and in the success of their common action. It is almost impossible to persuade a peasant community which has preserved its primary-group character that its action is wrong or doomed to failure except by breaking it up and discussing the matter separately with each individual. This socio-psychological feature explains the daring with which a peasant group, once resolved to vindicate its claims, often starts and pursues the most radical revolutionary action without apparently the slightest chance of success. It also shows whence comes that feeling of solidarity of wrongs and demands, that consciousness of acting not for one's self alone but for the group, which distinguishes revolution from personal revolt. Later, with increasing acquaintance with the external political and social conditions, the primary peasant community loses its naïve faith in its own righteousness and power; but then, as the contacts between communities grow, there develops a super-communal solidarity, the primary group conceives itself as part of a wider social body, class or nation, and the same unlimited faith is transferred to this new "great community."

We hardly need to emphasize the fact that these two fundamental attitudes underlying the revolutionary movements of the peasants—the tendency to advance and the consciousness of social power and moral righteousness of the community—are by no means socially destructive attitudes; on the contrary, if properly directed, they are the most efficient factors of social reconstruction.

# 14

# THE INDIVIDUALIZATION
# OF BEHAVIOR

THE GROUP has to provide a system of behavior for many persons at once, a code which applies to everybody and lasts longer than any individual or generation. Consequently the group has two interests in the individual—to suppress wishes and activities which are in conflict with the existing organization, or which seem the starting point of social disharmony, and to encourage wishes and actions which are required by the existing social system. And if the group performs this task successfully, as it does among savages, among Mohammedans, and as it did until recently among European peasants, no appreciable change in the moral code or in the state of culture is observable from generation to generation. In small and isolated communities there is little tendency to change or progress because the new experience of the individual is sacrificed for the sake of the security of the group.

But by a process, an evolution, connected with mechanical inventions, facilitated communication, the diffusion of print, the growth of cities, business organization, the capitalistic system, specialized occupations, scientific research, doctrines of freedom, the evolutionary view of life, etc., the family and community

---

Reprinted from *The Unadjusted Girl* (Boston: Little, Brown & Co., 1928), pp. 70–97.

influences have been weakened and the world in general has been profoundly changed in content, ideals, and organization.

Young people leave home for larger opportunities, to seek new experience, and from necessity. Detachment from family and community, wandering, travel, "vagabondage" have assumed the character of normality. Relationships are casualized and specialized. Men meet professionally, as promoters of enterprises, not as members of families, communities, churches. Girls leave home to work in factories, stores, offices, and studios. Even when families are not separated they leave home for their work.

Every new invention, every chance acquaintanceship, every new environment, has the possibility of redefining the situation and of introducing change, disorganization or different type organization into the life of the individual or even of the whole world. Thus, the invention of the check led to forgery; the sulphur match to arson; at present the automobile is perhaps connected with more seductions than happen otherwise in cities altogether; an assassination precipitated the World War; motion pictures and the *Saturday Evening Post* have stabilized and unstabilized many existences, considered merely as opportunity for new types of career. The costly and luxurious articles of women's wear organize the lives of many girls (as designers, artists, and buyers) and disorganize the lives of many who crave these pretty things.

In the small and spatially isolated communities of the past, where the influences were strong and steady, the members became more or less habituated to and reconciled with a life of repressed wishes. The repression was demanded of all, the arrangement was equitable, and while certain new experiences were prohibited, and pleasure not countenanced as an end in itself, there remained satisfactions, not the least of which was the suppression of the wishes of others. On the other hand the modern world presents itself as a spectacle in which the observer is never sufficiently participating. The modern revolt and unrest are due to the contrast between the paucity of fulfillment of the wishes of the individual and the fullness, or apparent fullness, of life around him. All age levels have been affected by the feeling that much, too much, is being missed in life. This unrest is felt most by those who have heretofore been most excluded from general participation in life—the mature woman and the young girl. Sometimes it expresses itself in despair and depression, sometimes in breaking all bounds. Immigrants form a particular class in this respect. They sometimes repudiate the old system completely in their haste to get into the new. There are cases where the behavior of immigrants, expressing natural but random and unregulated impulses, has been called insane by our courts.

The following case represents despair, the next revolt, and the last two, extraordinarily wild behavior.

There is a saying about the peacock, "When she looks at her feathers she laughs, and when she looks at her feet she cries." I am in the same situation.

My husband's career, upon which I spent the best years of my life, is established favorably; our children are a joy to me as a mother; nor can I complain about our material circumstances. But I am dissatisfied with myself. My love for my children, be it ever so great, cannot destroy myself. A human being is not created like a bee which dies after accomplishing its only task.

Desires, long latent, have been aroused in me and become more aggressive the more obstacles they encounter. . . . I now have the desire to go about and see and hear everything. I wish to take part in everything—to dance, skate, play the piano, sing, go to the theatre, opera, lectures and generally mingle in society. As you see, I am no idler whose purpose is to chase all sorts of foolish things, as a result of loose ways. This is not the case.

My present unrest is a natural result following a long period of hunger and thirst for non-satisfied desires in every field of human experience. It is the dread of losing that which never can be recovered —youth and time which do not stand still—an impulse to catch up with the things I have missed. . . . If it were not for my maternal feeling I would go away into the wide world.[1]

I had been looking for Margaret, for I knew she was a striking instance of the "unadjusted" who had within a year come with a kind of aesthetic logic to Greenwich Village. She needed something very

[1] *Forward*, March 11, 1921.

badly. What I heard about her which excited me was that she was twenty years old, unmarried, had never lived with a man or had any of that experience, had worked for a year on a socialist newspaper, and a socialist magazine, was a heavy drinker and a frequenter of Hell Hole, that she came from a middle-class family but preferred the society of the outcasts to any other. Greenwich Village is not composed of outcasts, but it does not reject them, and it enables a man or woman who desires to know the outcast to satisfy the desire without feeling cut off from humanity. Hell Hole is a saloon in the back room of which pickpockets, grafters, philosophers, poets, revolutionists, stool-pigeons, and the riffraff of humanity meet. Margaret loves this place and the people in it—so they told me—and there she did and said extreme things in which there was a bitter fling at decent society.

So that night, when she came with Christine, I invited her to go with me to Hell Hole to have a drink. She drank whiskey after whiskey and showed no effect. As soon as we were seated in the back room alone she started to tell me about herself. I forget what unessential thing I said to get her started. She knew by instinct what I desired and she told me her story with utter frankness, and with a simple, unaggressive self-respect.

"I belong to what is called a respectable, middle-class family. My father is a prominent newspaper man. Whenever I was ill, as a child, he gave me whiskey instead of medicine. This began at the age of four. One of my childish amusements was to mix cordials and water to entertain my little friends with. We lived in the city, and I had from four years of age the run of the streets. At six or eight I knew everything—about sex, about hard street life. I knew it wrong, of course, for I saw it but did not feel it. I felt wrong about it all, and feared it, wasn't a part of it, except as an observer. I saw no beauty or friendliness in sex feeling. I think it was this that kept me away later from physical intimacy with men; it couldn't appeal to me after my early life in the street. I know it doesn't always happen so, but it did with me.

"When I got to be thirteen years old my father reversed his attitude towards me; before then, all freedom; after that, all restraint. I was completely shut in. Soon after that I became religious and joined the church. I had a long pious correspondence with another girl and used to brood all the time about God and about my transcendental duties. This lasted till I was sixteen, and then life, ordinary external life, came back with a rush and I couldn't stand my exclusive inner world and outward restraint any longer, and I wanted to go away from home. So I worked hard in the High School and got a $300 scholarship in Latin and Greek. With this I went to a Western College and stayed there two years, working my own way and paying my expenses. I read a lot at this time, and liked revolutionary literature; read socialism, and poetry that was full of revolt. I took to anything which expressed a reaction against the conditions of my life at home.

"I stood well in my studies, and suppose I might have completed the college course, except that I got into trouble with the authorities, for very slight reasons, as it seems to me. I smoked cigarettes, a habit I had formed as a child, and that of course was forbidden. It was also forbidden to enter the neighboring cemetery, I don't know why. One day I smoked a cigarette in the graveyard—a double offense—and then, in the playfulness of my spirit, I wrote a poem about it and published it in the college paper. In this paper I had already satirized the Y. W. C. A. A few other acts of that nature made me an undesirable member of the college and my connection with it ceased.

"After an unhappy time at home—my father and I could not get on together; ever since my early childhood he had been trying to 'reform' me—I got a job on the socialist *Call*, a New York daily newspaper, at $—— a week. It was hard work all day, but I liked it and I didn't drink—I didn't want to—and lived on the money without borrowing. Later I went on the *Masses*, and there I was well off. [Then I went to Washington to picket for the suffragists and got a jail sentence, and when I returned the *Masses* had been suspended.] It was at that time that I began to go with the Hudson Dusters [a gang of criminals] and to drink heavily. Greenwich Village seemed to think it was too good for me, or I too bad for it. Most of the women were afraid to associate with me. Only the Hudson Dusters, or people like them, seemed really human to me. I went, in a kind of despair, to the water-front, and stayed three days and nights in the back room of a low saloon, where there were several old prostitutes. And I liked them. They seemed human, more so than other people. And in this place were working men. One man, with a wife and children, noticed I was going there and didn't seem to belong to them, and he asked me to go home with him and live with his family; and he meant it, and meant it decently.

"I want to know the down and outs," said Margaret with quiet, almost fanatical intenseness. "I find kindness in the lowest places, and more than kindness sometimes—something, I don't know what it is, that I want."[2]

There came a day when my wife heard that there was an Atlantic City not far from Philadelphia. So I granted her wish and rented a nice room for her in a hotel there and sent her with the two children to that seashore. . . .

The next summer I did not make out so well and could not afford to send my wife to the country, but she absolutely demanded to be sent even if I had to "hang and bring." . . . My protestations and explanations were of no avail. She went to Atlantic City and hired a room in the same hotel. . . .

I took my wife's behavior to heart and became ill. Some of my friends advised me to teach her a lesson and desert her, so that she would mend her ways in the future. They assured me that they would take care of my family, to keep them from starving. I was persuaded by them and left Philadelphia for a distant town.

My wife in Atlantic City, seeing that I sent her no money, returned home. Upon learning what had happened, she promptly sold the furniture, which had cost $800, for almost nothing and went to New York. My friends notified me of all that had occurred in my absence, whereupon I came back.

I advertised in the papers and found my wife. My first question was about the children and she replied she did not know where they were. Upon further questioning she answered that she had brought the children with her from Philadelphia but as she could do nothing with them in her way she simply left them in the street.

After great efforts made through my lawyer, I succeeded in obtaining the release of my children from the Gerry Society, after paying for their two months' keep there. . . .

Since this unhappy occurrence, my wife has many times wrecked our home, selling the household goods while I was at work and leaving me alone with the children. Whenever she feels like satisfying her cravings, or whenever she cannot afford to buy herself enough pretty clothes and hats, she deserts me. One time she was gone 9 months and never saw the children during this period. . . .

I tried to make up with her every time and give her another

[2] Hutchins Hapgood: "At Christine's" (Manuscript).

## The Individualization of Behavior 237

chance. But her cordiality lasted only until she again took a craving for some rag, when she would again leave home. She was even mean enough once to leave me with a five months' old baby who needed nursing and the only way out seemed to be the river for me and the baby. . . .

I assure you that everything I have written is the truth. If you do not believe me, you may convince yourself at the Desertion Bureau where my case has been recorded several times.[3]

She was one of the thousands of girls who are drawn to the great city from small towns. She perished because of her thirst for adventure. . . . While stopping at the Hotel Buckingham she went out one evening and never returned. A chauffeur told the police that he met the girl on the evening of her death and that she had been on a tour of the cafés and cabarets with him and that at 2 o'clock in the morning Miss Dixon became ill. She was taken to the Harlem Hospital, where her case was diagnosed as morphine poisoning. . . .

She came of a fine Virginia family and was educated at a fashionable boarding school. Four years ago she was married to a Yale graduate. [A friend] who had known her all her life said, "She had just gone mad with love of pleasure, though at heart she was a thoroughbred and exceedingly fine. She decided to make her own living and took a small part in a couple of shows. The discipline and routine were too much for her and she gave it up and went back to [her husband] from time to time. But always the lure of New York seemed to hold her in a spell."[4]

The world has become large, alluring, and confusing. Social evolution has been so rapid that no agency has been developed in the larger community of the state for regulating behavior which would replace the failing influence of the community and correspond completely with present activities. There is no universally accepted body of doctrines or practices. The churchman, for example, and the scientist, educator, or radical leader are so far apart that they cannot talk together. They are, as the Greeks expressed it, in different "universes of discourses."

3   *Forward*, December 8, 1920.
4   Newspaper item.

Dr. Austin O'Malley writes rather passionately about the control of births, in the Catholic weekly, "America." Says Dr. O'Malley: "The most helpless idiot is as far above a non-existent child as St. Bridget is above a committee on birth control." Let us pause over the idiot and the non-existent child. Must we say that all potential children should be born? Are we to take a firm stand against celibacy, which denies to so many possible children the right to be baptized? And will Dr. O'Malley tell us which is the greater virtue, to bear children that they may be baptized, or to have no children for the glory of one's own soul? This solicitude over the non-existent child has certain drawbacks. How large a family, in fact, does Dr. O'Malley desire a woman to bear? May she stop after the fourteenth infant, or must she say to herself: "There are still non-existent children, some of them helpless idiots; perhaps I will bear them that they may be baptized."[5]

Or, if we should submit any series of behavior problems to a set of men selected as most competent to give an opinion we should find no such unanimity as prevailed in a village community. One set of opinions would be rigoristic and hold that conformity with the existing code is advisable under all circumstances; another pragmatic, holding that the code may sometimes be violated. For example, in 1919, the United States Interdepartmental Social Hygiene Board authorized the Psychological Laboratory of the Johns Hopkins University to make an investigation of the "informational and educative effect upon the public of certain motion-picture films," and in this connection a questionnaire was sent to "medical men and women who have had most to do with problems in sex education and the actual treatment of venereal infections." From the manuscript of this investigation I give below some of the replies received to question 13.

*Question 13. Do you consider that absolute continence is always to be insisted upon? Or may it be taught that under certain conditions intercourse in the unmarried is harmless or beneficial?*

Dr. A. I know of no harm from absolute continence. Intercourse in the unmarried cannot be justified on any grounds of health or morals.

[5] Editorial in *The New Republic*, June 19, 1915.

## The Individualization of Behavior 239

Dr. B. No. For some absolute continence would be easy, for others, impossible. It is an individual problem to be decided by the individual, with or without advice.

Under certain conditions in the unmarried, male or female, intercourse is harmless or beneficial; under other conditions it is harmful and injurious (irrespective of venereal disease).

Dr. C. I think it is harmless and beneficial. But our standards are against it. And who could possibly conscientiously teach such a thing, no matter what he thought?

Dr. D. Certainly not. It is probably well to teach young people that continence before marriage is in general very desirable, as contrasted with the results of incontinence.

Dr. E. It is best to teach conformity to custom.

Dr. F. Absolute continence should always be insisted upon.

Dr. G. I know of no condition where one is justified in advising the unmarried that intercourse is harmless or beneficial.

Dr. H. Absolute continence.

Dr. I. No. [Continence is not always to be insisted upon.]

Dr. J. The first should not be insisted on any more than the latter should be recommended. . . .

Dr. K. The latter may be taught.

Dr. L. Not convinced either way.

Dr. M. Absolute continence should be preached as a doctrine to the unmarried, and let the individual adjust himself to this stern law according to his lights.[6]

Fifty-one replies were received to this question. Twenty-four were, in substance, "not permissible"; fifteen, "permissible"; four, "in doubt"; eight were indefinite, as, for example: "Adults will probably decide this for themselves."

As another example of a general defining agency, the legal system of the state does not pretend to be more than a partial set of negative definitions. An English jurist has thus described the scope of the law: "If A is drowning and if B is present, and if B by reaching out his hand can save A, and if B does not do this, and if A drowns, then B has committed no offense." All that the law requires of B is that he shall not push A into the

[6] These materials, edited by John B. Watson and K. S. Lashley, have been printed in part in *Mental Hygiene,* 4: 769–847.

water. The law is not only far from being a system capable of regulating the total life of men, but it does not even regulate the activities it is designed to regulate.

A misdemeanor may be much more heinous than a felony. The adulterator of drugs or the employer of child labor may well be regarded as vastly more reprehensible than the tramp who steals part of the family wash. So far as that goes there is an alarming multitude of acts and omissions not forbidden by statute or classified as crimes which are to all intents . . . fully as criminal as those designated as such by law. . . . For example, to push a blind man over the edge of the cliff so that he is killed . . . is murder, but to permit him to walk over it is no crime at all. It is a crime to defame the character of a woman if you write on a slip of paper, but no crime at all in the state of New York if you rise in a crowded hall and ruin her forever by word of mouth. It is a crime to steal a banana off a fruit stand, but no crime at all to borrow ten thousand dollars from a man whose entire fortune it is, although you have no expectation of returning it. . . . It is a crime to ruin a girl of 17 years and 11 months, but not to ruin a girl of 18. . . . Lying is not a crime, but lying under oath is a crime, provided it relates to a *material* matter, and what is a material matter jurists do not agree on. . . . Many criminals, even guilty of homicide, are as white as snow in comparison with others who have never transgressed the literal wording of the penal statute. "We used to have so and so for our lawyer," remarked the president of a street-railway corporation. "He was always telling us what we couldn't do. Now we have Blank and pay him $100,000 a year to tell us how we can do the same things."[7]

The definition of the situation is equivalent to the determination of the vague. In the Russian *mir* and the American rural community of fifty years ago nothing was left vague, all was defined. But in the general world movement to which I have referred, connected with free communication in space and free communication of thought, not only particular situations but the most general situations have become vague. Some situations were once defined and have become vague again; some have arisen and have never been defined. Whether this country shall partici-

[7] A. Train: *The Prisoner at the Bar*, p. 6.

pate in world politics, whether America is a refuge for the oppressed of other nationalities, whether the English should occupy India or the Belgians Africa, whether there shall be Sunday amusements, whether the history of the world is the unfolding of the will of God, whether men may drink wine, whether evolution may be taught in schools, whether marriage is indissoluble, whether sex life outside of marriage is permissible, whether children should be taught the facts of sex, whether the number of children born may be voluntarily limited—these questions have become vague. There are rival definitions of the situation, and none of them is binding.

In addition to the vagueness about these general questions there is an indeterminateness about particular acts and individual life-policies. It appears that the behavior of the young girl is influenced partly by the traditional code, partly by undesigned definitions of the situation derived from those incidents in the passing show of the greater world which suggest to her pleasure and recognition. If any standard prevails or characterizes a distinguished social set this is in itself a definition of the situation. Thus in a city the shop windows, the costumes worn on the streets, the newspaper advertisements of ladies' wear, the news items concerning objects of luxury define a proper girl as one neatly, fashionably, beautifully, and expensively gowned, and the behavior of the girl is an adaptation to this standard.

Supreme Court Justice Tierney remarked in the course of a trial between two women over the purchase of silk lingerie and paradise feathers yesterday, "The workings of the feminine mind are beyond me." . . .

The articles which Mrs. Small admits buying and the prices asked by Mme. Nicole are as follows:

Six suits of silk underwear, $780; six suits linen underwear, $780; six pairs silk stockings, $180; paradise feathers for fan, $1,480; handle for fan, $720.[8]

My sweetheart remarked that she would like to have a great deal of money. When I asked her what she would do with it, she replied that she would buy herself a lot of beautiful dresses. When I said

[8] *New York World*, February 4, 1922.

that it was all right to have them but it ought to be all right without them too, she protested that she loved fine clothes and this to such extent, that—

Here she made a remark which I am ashamed to let pass my lips. I would sooner have welcomed an open grave than to have heard those words. She said that she would sell her body for a time in order to procure nice clothes for herself.

And since that day I go around like a mad person. I neither eat nor sleep. In short, I am no more a man.

She afterward excused herself, claiming that it was said in a joke, and that as long as one talks without actually doing it there is no harm in it. But this is not reassuring to me. I have a premonition that she would go further than mere talk after marriage, for if she carries such notions in her head now, what might happen after we are married.[9]

Intermediate between the home and work (or the school) there are certain organized influences for giving pleasure and information—the motion picture, the newspaper, the light periodical—which define the situation is equivocal terms. They enter the home and are dependent upon its approval, and are therefore obliged to present life in episodes which depict the triumph of virtue. But if they limited themselves to this they would be dull. The spectacle therefore contains a large and alluring element of sin over which virtue eventually triumphs. The moral element is preserved nominally but the real interest and substance is something else.

A young girl may be taught at home and church that chastity is a virtue, but the newspapers and the movies feature women in trouble along this line, now painting them as heroines, now sobbing over their mystery and pathos. Apparently *they* get all the attention and attention is the life blood of youth. The funny papers ridicule marriage, old maids and bashful men. The movies, magazines, street conversation and contemporary life are filled with the description of lapses that somehow turn out safely and even luxuriously. If the modern young girl practises virtue she may not believe in it. The

[9] *Forward,* May 4, 1920.

## The Individualization of Behavior 243

preliminaries to wrong-doing are apparently the accepted manners of the time. When the girl herself lapses it is frequently because of lack of a uniform, authoritative definition of the social code.[10]

Among well-to-do girls a new type has been differentiated, characterized by youth, seeming innocence, sexual sophistication and a relatively complete depudorization.

The modern age of girls and young men is intensely immoral and immoral seemingly without the pressure of circumstances. At whose door we may lay the fault, we cannot tell. Is it the result of what we call "the emancipation of woman," with its concomitant freedom from chaperonage, increased intimacy between the sexes in adolescence, and a more tolerant viewpoint toward all things unclean in life? This seems the only logical forbear of the present state. And are the girls causing it now, or the men? Each sex will lay the blame on the heads, or passions, of the other, and perhaps both sexes are equally at fault.

Whosesoever the fault may be (and that is not such an important question, since both sexes are equally immoral), the whole character of social relations among younger people is lamentable. The modern dances are disgusting—the "toddle" and its variations and vibrations, the "shimmy" and its brazen pandering to the animal senses, and the worst offspring of jazz, the "camel-walk." There is but one idea predominant in these dances—one that we will leave unnamed.

It is not only in dancing that this immorality appears. The modern social bud drinks, not too much often, but enough; smokes considerably, swears unguardedly, and tells "dirty" stories. All in all, she is a most frivolous, passionate, sensation-seeking little thing.[11]

"Flappers" usually are girls who believe personality is physical, who consider all advice as abstract, who love continual change, who converse in generalities and who are in many higher institutions of learning.

To present a picture of the normal girl as she exists today is a daring venture. She has no average, she has no group tie. She is

[10] Miriam Van Waters: "The True Value of Correctional Education." Paper read at the 51st American Prison Conference, November 1, 1921.
[11] Editorial in the Brown University *Daily Herald* quoted in the *New York World*, February 3, 1921.

a stranger to herself—sometimes especially to members of her own family—and cannot be compared with her kind of a previous age.

We are tempted to think of her as living in a spirit of masquerade, so rapidly and completely can she assume different and difficult rôles of accomplishment.

She tantalizes us by the simpleness of her artfulness and yet unrealness. We find her light-hearted, which is the privilege of youth. She believes with Stevenson that to have missed the joy is to have missed it all. We find her harboring secrets and imbedded emotions which are her hidden treasure in the mysterious discovery of herself as a private individual. If we do not understand these symptoms we call it temperament and try to dispose of the girl as difficult or as needing discipline.[12]

Formerly the fortunes of the individual were bound up with those of his family and to some degree with those of the community. He had his security, recognition, response, and new experience in the main as group member. He could not rise or fall greatly above or below the group level. Even the drunkard and the "black sheep" had respect in proportion to the standing of his family. And correspondingly, if a family member lost his "honor," the standing of the whole family was lowered.

Individualism, on the other hand, means the personal schematization of life—making one's own definitions of the situation and determining one's own behavior norms. Actually there never has been and never will be anything like complete individualization, because no one lives or can live without regard to a public. Anything else would be insanity. But in their occupational pursuits men have already a degree of individualization, decide things alone and in their own way. They take risks, schematize their enterprises, succeed or fail, rise higher and fall lower. A large element of individualism has entered into the marriage relation also. Married women are now entering the occupations freely and from choice, and carrying on amateur interests which formerly were not thought of as going with marriage. And this is evidently a good thing, and stabilizes marriage. Marriage alone

[12] Mary Ide Bentley, Address at Berkeley, California. *New York Sun*, February 7, 1922.

## The Individualization of Behavior

is not a life, particularly since the decline of the community type of organization. The cry of despair in the first document is from a woman who limited her life to marriage, probably by her own choice, and is now apparently too old to have other interests. But on the other hand the following document is a definition of marriage as exclusively a device for the realization of personal wishes and the avoidance of responsibility.

Girls, get married! Even if your marriage turns out badly, you are better off than if you had stayed single. I know half a dozen women whose first marriages were failures. They got rid of their first husbands easily and have made much better marriages than they could have made if they had stayed single. Their new husbands idolize them. One of my women acquaintances who has been married four times is the most petted wife I know.

My own marriage has turned out well. Everything seemed against it. I was well known in my profession, and when I married I was making as much money as my husband. We were of different religions. He drank.

But he had one big quality. He was generous. Since our marriage he has refused to let me work. Girls, be sure the man you pick is generous. Look out for a tightwad. If a man is liberal with his money he is sure to be easy to get along with. Liberal men in money matters do not annoy their wives in the other concerns of life. . . .

But even if my marriage had turned out badly, I would have been better off than if I had neglected the opportunity to become married. I met new friends through my husband. If I had divorced him at any time, I know many of his men friends would have courted me. There is something about the magic letters "Mrs." that gives a woman an added attraction in the eyes of men. There is a middle-aged widow in our apartment house that has more men taking her to theatres and dances than all the flappers and unmarried young women. . . .

I often wonder what men get married for. They take heavy financial responsibilities. They mortgage their free time to one woman. What a wife's clothes cost them would enable them to enjoy expensive amusements, extensive travel and better surroundings generally. Then, too, a bachelor, no matter what his age or social position, gets more attention socially than a married man. Children, too, give less pleasure and service to a father than a mother.

But for women, marriage is undoubtedly a success. It raises their position in the community. In most cases, it releases them from the danger of daily necessary work and responsibility. It brings them more attention from other men. Even when incompatibility intervenes, alimony provides separate support without work. In such cases, it also provides a more strategic position for a new and better marriage.[13]

In the same connection, the following cases show the growing tendency toward individualized definitions of sexual relations outside of marriage. In the first of the three following cases an immigrant girl explicitly organizes her life on the basis of prostitution instead of work. In the next the girls commercialize a series of betrothals. In the third the girl has worked out her own philosophy of love and calls herself a missionary prostitute.

[When I left Europe] my little sister's last words were, "Here, in hell, I will dream through the nights that far, far, across the ocean, my loving brother lives happily." And my last words were, "I shall forget my right hand if I ever forget you."

I suffered not a little in the golden land. . . . Five years passed. I loyally served the God of gold, saved some money and sent for my sister. For three years I believed myself the happiest of men. . . . My sister bloomed like a rose in May and she was kind and motherly to me. We were tied by a bond of the highest love and on my part that love had until now remained the same. But listen what a terrible thing occurred.

About a year ago I noticed a marked change in my sister—both physically and spiritually. She grew pale, her eyes lost their fire and her attitude toward me changed also. She began to neglect her work (I taught her a good trade), until half a year ago she entirely gave up the work. This angered me very much and I began to shadow her in order to discover the mystery in her life, for she had recently avoided talking to me, particularly of her life. I concluded that she kept company with a boy and that caused her trouble.

But I soon noticed that she was wearing such expensive things that a boy could not afford to buy them. She had a couple of diamond rings and plenty of other jewelry. I investigated until I discovered, oh, horrible! that my sister was a prostitute. . . .

[13] *New York American*, September 27, 1920.

You can understand that I want to drag her out of the mire, but ... she tells me that I do not understand life. She cannot conceive why it should be considered indecent to sell one's body in this manner. When I point out to her the end that awaits her she says in the first place it is not more harmful than working by steam for twelve to fourteen hours; in the second place, even if it were so, she enjoys life more. One must take as much as possible out of life. When I call her attention to the horrible degradation she replies that in the shop, too, we are humiliated by the foreman, and so on. . . .

I know that if I could convince her that I am right, she would be willing to emerge from the swamp, but I am unfortunately too inadequate in words, she being a good speaker, and I am usually defeated.[14]

I read in the "Bintel" the letter of a young man who complained that his fiancée extorted presents from him and that when, as a result of unemployment, he was unable to buy her everything she demanded, she began to make trouble for him—that she was evidently playing to have him desert her and leave her the property she had extorted.

Well, I am a woman myself, and can bear testimony that there are unfortunately such corrupted characters among my sex, who rob young men in this disgraceful manner. With these girls it is a business to "trim" innocent and sincere young men and then leave them. To them it is both business and pleasure. It gives them great joy to catch a victim in their outspread net and press as much of his hard-earned money out of him as possible.

I know a girl who . . . extracted from her naïve victim everything she laid her eyes on. When he stopped buying her so many things she began to treat him so shamefully that the poor boy was compelled to run away to another town, leaving all his gifts with the girl. The poor fellow was not aware that his so-called fiancée merely tricked him into buying her all kinds of jewelry and finery. He was afraid she would sue him for breach of promise and this fear caused him to leave town.

And don't think for a moment that that girl is ashamed of her deed. Not at all. She even boasts of her cleverness in turning the

[14] *Forward,* January 1, 1920.

heads of young men and their pockets inside out. She expects to be admired for that. . . .

I attempted to explain to her that she is a common swindler and thief, but she replied that not only is it not wrong but a philanthropical act. Her argument was that there are many men who betray innocent girls and it is therefore no more than right that girls should betray men also.[15]

[After the marriage of a brilliant man who had flirted with her but never mentioned marriage] she went on the stage, and was immoral in an unhappy sort of way. She met a young artist whose struggles for success aroused her pity and motherly instinct. With the memory of her faithless lover uppermost she plunged into a passionate realization of sex, more to drown her feelings than anything else. She roused the best in this boy, made a man of him, and steadied him. With her sexual tempests there came an after-calm when she forbade any familiarity. This was not studied but an instinct. She hated men, yet they fascinated her, and she them.

She studied stenography and worked as private secretary in a theatrical company. She tried to face life with work as her only outlet, but the restlessness of her grief made her crave excitement. She made friends easily, but her sexual appeal made it difficult for her to fit into a commonplace social atmosphere. She married the artist to the girl he loved, after a terrible struggle to make him realize it was not herself he loved. Later he came and thanked her. "The quiet women make the best wives," he said, "but my wife would not have loved me if you had not made me into a man. She cannot, however, give me what I get from you. I wish I could come to you once in a while?"

She said yes, and he came. That was five years ago and that is why she calls herself a prostitute. Her women friends have no idea she is not the quiet, dignified woman she appears to be, and men, many of them married men, want her for their own. She has no use for the man about town; only the man with brains or talent fascinates her at all. She says, "I suppose every one would think me a sinner; I am. I deliberately let a married man stay with me for a time. It is an art. I have learned to know their troubles. They tell me they

[15] *Forward*, December 15, 1920.

## The Individualization of Behavior 249

are unhappy with their wives, wish to go away, are desperate with the monotony of existence. It is generally that they are not sexually mated, or the wife has no sex attraction. Of course she loves him, and he her. I give them what they need. It is weary for the brain to understand men, it is harder on me mentally than physically. I control them only because I have self-restraint. I send them away soon. They are furious; they storm and rage and threaten they will go to some other woman. What do I care? They know it and I send them back to their wives. They will go to her; they would not go to any other woman. That is where I do good. This sex business is a strange thing. I am a missionary prostitute. I only do this once in a while, when I think a man needs me and he is one who will come under my influence. I know I have managed to avert the downfall of several households. If the wives know? Never mind; they don't. I am not coarse; I can be a comrade to a man and doubt if I harm him. I make him sin in the general acceptance of the term, the common interpretation of God's commandments. How do we know God didn't mean us to use all the powers he gave us?[16]

In the two cases following, adjustment to life is highly individualized but moral and social. The one is a response adjustment, recognizing freedom for new experience, particularly for creative work, and in the other marriage is based on the inherent values of the relationship, and on nothing else.

Being firmly of the opinion that nine out of ten of the alliances I saw about me were merely sordid endurance tests, overgrown with a fungus of familiarity and contempt, convinced that too often the most sacred relationship wears off like a piece of high sheen satin damask, and in a few months becomes a breakfast cloth, stale with soft-boiled egg stains, I made certain resolutions concerning what my marriage should not be.

First of all, I am anxious to emphasize that my marriage was neither the result of a fad or an ism, but simply the working out of a problem according to the highly specialized needs of two professional people.

We decided to live separately, maintaining our individual studio-apartments and meeting as per inclination and not duty. We decided

[16] Edith L. Smith, in collaboration with Hugh Cabot, "A Study in Sexual Morality," *Social Hygiene* 2: 537.

that seven breakfasts a week opposite one another might prove irksome. Our average is two. We decided that the antediluvian custom of a woman casting aside the name that had become as much a part of her personality as the color of her eyes had neither rhyme or reason. I was born Fannie Hurst and expect to die Fannie Hurst. We decided that in the event of offspring the child should take the paternal name until reaching the age of discretion, when the final decision would lie with him.

My husband telephones me for a dinner appointment exactly the same as scores of other friends. I have the same regard for his plans. We decided that, since nature so often springs a trap as her means to inveigle two people into matrimony, we would try our marriage for a year and at the end of that period go quietly apart, should the venture prove itself a liability instead of an asset. . . .

On these premises, in our case at least, after a five-year acid test, the dust is still on the butterfly wings of our adventure. The dew is on the rose.[17]

I am a college graduate, 27, married five years and the mother of a three-year-old boy. I have been married happily, and have been faithful to my husband.

At six I had decided upon my husband. Jack was his name; he was a beautiful boy, fair, blue eyes, delicate and poetic looking. He was mentally my superior, he loved poetry and wrote good verses. He read a great deal and talked well. He loved me and I loved him, yet there was no demonstration of it in embraces. We played together constantly, and we spoke of the time when we might marry. His great desire was to have a colored child with light hair and blue eyes for a daughter, and we had agreed upon it. All of our plans were spoken about before our parents, there was no effort made to hide our attachment. I was by nature rough and a great fighter, Jack was calm and serious, and at times I fought his battles for him. I was maternal towards him. His mother died during our friendship, and I tried to take her place. It was a pure love, nothing cheap or silly. He was killed in the Iroquois Fire and my life was dreary for a long time. I remember the hopeless feeling I experienced when I heard the news. I did not weep, I turned to my mother and said, "I don't want to live any longer."

[17] *New York World,* May 4, 1920.

We had always been allowed to sit across from each other at school, and after Jack's death, I was granted permission to keep his seat vacant for the rest of the year, and I kept a plant on the desk which I tended daily as a memorial to my friend.

. . . In college, a coeducational school, I was not allowed to remain ignorant long. I was young and healthy and a real *Bachfisch* in my enthusiastic belief in goodness. I was fortunate in having a level-headed senior for my best friend. She saw an upper classman [girl] falling in love with me, and she came to me with the news. Then she saw how innocent I was and how ignorant, and my sex education was begun. She told me of marriage, of mistresses, of homosexuality. I was sick with so much body thrown at me at once, and to add to the unpleasantness some one introduced me to Whitman's poetry. I got the idea that sex meant pain for women, and I determined never to marry.

But the next year I felt very differently about sex. I was used to the knowledge and I went with a crowd of girls who were wise, and I had a crush. I had never been stirred before, but I was by her. She told me her ambitions, and I told her mine; it was the first time I had ever been a person to any one, and I was her loyal loving friend. I kissed her intimately once and thought that I had discovered something new and original. We read Maupassant together and she told me the way a boy had made love to her. Everything was changed, love was fun, I was wild to taste it. I cultivated beaux, I let them kiss me and embrace me, and when they asked me to live with them, I was not offended but pleased. I learned my capacity, how far I could go without losing my head, how much I could drink, smoke, and I talked as freely as a person could. I discussed these adventures with the other girls, and we compared notes on kisses and phrases, and technique. We were healthy animals and we were demanding our rights to spring's awakening. I never felt cheapened, nor repentant, and I played square with the men. I always told them I was not out to pin them down to marriage, but that this intimacy was pleasant and I wanted it as much as they did. We indulged in sex talk, birth control, luetic infection, mistresses; we were told of the sins of our beaux, and I met one boy's mistress, an old university girl. This was life. I could have had complete relations with two of these boys if there had been no social stigma attached, and enjoyed it for a time. But instead I consoled myself with thinking that I still had time to give up my virginity, and that when I did I wanted as much as I could get for it in the way of passionate love. Perhaps the thing that saved me from falling in love was a sense of humor. That part of me always watched the rest of me pretend to be swooning, and I never really closed my eyes. But there was a lot of unhealthy sex going around because of the artificial cut off. We thought too much about it; we all tasted homosexuality in some degree. We never found anything that could be a full stop because there was no gratification.

During this period of stress and heat I met a man, fine, clean, mature and not seemingly bothered with sex at all. I kissed him intimately too, but it was very different. He had great respect for me, and he believed in me. I respected him, admired his artistic soul and his keen mind. There was no sex talk with him, it was music and world-views and philosophy. He never made any rash statements, nor false steps. He could sense a situation without touching it, and I felt drawn to him. I knew he had never been with a woman and he told me once that he could never express more than he felt for a person, and could sustain. After five years of friendship we married. There was no great flair to it; it was an inner necessity that drove us to it; we could no longer escape each other. We tried to figure it out, but the riddle always said marry. Sexually I had more experience than he, I was his first mistress, his wife, his best friend, and his mother, and no matter what our moods were, in one of these capacities I was needed by him. Our adjustment was difficult; he had lived alone for thirty years. I was used to having my own way, and he was a very sensitive man, nervous, sure of his opinion, and we quarreled for a while, but never very bitterly. Sexually we were both afraid of offending the other and so that was slow. But in four months we had found our heads again and were well adjusted. He was, and is, the best friend I ever had. I love him more as I know him longer. We can share everything, we are utterly honest and frank with each other, we enjoy our sex life tremendously as well as our friendship. But it was difficult for us to abandon ourselves. To allow any one to know you better than you know yourself is a huge and serious thing and calls for time and love and humor.

I have never known any one as fine as my husband. He is generous, honest, keen, artistic, big, liberal, everything that I most want in a person. I have never been tired of him. I feel confident that he loves me more now than ever before and that he thinks me very fine, a good sport. We have been thrown together a great deal through poverty, and I feel that we are alone in the world and facing it together, a not too friendly world at that. Yet with all this love and closeness, I don't feel that I possess my husband, nor that he does me. I am still the same old girl, the same personality, and my first duty is to develop my own gifts. I have no feeling of permanency with him because we are legally married, but at present a separation is unthinkable. I am worth more to myself with him, and life is infinitely sweeter and richer within the home than any other place.

But if I had married the average American husband who plays the business game as a religion, then I should long ago have been unfaithful to him. I could never disclose myself and be happy with a man who had any interest more important to him than our relationship.

As long as our relationship continues as it is I think we will both be faithful to each other. But I need to have freedom to move about now with all this. And perhaps part of my happiness consists in the fact that I do have freedom. I have had intimate friendships with other men since I am married, kissed them, been kissed, been told that they would like to have me with them. But none of this seems to touch my relation with my husband. I want, and I need to be, intimate on my own hook in my own way with other people. I don't honestly know whether I would take a lover or not. If my husband gave me the assurance that he would take me back, on the old basis, I think I would try it to see if it's as great as it's said to be. But if I had to give up my husband, I would not. I need him as I need my eyes and hands. He is the overtone in the harmony, and I am that for him. I like to experiment, but from past experience I believe the cost would be greater than the gain. I am free at home as I am not anywhere else. I love it, I express myself freely and completely emotionally, and the only reason I could have for being unfaithful would be experimentation. And if I were unfaithful I should have to tell my husband the whole affair; I could not enjoy it otherwise. I have no feeling against it, and no urge towards it. I can honestly say that I am a happy woman, that I have every opportunity to develop my potentialities in my present relation, that I am free as any one can be, that my husband is superior, as a mate for me, to any one I have ever seen. I regret nothing of the past; it could have been improved tremendously, but it was pleasant and human.[18]

[18] Autobiography (Manuscript).

# V. Methodology and Method

# 15

# METHODOLOGICAL NOTE:
# ATTITUDE AND VALUE

Now THERE are two fundamental practical problems which have constituted the center of attention of reflective social practice in all times. These are (1) the problem of the dependence of the individual upon social organization and culture, and (2) the problem of the dependence of social organization and culture upon the individual. Practically, the first problem is expressed in the question, How shall we produce with the help of the existing social organization and culture the desirable mental and moral characteristics in the individuals constituting the social group? And the second problem means in practice, How shall we produce, with the help of the existing mental and moral characteristics of the individual members of the group, the desirable type of social organization and culture?[1]

If social theory is to become the basis of social technique and to solve these problems really, it is evident that it must in-

---

Reprinted from *The Polish Peasant in Europe and America* (New York: Alfred A. Knopf, 1927; New York: Dover Publications, 1958), I, 20–44, 74–86.

1  Of course a concrete practical task may include both problems, as when we attempt, by appealing to the existing attitudes, to establish educational institutions which will be so organized as to produce or generalize certain desirable attitudes.

clude both kinds of data involved in them—namely, the objective cultural elements of social life and the subjective characteristics of the members of the social group—and that the two kinds of data must be taken as correlated. For these data we shall use now and in the future the terms "social values" (or simply "values") and "attitudes."

By a social value we understand any datum having an empirical content accessible to the members of some social group and a meaning with regard to which it is or may be an object of activity. Thus, a foodstuff, an instrument, a coin, a piece of poetry, a university, a myth, a scientific theory, are social values. Each of them has a content that is sensual in the case of the foodstuff, the instrument, the coin; partly sensual, partly imaginary in the piece of poetry, whose content is constituted, not only by the written or spoken words, but also by the images which they evoke, and in the case of the university, whose content is the whole complex of men, buildings, material accessories, and images representing its activity; or, finally, only imaginary in the case of a mythical personality or a scientific theory. The meaning of these values becomes explicit when we take them in connection with human actions. The meaning of the foodstuff is its reference to its eventual consumption; that of an instrument, its reference to the work for which it is designed; that of a coin, the possibilities of buying and selling or the pleasures of spending which it involves; that of the piece of poetry, the sentimental and intellectual reactions which it arouses; that of the university, the social activities which it performs; that of the mythical personality, the cult of which it is the object and the actions of which it is supposed to be the author; that of the scientific theory, the possibilities of control of experience by idea or action that it permits. The social value is thus opposed to the natural thing, which has a content but, as a part of nature, has no meaning for human activity, is treated as "valueless"; when the natural thing assumes a meaning, it becomes thereby a social value. And naturally a social value may have many meanings, for it may refer to many different kinds of activity.

By attitude we understand a process of individual consciousness which determines real or possible activity of the individual in the social world. Thus, hunger that compels the consumption of the foodstuff; the workman's decision to use the tool; the tendency of the spendthrift to spend the coin; the poet's feelings and ideas expressed in the poem and the reader's sympathy and admiration; the needs which the institution tries to satisfy and the response it provokes; the fear and devotion manifested in the cult of the divinity; the interest in creating, understanding, or applying a scientific theory and the ways of thinking implied in it—all these are attitudes. The attitude is thus the individual counterpart of the social value; activity, in whatever form, is the bond between them. By its reference to activity and thereby to individual consciousness the value is distinguished from the natural thing. By its reference to activity and thereby to the social world the attitude is distinguished from the psychical state. In the examples quoted above we were obliged to use with reference to ideas and volitions words that have become terms of individual psychology by being abstracted from the objective social reality to which they apply, but originally they were designed to express attitudes, not psychological processes. A psychological process is an attitude treated as an object in itself, isolated by a reflective act of attention, and taken first of all in connection with other states of the same individual. An attitude is a psychological process treated as primarily manifested in its reference to the social world and taken first of all in connection with some social value. Individual psychology may later re-establish the connection between the psychological process and the objective reality which has been severed by reflection; it may study psychological processes as conditioned by the facts going on in the objective world. In the same way social theory may later connect various attitudes of an individual and determine his social character. But it is the original (usually unconsciously occupied) standpoints which determine at once the subsequent methods of these two sciences. The psychological process remains always fundamentally a *state of somebody;* the attitude remains always fundamentally an attitude *toward something.*

Taking this fundamental distinction of standpoint into account, we may continue to use for different classes of attitudes the same terms which individual psychology has used for psychological processes, since these terms constitute the common property of all reflection about conscious life. The exact meaning of all these terms from the standpoint of social theory must be established during the process of investigation, so that every term shall be defined in view of its application and its methodological validity tested in actual use. It would be therefore impractical to attempt to establish in advance the whole terminology of attitudes.

But when we say that the data of social theory are attitudes and values, this is not yet a sufficient determination of the object of this science, for the field thus defined would embrace the whole of human culture and include the object-matter of philology and economics, theory of art, theory of science, etc. A more exact definition is therefore necessary in order to distinguish social theory from these sciences, established long ago and having their own methods and their own aims.

This limitation of the field of social theory arises quite naturally from the necessity of choosing between attitudes or values as fundamental data—that is, as data whose characters will serve as a basis for scientific generalization. There are numerous values corresponding to every attitude, and numerous attitudes corresponding to every value; if, therefore, we compare different actions with regard to the attitudes manifested in them and form, for example, the general concept of the attitude of solidarity, this means that we have neglected the whole variety of values which are produced by these actions and which may be political or economical, religious or scientific, etc. If, on the contrary, we compare the values produced by different actions and form, for example, the general concepts of economic or religious values, this means that we have neglected the whole variety of attitudes which are manifested in these actions. Scientific generalization must always base itself upon such characters of its data as can be considered essential to its purposes, and the essential characters of human actions are completely different when we treat them from the standpoint of attitudes and when we are interested in them as values. There is therefore no possibility of giving to attitudes and values the same importance in a methodical scientific investigation; either attitudes must be subordinated to values or the contrary.

Now in all the sciences which deal with separate domains of human culture like language, art, science, economics, it is the attitudes which are subordinated to values—a standpoint which results necessarily from the very specialization of these sciences in the study of certain classes of cultural values. For a theorician of art or an economist an attitude is important and is taken into consideration only in so far as it manifests itself in changes introduced into the sphere of aesthetic or economic values, and is defined exclusively by these changes—that is, by the pre-existing complex of objective data upon which it acted and by the objective results of this activity. But unless there is a special class of cultural values which are not the object-matter of any other science, and unless there are special reasons for assigning this class to social theory—a problem which we shall discuss presently—the latter cannot take the same standpoint and subordinate attitudes to values, for this would mean a useless duplication of existing sciences. There may be, as we shall see, some doubts whether such groups of phenomena as religion or morality should be for special reasons included in the field of social theory or should constitute the object-matter of distinct sciences; but there is no doubt that language and literature, art and science, economics and technique, are already more or less adequately treated by the respective disciplines and, while needing perhaps some internal reforms, do not call for a supplementary treatment by sociology or "folk-psychology" (Wundt).

But there is also no doubt that a study of the social world from the opposite standpoint—that is, taking attitudes as special object-matter and subordinating values to them—is necessary, and that an exact methodology of such a study is lacking. Ethics, psychology, ethnology, sociology, have an interest in this field and each has occupied it in a fragmentary and unmethodical way. But in ethics the study of attitudes has been subordinated to the problem of ideal norms of behavior, not treated as an end in itself, and under these conditions no adequate method of a purely theoretic investigation can be worked out. Ethnology has contributed valuable data for the study of attitudes and values as found in the various social groups, particularly the "lower" races, but its work is mainly descriptive. Of the sociological method in the exact sense of the term we shall speak presently. Psychology is, however, the science which has been definitely identified with the study of consciousness, and the main question at this point is how far psychology has covered or is capable of covering the field of attitudes.

As we have indicated above, the attitude is not a psychological datum in the sense given to this term by individual psychology, and this is true regardless of the differences between psychological schools. Concretely speaking, any method of research which takes the individual as a distinct entity and isolates him from his social environment, whether in order to determine by introspective analysis the content and form of his conscious processes, or in order to investigate the organic facts accompanying these processes, or, finally, in order to study experimentally his behavior as reaction to certain stimuli, finds necessarily only psychical, physical, or biological facts essentially and indissolubly connected with the individual as a psychical, physical, or generally biological reality. In order to reach scientific generalizations, such a method must work on the assumption of the universal permanence and identity of human nature as far as expressed in these facts; that is, its fundamental concepts must be such as to apply to all human beings, some of them even to all conscious beings, and individual differences must be reconstructed with the help of these concepts as variations of the same fundamental background, due to varying intensities, qualities, and combinations of essentially the same universal processes. Indeed, as every psychological fact is a state of the individual as fundamental reality, the uniformity of these facts depends on the permanence and uniformity of such individual realities. The central field of individual psychology is therefore constituted by the most elementary conscious phenomena, which are the only ones that can be adequately treated as essentially identical in all conscious beings; phenomena which are

## Attitude and Value  263

limited to a certain number of individuals either must be treated as complex and analyzed into elementary and universal elements, or, if this cannot be done, then their content, varying with the variation of social milieu, must be omitted and only the *form* of their occurrence reconstructed as presumably the same wherever and whenever they happen.

But psychology is not exclusively individual psychology. We find numerous monographs listed as psychological, but studying conscious phenomena which are not supposed to have their source in "human nature" in general, but in special social conditions, which can vary with the variation of these conditions and still be common to all individuals in the same conditions, and which are therefore treated, not as mere states of individual beings, but as self-sufficient data to be studied without any necessary assumptions about the psychological, physiological, or biological constitution of the individuals composing the group. To this sphere of psychology belong all investigations that concern conscious phenomena particular to races, nationalities, religious, political, professional groups, corresponding to special occupations and interests, provoked by special influences of a social milieu, developed by educational activities and legal measures, etc. The term "social psychology" has become current for this type of investigation. The distinction of social from individual psychology and the methodological unity of social psychology as a separate science have not been sufficiently discussed, but we shall attempt to show that social psychology is precisely the science of attitudes and that, while its methods are essentially different from the methods of individual psychology, its field is as wide as conscious life.

Indeed, every manifestation of conscious life, however simple or complex, general or particular, can be treated as an attitude, because every one involves a tendency to action, whether this action is a process of mechanical activity producing physical changes in the material world, or an attempt to influence the attitudes of others by speech and gesture, or a mental activity which does not at the given moment find a social expression, or even a mere process of sensual apperception. And all the objects of these actions can be treated as *social* values, for they all have some content which is or may be accessible to other individuals—even a personal "idea" can be communicated to others—and a meaning by which they may become the objects of the activity of others. And thus social psychology, when it undertakes to study the conscious phenomena found in a given social group, has no reasons a priori which force it to limit itself to a certain class of such phenomena to the exclusion of others; any manifestation of the conscious life of any member of the group is an attitude when taken in connection with the values which constitute the sphere of experience of this group, and this sphere includes data of the natural environment as well as artistic works or religious beliefs, technical products and economic relations as well as scientific theories. If, therefore, monographs in social psychology limit themselves to such special problems as, for example, the study of general conscious phenomena produced in a social group by certain physical, biological, economic, political influences, by common occupation, common religious beliefs, etc., the limitation may be justified by the social importance of these phenomena or even by only a particular interest of the author, but it is not necessitated by the nature of social psychology, which can study among the conscious phenomena occurring within the given social group, not only such as are peculiar to this group as a whole, but also, on the one hand, such as individual psychology assumes to be common to all conscious beings, and, on the other hand, such as may be peculiar to only one individual member of the group.

But of course not all the attitudes found in the conscious life of a social group have the same importance for the purposes of social psychology at a given moment, or even for its general purposes as a science of the social world. On the one hand, the task of every science in describing and generalizing the data is to reduce as far as possible the limitless complexity of experience to a limited number of concepts, and therefore those elements of reality are the most important which are most generally found in that part of experience which constitutes the object-matter of a science. And thus for social psychology the importance of an attitude is proportionate to the number and variety of actions in which this attitude is manifested. The more generally an attitude is

*Attitude and Value* 265

shared by the members of the given social group and the greater the part which it plays in the life of every member, the stronger the interest which it provokes in the social psychologist, while attitudes which are either peculiar to a few members of the group or which manifest themselves only on rare occasions have as such a relatively secondary significance, but may become significant through some connection with more general and fundamental attitudes.[2]

On the other hand, scientific generalizations are productive and valuable only in so far as they help to discover certain relations between various classes of the generalized data and to establish a systematic classification by a logical subordination and co-ordination of concepts; a generalization which bears no relation to others is useless. Now, as the main body of the materials of social psychology is constituted by *cultural* attitudes, corresponding to variable and multiform *cultural* values, such elementary *natural* attitudes as correspond to stable and uniform *physical* conditions —for example, attitudes manifested in sensual perception or in the action of eating—in spite of their generality and practical importance for the human race, can be usefully investigated within the limits of this science only if a connection can be found between them and the cultural attitudes—if, for example, it can be shown that sensual perception or the organic attitude of disgust varies within certain limits with the variation of social conditions. As long as there is no possibility of an actual subordination or co-ordination as between the cultural and the natural attitudes, the natural attitudes have no immediate interest for social psychology, and their investigation remains a task of individual psychology. In other words, those conscious phenomena corresponding to the physical world can be introduced into social psychology

[2] In connection, indeed, with the problems of both the creation and the destruction of social values, the most exceptional and divergent attitudes may prove the most important ones, because they may introduce a crisis and an element of disorder. And to the social theorist and technician the disorderly individual is of peculiar interest as a destroyer of values, as in the case of the anti-social individual, and as a creator of values, as in the case of the man of genius.

only if it can be shown that they are not purely "natural"—independent of social conditions—but also in some measure cultural—influenced by social values.

Thus, the field of social psychology practically comprises first of all the attitudes which are more or less generally found among the members of a social group, have a real importance in the life-organization of the individuals who have developed them, and manifest themselves in social activities of these individuals. This field can be indefinitely enlarged in two directions if the concrete problems of social psychology demand it. It may include attitudes which are particular to certain members of the social group or appear in the group only on rare occasions, as soon as they acquire for some reason a social importance; thus, some personal sexual idiosyncrasy will interest social psychology only if it becomes an object of imitation or of indignation to other members of the group or if it helps to an understanding of more general sexual attitudes. On the other hand, the field of social psychology may be extended to such attitudes as manifest themselves with regard, not to the social, but to the physical, environment of the individual, as soon as they show themselves affected by social culture; for example, the perception of colors would become a socio-psychological problem if it proved to have evolved during the cultural evolution under the influence of decorative arts.

Social psychology has thus to perform the part of a general science of the subjective side of social culture which we have heretofore usually ascribed to individual psychology or to "psychology in general." It may claim to be *the* science of consciousness as manifested in culture, and its function is to render service, as a general auxiliary science, to all the special sciences dealing with various spheres of social values. This does not mean that social psychology can ever supplant individual psychology; the methods and standpoints of these two sciences are too different to permit either of them to fulfil the function of the other, and, if it were not for the traditional use of the term "psychology" for both types of research, it would be even advisable to emphasize this difference by a distinct terminology.

But when we study the life of a concrete social group we find a certain very important side of this life which social psychology cannot adequately take into account, which none of the special sciences of culture treats as its proper object-matter, and which during the last fifty years has constituted the central sphere of interest of the various researches called *sociology*. Among the attitudes prevailing within a group some express themselves only in individual actions—uniform or multiform, isolated or combined —but only in actions. But there are other attitudes—usually, though not always, the most general ones—which, besides expressing themselves directly, like the first, in actions, find also an indirect manifestation in more or less explicit and formal *rules* of behavior by which the group tends to maintain, to regulate, and to make more general and more frequent the corresponding type of actions among its members. These rules—customs and rituals, legal and educational norms, obligatory beliefs and aims, etc.— arouse a twofold interest. We may treat them, like actions, as manifestations of attitudes, as indices showing that, since the group demands certain kinds of actions, the attitude which is supposed to manifest itself in these actions is shared by all those who uphold the rule. But, on the other hand, the very existence of a rule shows that there are some, even if only weak and isolated, attitudes which do not fully harmonize with the one expressed in the rule, and that the group feels the necessity of preventing these attitudes from passing into action. Precisely as far as the rule is consciously realized as binding by individual members of the group from whom it demands a certain adaptation, it has for every individual a certain content and a certain meaning and is a value. Furthermore, the action of an individual viewed by the group, by another individual, or even by himself in reflection, with regard to this action's agreement or disagreement with the rule, becomes also a value to which a certain attitude of appreciation or depreciation is attached in various forms. In this way rules and actions, taken, not with regard to the attitudes *expressed* in them, but with regard to the attitudes *provoked* by them, are quite analogous to any other values—economic, artistic, scientific, religious, etc. There may be many various attitudes corresponding to a rule or action as objects of individual reflection and appreciation, and a certain attitude—such as, for example, the desire for personal freedom or the feeling of social righteousness—may bear positively or negatively upon many rules and actions, varying from group to group and from individual to individual. These values cannot, therefore, be the object-matter of social psychology; they constitute a special group of objective cultural data alongside the special domains of other cultural sciences like economics, theory of art, philology, etc. The rules of behavior, and the actions viewed as conforming or not conforming with these rules, constitute with regard to their objective significance a certain number of more or less connected and harmonious systems which can be generally called *social institutions*, and the totality of institutions found in a concrete social group constitutes the *social organization* of this group. And when studying the social organization as such we must subordinate attitudes to values as we do in other special cultural sciences; that is, attitudes count for us only as influencing and modifying rules of behavior and social institutions.

Sociology, as theory of social organization, is thus a special science of culture like economics or philology, and is in so far opposed to social psychology as the general science of the subjective side of culture. But at the same time it has this in common with social psychology: that the values which it studies draw all their reality, all their power to influence human life, from the social attitudes which are expressed or supposedly expressed in them; if the individual in his behavior is so largely determined by the rules prevailing in his social group, it is certainly due neither to the rationality of these rules nor to the physical consequences which their following or breaking may have, but to his consciousness that these rules represent attitudes of his group and to his realization of the *social* consequences which will ensue for him if he follows or breaks the rules. And therefore both social psychology and sociology can be embraced under the general term of social theory, as they are both concerned with the relation between the individual and the concrete social group, though their standpoints on this common ground are quite opposite, and though their fields are not equally wide, social psychology comprising the attitudes of the individual toward *all* cultural values of the given social group, while sociology can study only one type of these values—social rules—in their relation to individual attitudes.

We have seen that social psychology has a central field of interest including the most general and fundamental cultural attitudes found within concrete societies. In the same manner there is a certain domain which constitutes the methodological center of sociological interest. It includes those rules of behavior which concern more especially the active relations between individual members of the group and between each member and the group as a whole. It is these rules, indeed, manifested as mores, laws, and group-ideals and systematized in such institutions as the family, the tribe, the community, the free association, the state, etc., which constitute the central part of social organization and provide through this organization the essential conditions of the existence of a group as a distinct cultural entity and not a mere agglomeration of individuals; and hence all other rules which a given group may develop and treat as obligatory have a secondary sociological importance as compared with these. But this does not mean that sociology should not extend its field of investigation beyond this methodological center of interest. Every social group, particularly on lower stages of cultural evolution, is inclined to control all individual activities, not alone those which attain directly its fundamental institutions. Thus we find social regulations of economic, religious, scientific, artistic activities, even of technique and speech, and the break of these regulations is often treated as affecting the very existence of the group. And we must concede that, though the effect of these regulations on cultural productivity is often more than doubtful, they do contribute as long as they last to the unity of the group, while, on the other hand, the close association which has been formed between these rules and the fundamental social institutions without which the group cannot exist has often the consequence that cultural evolution which destroys the influence of these secondary regulations may actually disorganize the group. Precisely as far as these social rules concerning special cultural activities are in the above-determined way connected with the rules which bear on social relations they acquire an interest for sociology. Of course it can be determined only a posteriori how far the field of sociology should be extended beyond the investigation of fundamental social institutions, and the situation varies from group to group and from period to period. In all civilized societies some part of every cultural activity—religious, economic, scientific, artistic, etc.—is left outside of social regulation, and another, perhaps even larger, part, though still subjected to social rules, is no longer supposed to affect directly the existence or coherence of society and actually does not affect it. It is therefore a grave methodological error to attempt to include generally in the field of sociology such cultural domains as religion or economics on the ground that in certain social groups religious or economic norms are considered—and in some measure even really are—a part of social organization, for even there the respective values have a content which cannot be completely reduced to social rules of behavior, and their importance for social organization may be very small or even none in other societies or at other periods of evolution.

The fundamental distinction between social psychology and sociology appears clearly when we undertake the comparative study of special problems in various societies, for these problems naturally divide themselves into two classes. We may attempt to explain certain attitudes by tracing their origin and trying to determine the laws of their appearance under various social circumstances, as, for example, when we investigate sexual love or feeling of group-solidarity, bashfulness or showing off, the mystical emotion or the aesthetic amateur attitude, etc. Or we may attempt to give an explanation of social institutions and try to subject to laws their appearance under various socio-psychological conditions, as when our object-matter is marriage or family, criminal legislation or censorship of scientific opinions, militarism or parliamentarism, etc. But when we study monographically a concrete social group with all its fundamental attitudes and values, it is difficult to make a thoroughgoing separation of socio-psychological and sociological problems, for any concrete body of material contains both. Consequently, since the present work is precisely a monograph of a concrete social group, we cannot go into a detailed analysis of methodological questions concerning exclusively the socio-psychological or sociological investigation in particular, but must limit ourselves to such general methodological indications as concern both.

The chief problems of modern science are problems of causal explanation. The determination and systematization of data is only the first step in scientific investigation. If a science wishes to lay the foundation of a technique, it must attempt to understand and to control the process of *becoming*. Social theory cannot avoid this task, and there is only one way of fulfilling it. Social becoming, like natural becoming, must be analyzed into a plurality of facts, each of which represents a succession of cause and effect. The idea of social theory is the analysis of the totality of social becoming into such causal processes and a systematization permitting us to understand the connections between these processes. No arguments a priori trying to demonstrate the impossibility of application of the principle of causality to conscious human life in general can or should halt social theory in tending to this idea, whatever difficulties there may be in the way, because as a matter of fact we continually do apply the principle of causality to the social world in our activity and in our thought, and we shall always do this as long as we try to control social becoming in any form. So, instead of fruitlessly discussing the justification of this application in the abstract, social theory must simply strive to make it more methodical and perfect in the concrete—by the actual process of investigation.

But if the general philosophical problem of free will and determinism is negligible, the particular problem of the best possible method of causal explanation is very real. Indeed, its solution is the fundamental and inevitable introductory task of a science which, like social theory, is still in the period of formation. The great and most usual illusion of the scientist is that he simply takes the facts as they are, without any methodological prepossessions, and gets his explanation entirely a posteriori from pure experience. A fact by itself is already an abstraction; we isolate a certain limited aspect of the concrete process of becoming, rejecting, at least provisionally, all its indefinite complexity. The question is only whether we perform this abstraction methodically or not, whether we know what and why we accept and reject, or simply take uncritically the old abstractions of "common sense." If we want to reach scientific explanations, we must keep in mind that our facts must be determined in such a way as to permit of their subordination to general laws. A fact which cannot be treated as a manifestation of one or several laws is inexplicable causally. When, for example, the historian speaks of the causes of the present war, he must assume that the war is a combination of the effects of many causes, each of which may repeat itself many times in history and must have always the same effect, although such a combination of these causes as has produced the present war may never happen again. And only if social theory succeeds in determining causal laws can it become a basis of social technique, for technique demands the possibility of foreseeing and calculating the effects of given causes, and this demand is realizable only if we know that certain causes will always and everywhere produce certain effects.

Now, the chief error of both social practice and social theory has been that they determined, consciously or unconsciously, social facts in a way which excluded in advance the possibility of their subordination to any laws. The implicit or explicit assumption was that a social fact is composed of two elements, a cause which is either a social phenomenon or an individual act, and an effect which is either an individual act or a social phenomenon. Following uncritically the example of the physical sciences, which always tend to find the one determined phenomenon which is the necessary and sufficient condition of another phenomenon, social theory and social practice have forgotten to take into account one essential difference between physical and social reality, which is that, while the effect of a physical phenomenon depends exclusively on the objective nature of this phenomenon and can be calculated on the ground of the latter's empirical content, the effect of a social phenomenon depends in addition on the subjective standpoint taken by the individual or the group toward this phenomenon and can be calculated only if we know, not only the objective content of the assumed cause, but also the meaning which it has at

*Attitude and Value* 273

the given moment for the given conscious beings. This simple consideration should have shown to the social theorist or technician that a social cause cannot be simple, like a physical cause, but is compound, and must include both an objective and a subjective element, a value *and* an attitude. Otherwise the effect will appear accidental and incalculable, because we shall have to search in every particular case for the reasons why this particular individual or this particular society reacted to the given phenomenon in this way and not in any other way.

In fact, a social value, acting upon individual members of the group, produces a more or less different effect on every one of them; even when acting upon the same individual at various moments it does not influence him uniformly. The influence of a work of art is a typical example. And such uniformities as exist here are quite irrelevant, for they are not absolute. If we once suppose that a social phenomenon is the cause—which means a necessary and sufficient cause, for there are no "insufficient" causes—of an individual reaction, then our statement of this causal dependence has the logical claim of being a scientific law from which there can be no exceptions; that is, every seeming exception must be explained by the action of some other cause, an action whose formulation becomes another scientific law. But to explain why in a concrete case a work of art or a legal prescription which, according to our supposed law, should provoke in the individual a certain reaction $A$ provokes instead a reaction $B$, we should have to investigate the whole past of this individual and repeat this investigation in every case, with regard to every individual whose reaction is not $A$, without hoping ever to subordinate those exceptions to a new law, for the life-history of every individual is different. Consequently social theory tries to avoid this methodological absurdity by closing its eyes to the problem itself. It is either satisfied with statements of causal influences which hold true "on the average," "in the majority of cases"—a flat self-contradition, for, if something *is a cause,* it must have by its very definition, always and necessarily *the same effect,* otherwise it is not a cause at all. Or it tries to analyze phenomena acting upon individuals and individual reactions to them into simpler elements, hoping thus to find simple facts, while the trouble is not with the complexity of data, but with the complexity of the context on which these data act or in which they are embodied—that is, of the human personality. Thus, as far as the complexity of social data is concerned, the principle of gravitation and the smile of Mona Lisa are simple in their objective content, while their influence on human attitudes has been indefinitely varied; the complex system of a graphomaniac or the elaborate picture of a talentless and skilless man provokes much more uniform reactions. And, on the individual side, the simple attitude of anger can be provoked by an indefinite variety of social phenomena, while the very complicated attitude of militant patriotism appears usually only in very definite social conditions.

But more than this. Far from obviating the problem of individual variations, such uniformities of reaction to social influences as can be found constitute a problem in themselves. For with the exception of the elementary reactions to purely physical stimuli, which may be treated as identical because of the identity of "human nature" and as such belong to individual psychology, all uniformities with which social psychology has to deal are the product of social conditions. If the members of a certain group react in an identical way to certain values, it is because they have been socially trained to react thus, because the traditional rules of behavior predominant in the given group impose upon every member certain ways of defining and solving the practical situations which he meets in his life. But the very success of this social training, the very fact that individual members do accept such definitions and act in accordance with them, is no less a problem than the opposite fact—the frequent insuccess of the training, the growing assertion of the personality, the growing variation of reaction to social rules, the search for personal definitions—which characterizes civilized societies. And thus, even if we find that all the members of a social group react in the same way to a certain value, still we cannot assume that this value alone is the cause of this reaction, for the latter is also conditioned by the uniformity of attitudes prevailing in the group; and this uniformity itself cannot be taken as granted and omitted—as we omit the uniformity of environing conditions in a physical fact—because it is the particular effect of certain social rules acting upon the members of the group who, because of certain predispositions, have accepted these rules, and this effect may be at any moment counterbalanced by the action of different causes, and is in fact counterbalanced more and more frequently with the progress of civilization.

In short, when social theory assumes that a certain social value is of itself the cause of a certain individual reaction, it is then forced to ask: "But why did this value produce this particular effect when acting on this particular individual or group at this particular moment?" Certainly no scientific answer to such a question is possible, since in order to explain this "why" we should have to know the whole past of the individual, of the society, and of the universe.

Analogous methodological difficulties arise when social theory attempts to explain a change in social organization as a result of the activity of the members of the group. If we treat individual activity as a *cause* of social changes, every change appears as inexplicable, particularly when it is "original," presents many new features. Necessarily this point is one of degree, for every product of individual activity is in a sense a new value and in so far original as it has not existed before this activity, but in certain cases the importance of the change brought by the individual makes its incalculable and inexplicable character particularly striking. We have therefore almost despaired of extending consistently the principle of causality to the activities of "great men," while it still seems to us that we do understand the everyday productive activity of the average human individual or of the "masses." From the methodological standpoint, however, it is neither more nor less difficult to explain the greatest changes brought into the social world by a Charles the Great, a Napoleon, a Marx, a Bismarck than to explain a small change brought by a peasant who starts a lawsuit against his relatives or buys a piece of land to increase his farm. The work of the great man, like that of the ordinary man, is the result of his tendency to modify the existing conditions, of his attitude toward his social environment which makes him reject certain existing values and produce certain new values. The difference is in the values which are the object of the activity, in the nature, importance, complexity, of the social problems put and solved. The change in social organization produced by a great man may be thus equivalent to an accumulation of small changes brought by millions of ordinary men, but the idea that a creative process is more explicable when it lasts for several generations than when it is performed in a few months or days, or that by dividing a creative process into a million small parts we destroy its irrationality, is equivalent to the conception that by a proper combination of mechanical elements in a machine we can produce a *perpetuum mobile*.

The simple and well-known fact is that the social results of individual activity depend, not only on the action itself, but also on the social conditions in which it is performed; and therefore the cause of a social change must include both individual and social elements. By ignoring this, social theory faces an infinite task whenever it wants to explain the simplest social change. For the same action in different social conditions produces quite different results. It is true that if social conditions are sufficiently stable the results of certain individual actions are more or less determinable, at least in a sufficient majority of cases to permit an approximate practical calculation. We know that the result of the activity of a factory-workman will be a certain technical product, that the result of the peasant's starting a lawsuit against a member of his family will be a dissolution of family bonds between him and this member, that the result of a judge's activity in a criminal case will be the condemnation and incarceration of the offender if he is convicted. But all this holds true only if social conditions remain stable. In case of a strike in the factory, the workman will not be allowed to finish his product; assuming that the idea of family solidarity has ceased to prevail in a peasant group, the lawsuit will not provoke moral indignation; if the action upon which the judge has to pronounce this verdict ceases to be treated as a crime because of a change of political conditions or of public opinion, the offender, even if convicted, will be set free. A method which permits us to determine only cases of stereotyped activity and leaves us helpless in face of changed conditions is not a scientific method at all, and becomes even less and less practically useful with the continual increase of fluidity in modern social life.

Moreover, social theory forgets also that the uniformity of results of certain actions is itself a problem and demands explanation exactly as much as do the variations. For the stability of social conditions upon which the uniformity of results of individual activity depends is itself a product of former activities, not an original natural status which might be assumed as granted. Both its character and its degree vary from group to group and from epoch to epoch. A certain action may have indeed determined and calculable effects in a certain society and at a certain period, but will have completely different effects in other societies and at other periods.

And thus social theory is again confronted by a scientifically absurd question. Assuming that individual activity in itself is the cause of social effects, it must then ask: "Why does a certain action produce this particular effect at this particular moment in this particular society?" The answer to this question would demand a complete explanation of the whole status of the given society at the given moment, and thus force us to investigate the entire past of the universe.

The fundamental methodological principle of both social psychology and sociology—the principle without which they can never reach scientific explanation—is therefore the following one:

*The cause of a social or individual phenomenon is never another social or individual phenomenon alone, but always a combination of a social and an individual phenomenon.*

Or, in more exact terms:

*The cause of a value or of an attitude is never an attitude or a value alone, but always a combination of an attitude and a value.*[3] . . .

---

[3] It may be objected that we have neglected to criticize the conception according to which the cause of a social phenomenon is to be sought, not in an individual, but exclusively in another social phenomenon (Durk-

As to the present work, it evidently cannot in any sense pretend to establish social theory on a definitely scientific basis. It is clear from the preceding discussion that many workers and much time will be needed before we free ourselves from the traditional ways of thinking, develop a completely efficient and exact working method, and reach a system of scientifically correct generalizations. Our present very limited task is the preparation of a certain body of materials, even if we occasionally go beyond it and attempt to reach some generalizations.

Our object-matter is one class of modern society in the whole concrete complexity of its life. The selection of the Polish peasant society, motivated at first by somewhat incidental reasons, such as the intensity of the Polish immigration and the facility of getting materials concerning the Polish peasant, has proved during the investigation to be a fortunate one. The Polish peasant finds himself now in a period of transition from the old forms of social organization that had been in force, with only insignificant changes, for many centuries, to a modern form of life. He has preserved enough of the old attitudes to make their sociological reconstruction possible, and he is sufficiently advanced upon the new way to make a study of the development of modern attitudes particularly fruitful. He has been invited by the upper classes to collaborate in the construction of Polish national life, and in certain lines his development is due to the conscious educational efforts of his leaders—the nobility, the clergy, the middle class. In this respect he has the value of an experiment in social technique; the successes, as well as the failures, of this educational activity of the upper classes are very significant for social work. These efforts of the upper classes themselves have a particular sociological impor-

---

heim). But a criticism of this conception is implied in the previous discussion of the data of social theory. As these data are both values and attitudes, a fact must include both, and a succession of values alone cannot constitute a fact. Of course much depends also on what we call a "social" phenomenon. An attitude may be treated as a social phenomenon as opposed to the "state of consciousness" of individual psychology; but it is individual, even if common to all members of a group, when we oppose it to a value.

tance in view of the conditions in which Polish society has lived during the last century. As a society without a state, divided among three states and constantly hampered in all its efforts to preserve and develop a distinct and unique cultural life, it faced a dilemma—either to disappear or to create such substitutes for a state organization as would enable it to resist the destructive action of the oppressing states; or, more generally, to exist without the framework of a state. These substitutes were created, and they are interesting in two respects. First, they show, in an exceptionally intensified and to a large extent isolated form, the action of certain factors of social unity which exist in every society but in normal conditions are subordinated to the state organization and seldom sufficiently accounted for in sociological reflection. Secondly, the lack of permanence of every social institution and the insecurity of every social value in general, resulting from the destructive tendencies of the dominating foreign states, bring with them a necessity of developing and keeping constantly alive all the activities needed to reconstruct again and again every value that had been destroyed. The whole mechanism of social creation is therefore here particularly transparent and easy to understand, and in general the rôle of human attitudes in social life becomes much more evident than in a society not living under the same strain, but able to rely to a large extent upon the inherited formal organization for the preservation of its culture and unity.

We use in this work the inductive method in a form which gives the least possible place for any arbitrary statements. The basis of the work is concrete materials, and only in the selection of these materials some necessary discrimination has been used. But even here we have tried to proceed in the most cautious way possible. . . .

The general character of the work is mainly that of a systematization and classification of attitudes and values prevailing in a concrete group. Every attitude and every value, as we have said above, can be really understood only in connection with the whole social life of which it is an element, and therefore this method is the only one that gives us a full and systematic acquaintance with all the complexity of social life. But it is evident that this monograph must be followed by many others if we want our acquaintance with social reality to be complete. Other Slavic groups, particularly the Russians; the French and the Germans, as representing different types of more efficient societies; the Americans, as the most conspicuous experiment in individualism; the Jews, as representing particular social adaptations under peculiar social pressures; the Oriental, with his widely divergent attitudes and values; the Negro, with his lower cultural level and unique social position—these and other social groups should be included in a series of monographs, which in its totality will give for the first time a wide and secure basis for any sociological generalizations whatever. Naturally the value of every monograph will increase with the development of the work, for not only will the method continually improve, but every social group will help to understand every other.

In selecting the monographic method for the present work and in urging the desirability of the further preparation of large bodies of materials representing the total life of different social groups, we do not ignore the other method of approaching a scientific social theory and practice—the study of special problems, of isolated aspects of social life. And we are not obliged even to wait until all the societies have been studied monographically, in their whole concrete reality, before beginning the comparative study of particular problems. Indeed, the study of a single society, as we have undertaken it here, is often enough to show what rôle is played by a particular class of phenomena in the total life of a group and to give us in this way sufficient indications for the isolation of this class from its social context without omitting any important interaction that may exist between phenomena of this class and others, and we can then use these indications in taking the corresponding kinds of phenomena in other societies as objects of comparative research.

By way of examples, we point out here certain problems suggested to us by the study of the Polish peasants for which this study affords a good starting-point.[4]

1. *The problem of individualization.* How far is individualization compatible with social cohesion? What are the forms of individualization that can be considered socially useful or socially harmful? What are the forms of social organization that allow for the greatest amount of individualism?

We have been led to the suppositions that, generally speaking, individualization is the intermediary stage between one form of social organization and another; that its social usefulness depends on its more or less constructive character—that is, upon the question whether it does really lead to a new organization and whether the latter makes the social group more capable of resisting disintegrating influences; and that, finally, an organization based upon a conscious co-operation in view of a common aim is the most compatible with individualism. The verification of these suppositions and their application to concrete problems of such a society as the American would constitute a grateful work.

2. *The problem of efficiency.* Relation between individual and social efficiency. Dependence of efficiency upon various individual attitudes and upon various forms of social organization.

The Polish society shows in most lines of activity a particularly large range of variation of individual efficiency with a relatively low scale of social efficiency. We have come to the conclusion that both phenomena are due to the lack of a sufficiently persistent and detailed frame of social organization, resulting from the loss of state-independence. Under these conditions individual efficiency depends upon individual attitudes much more than upon social conditions. An individual may be very efficient because there is little to hinder his activity in any line he selects, but he may also be very inefficient because there is little to push him or to help him. The total social result of individual activities under these conditions is relatively small, because social efficiency

[4] Points 2 and 8 following are more directly connected with materials on the middle and upper classes of Polish society which do not appear in the present work.

depends, not only on the average efficiency of the individuals that constitute the group, but also on the more or less perfect organization of individual efforts. Here, again, the application of these conclusions to other societies can open the way to important discoveries in this particular sphere by showing what is the way of conciliating the highest individual with the highest social efficiency.

3. *The problem of abnormality—crime, vagabondage, prostitution, alcoholism, etc.* How far is abnormality the unavoidable manifestation of inborn tendencies of the individual, and how far is it due to social conditions?

The priests in Poland have a theory with regard to their peasant parishioners that there are no incorrigible individuals, provided that the influence exercised upon them is skilful and steady and draws into play all of the social factors—familial solidarity, social opinion of the community, religion and magic, economic and intellectual motives, etc. And in his recent book on *The Individual Delinquent*, Dr. William Healy touches the problem on the same side in the following remark: "Frequently one wonders what might have been accomplished with this or that individual if he had received a more adequate discipline during his childhood." By our investigation of abnormal attitudes in connection with normal attitudes instead of treating them isolately, and by the recognition that the individual can be fully understood and controlled only if all the influences of his environment are properly taken into account, we could hardly avoid the suggestion that abnormality is mainly, if not exclusively, a matter of deficient social organization. There is hardly any human attitude which, if properly controlled and directed, could not be used in a socially productive way. Of course there must always remain a quantitative difference of efficiency between individuals, often a very far-going one, but we can see no reason for a permanent qualitative difference between socially normal and antisocial actions. And from this standpoint the question of the antisocial individual assumes no longer the form of the right of society to protection, but that of the right of the antisocial individual to be made useful.

4. *The occupational problem.* The modern division and organization of labor brings an enormous and continually growing quantitative prevalence of occupations which are almost completely devoid of stimulation and therefore present little interest for the workman. This fact necessarily affects human happiness profoundly, and, if only for this reason, the restoration of stimulation to labor is among the most important problems confronting society. The present industrial organization tends also to develop a type of human being as abnormal in its way as the opposite type of individual who gets the full amount of occupational stimulation by taking a line of interest destructive of social order—the criminal or vagabond. If the latter type of abnormality is immediately dangerous for the present state of society, the former is more menacing for the future, as leading to a gradual but certain degeneration of the human type—whether we regard this degeneration as congenital or acquired.

The analysis of this problem discloses very profound and general causes of the evil, but also the way of an eventual remedy. It is a fact too well known to be emphasized that modern organization of labor is based on an almost absolute prevalence of economic interests—more exactly, on the tendency to produce or acquire the highest possible amount of economic values—either because these interests are actually so universal and predominant or because they express themselves in social organization more easily than others—a point to be investigated. The moralist complains of the materialization of men and expects a change of the social organization to be brought about by moral or religious preaching; the economic determinist considers the whole social organization as conditioned fundamentally and necessarily by economic factors and expects an improvement exclusively from a possible historically necessary modification of the economic organization itself. From the sociological viewpoint the problem looks much more serious and objective than the moralist conceives it, but much less limited and determined than it appears to the economic determinist. The economic interests are only one class of human attitudes among others, and every attitude can be modified by an adequate social technique. The interest in the nature of work is frequently as strong as, or stronger than, the interest in the economic results of the work, and often finds an objective expression in spite of the fact that actual social organization has little place for it. The protests, in fact, represented by William Morris mean that a certain class of work has visibly passed from the stage where it was stimulating to a stage where it is not—that the handicrafts formerly expressed an interest in the work itself rather than in the economic returns from the work. Since every attitude tends to influence social institutions, we may expect that, with the help of social technique, an organization and a division of labor based on occupational interests may gradually replace the present organization based on demands of economic productivity. In other words, with the appropriate change of attitudes and values all work may become artistic work.

5. *The relation of the sexes.* Among the many problems falling under this head two seem to us of fundamental importance, the first mainly socio-psychological, the second mainly sociological: (1) In the relation between the sexes how can a maximum of reciprocal response be obtained with the minimum of interference with personal interests? (2) How is the general social efficiency of a group affected by the various systems of relations between man and woman?

We do not advance at this point any definite theories. But a few suggestions of a general character arise in connection with the study of a concrete society. In matters of reciprocal response we find among the Polish peasants the sexes equally dependent on each other, though their demands are of a rather limited and unromantic character, while at the same time this response is secured at the cost of a complete subordination of their personalities to a common sphere of group-interests. When the development of personal interests begins, this original harmony is disturbed, and the disharmony is particularly marked among the immigrants in America, where it often leads to a complete and radical disorganization of family life. There does not seem to be as yet any real solution in view. In this respect the situation of the Polish peasants may throw an interesting light upon the general situation of the cultivated classes of modern society. The difference between these two situations lies in the fact that among the peasants both man and woman begin almost simultaneously to develop personal claims, whereas in the cultivated classes the personal claims of the man have been developed and in a large measure satisfied long ago, and the present problem is almost exclusively limited to the woman. The situations are analogous, however, in so far as the difficulty of solution is concerned.

With regard to social efficiency, our Polish materials tend to show that, under conditions in which the activities of the woman can attain an objective importance more or less equal to those of the man, the greatest social efficiency is attained by a systematic collaboration of man and woman in external fields rather than by a division of tasks which limits the woman to "home and children." The line along which the peasant class of Polish society is particularly efficient is economic development and co-operation; and precisely in this line the collaboration of women has been particularly wide and successful. As far as a division of labor based upon differences of the sexes is concerned, there seems to be at least one point at which a certain differentiation of tasks would be at present in accordance with the demands of social efficiency. The woman shows a particular aptitude of mediation between the formalism, uniformity, and permanence of social organization and the concrete, various, and changing individualities. And, whether this ability of the woman is congenital or produced by cultural conditions, it could certainly be made socially very useful, for it is precisely the ability required to diminish the innumerable and continually growing frictions resulting from the misadaptations of individual attitudes to social organization, and to avoid the incalculable waste of human energy which contrasts so deplorably in our modern society with our increasingly efficient use of natural energies.

6. *The problem of social happiness.* With regard to this problem we can hardly make any positive suggestions. It is certain that both the relation of the sexes and the economic situation are among the fundamental conditions of human happiness, in the sense of making it and of spoiling it. But the striking point is that,

aside from abstract philosophical discussion and some popular psychological analysis, the problem of happiness has never been seriously studied since the epoch of Greek hedonism, and of course the conclusions reached by the Greeks, even if they were more scientific than they really are, could hardly be applied to the present time, with its completely changed social conditions. Has this problem been so much neglected because of its difficulty or because, under the influence of certain tendencies immanent in Christianity, happiness is still half-instinctively regarded as more or less sinful, and pain as meritorious? However that may be, the fact is that no things of real significance have been said up to the present about happiness, particularly if we compare them with the enormous material that has been collected and the innumerable important ideas that have been expressed concerning unhappiness. Moreover, we believe that the problem merits a very particular consideration, both from the theoretical and from the practical point of view, and that the sociological method outlined above gives the most reliable way of studying it.

7. *The problem of the fight of races (nationalities) and cultures.* Probably in this respect no study of any other society can give so interesting sociological indications as the study of the Poles. Surrounded by peoples of various degrees of cultural development—Germans, Austrians, Bohemians, Ruthenians, Russians, Lithuanians—having on her own territory the highest percentage of the most unassimilable of races, the Jews, Poland is fighting at every moment for the preservation of her racial and cultural status. Moreover, the fight assumes the most various forms: self-defense against oppressive measures promulgated by Russia and Germany in the interest of their respective races and cultures; self-defense against the peaceful intrusion of the Austrian culture in Galicia; the problem of the assimilation of foreign colonists—German or Russian; the political fight against the Ruthenians in Eastern Galicia; peaceful propaganda and efforts to maintain the supremacy of Polish culture on the vast territory between the Baltic and the Black seas (populated mainly by Lithuanians, White Ruthenians, and Ukranians), where the

*Attitude and Value* 287

Poles constitute the cultivated minority of estate-owners and intellectual bourgeoisie; various methods of dealing with the Jews —passive toleration, efforts to assimilate them nationally (not religiously), social and economic boycott. All these ways of fighting develop the greatest possible variety of attitudes.

And the problem itself assumes a particular actual importance if we remember that the present war is a fight of races and cultures, which has assumed the form of war because races and cultures have expressed themselves in the modern state-organization. The fight of races and cultures is the predominant fact of modern historical life, and it must assume the form of war when it uses the present form of state-organization as its means. To stop wars one must either stop the fight of races and cultures by the introduction of new schemes of attitudes and values or substitute for the isolated national state as instrument of cultural expansion some other type or organization.

8. Closely connected with the foregoing is *the problem of an ideal organization of culture.* This is the widest and oldest sociological problem, lying on the border between theory and practice. Is there one perfect form of organization that would unify the widest individualism and the strongest social cohesion, that would exclude any abnormality by making use of all human tendencies, that would harmonize the highest efficiency with the greatest happiness? And, if one and only one such organization is possible, will it come automatically, as a result of the fight between cultures and as an expression of the law of the survival of the fittest, so that finally "the world's history will prove the world's tribunal"? Or must such an organization be brought about by a conscious and rational social technique modifying the historical conditions and subordinating all the cultural differences to one perfect system? Or is there, on the contrary, no such unique ideal possible? Perhaps there are many forms of a perfect organization of society, and, the differentiation of national cultures being impossible to overcome, every nation should simply try to bring its own system to the greatest possible perfection, profiting by the experiences of others, but not imitating them. In this case

the fight of races and cultures could be stopped, not by the destruction of historical differences, but by the recognition of their value for the world and by a growing reciprocal acquaintance and estimation. Whatever may be the ultimate solution of this problem, it is evident that the systematic sociological study of various cultures, as outlined in this note and exemplified in its beginnings in the main body of the work, is the only way to solve it.

# 16

# THE RELATION OF RESEARCH
# TO THE SOCIAL PROCESS

IT IS recognized that the object of research in both the material and the social worlds is control, or it might be said to be the supplying of materials and situations for the satisfaction of human desires—the providing of what men want. There can be no question that there has been research since the world began. The bow and arrow, the spring trap, the invention of poisons, and so on, represent research by primitive man; and even the life of animals is a constant experimentation and a learning process.

What we have in mind at present is, of course, a more organized and continuous approach which we call scientific. From this standpoint the achievements in the physical and biological sciences have been positive and enormous. No one questions that medical research has modified the social process and secured greater control of one of the aspects of life, as when Koch discovered the tubercle bacillus; or Semmelweis in Vienna observed with solicitude and profound reflection that the mortality in surgical cases in one ward of his hospital was five times as great as in another, observed further that the operators in the ward of high mortality usually came directly from the dissecting rooms, concluded that they were carrying "cadaver" to the

---

*Reprinted* from W. F. G. Swann *et al., Essays on Research in the Social Sciences* (Washington: Brookings Institution, 1931), pp. 174-94.

wounds of the patients, and ordered them to wash their hands in chloride of lime; or when Bruce in British Uganda, seeking the cause of sleeping sickness, caused specimens of all insects from all localities to be sent in by the chiefs and the missionaries, made a spot map of the incidence of sleeping sickness and spot maps of the incidence of all the insects, and through superimposition discovered that the map of sleeping sickness and the map representing the tsetse fly coincided.

The physical and biological sciences have the advantage of experimentation and instrumentation, and are impeded by less resistance to change than is the field of social interaction. In the social sciences the problem is not mainly the control of the material world but of the behavior of individuals as members of a society. The subject matter of all the social sciences is in fact fundamentally behavior. And here experimentation with the human materials is limited, and resistance to change is more stubborn on account of the sanctity of custom and the rivalry of personal interests.

I find that I have been invited to be on this occasion "as much of an anthropologist, philosopher, sociologist, and aesthete as I care to make of myself at one time." Some of those things I don't want to be at all and I shall attempt to show, mainly by examples, the present approach to the control of behavior and the social process in the field with which I am most familiar, with so much of the methodological indications as may be involved.

The student of behavior whether social psychologist, sociologist, criminologist, or psychiatrist, is at present approaching the problem of behavior from the situational standpoint. The situation in which the person finds himself is taken as containing the configuration of the factors conditioning the behavior reaction. Of course, it is not the spatial material situation which is meant, but the situation of social relationships. It involves all the institutions and mores—family, gang, church, school, the press, the movies, and the attitudes and values of other persons with which his own come in conflict or co-operation. The individual always possesses a repertory of attitudes (tendencies to act) and values (goals toward which the action is directed), depending in each case on biological constitution on the one hand and social conditioning on the other. A study of the concrete situations which the individual encounters, into which he is forced, or which he creates will disclose the character of his adaptive strivings and the processes of adjustment. The study of the situation, the behavior in the situation, the changes brought about in the situation, and the resulting change in behavior represent the nearest approach the social scientist is able to make to the use of experiment in social research.

The situational approach is, of course, not a new procedure. It is the method in use by both the experimental physiologists and the psychologists who prepare situations, introduce the subject into the situation, observe the behavior reactions, change the situation, and observe the changes in the reactions. Child rendered one point in the situation more stimulating than others by applying an electric needle or other stimulus and made heads grow where tails would otherwise have grown. The situational character of the animal experimentation of the psychologists is well known. The rat, for example, in order to open a door, must not only stand on a platform placed in a certain position, but at the same time pull a string. A complete study of situations would give a complete account of the rat's attitudes, values, and intelligence.

I will first give some examples of the approaches which may be made from the situational standpoint in the field of social interaction. In connection with the problem of nature and nurture as conditioning intelligence, Freeman and his associates in Chicago placed six hundred children in foster homes and studied the results. They were apparently accepting a challenge of Terman who had said: "A crucial experiment would be to take a large number of very young children from the lower classes and after placing them in the most favorable environment obtainable, compare their later mental development with that of the children born into the best homes."[1] In this experiment comparisons were

[1] L. M. Terman *et al.*, *Mental and Physical Traits of a Thousand Gifted Children* (Genetic Studies in Genius, No. 1), p. 18.

made, in the case of one group, between results on intelligence tests which had been given before adoption and results after they had been in the foster home a number of years. Another comparison was made between children of the same family who had been placed in different homes, the home being rated on a scheme which took into consideration the material environment, evidence of culture, occupation of foster father, education and social activity of foster parents. Both of these comparisons had held heredity constant, letting the situation vary. A third comparison held environment constant, letting heredity vary, that is, it concerned itself with a comparison of the intelligence of the own children of the foster parents and of the foster children. The results, stated in a word, show that when two unrelated children are reared in the same home, differences in intelligence tend to decrease, and that when two related children are reared in different homes they tend to differ from one another in intelligence. This study was limited to the question of intelligence, but it is obvious that a fundamental study of behavior could be made by the same method. The adoption of children from "inferior" homes by persons living in "superior" homes provided a crude experimental situation. For some of these children, the "IQ" was known before adoption. After a period in the new environment the IQ was again obtained, and the changes compared with the average change in other children. For another group the IQ's were compared with own siblings and with foster siblings, for own parents with foster parents, and so on. This was, in effect, an experimental situation, in which both nature and nurture were allowed to vary and the numerical changes in IQ associated with such variation indicated. The very crude measurers of inferiority and superiority of environment tended to invalidate the results, but the method has further possibilities in the field of education and criminology.

Similarly, Healy and Bronner and their associates in Boston have studied the changes in behavior (cessation from delinquency) of a group of fifty juvenile offenders after placement in foster homes. These changes are compared with those occurring in delinquents given other forms of treatment. The experimental inadequacy lies in the factor of the selection of the delinquents (although Healy claims to have selected the less "promising" delinquents) and in the inability to define and measure the environmental factors producing the change. These two studies, in their defects as well as their positive value, point to the great importance of fundamental research which will lead to the further application of this method.

Burgess and Shaw have made regional surveys in Chicago disclosing an extraordinarily high rate of boy delinquency in the slum regions in comparison with the residential districts. Dividing the city into regions and following radii from the business district toward the suburbs and studying the delinquency in the boy population between eleven and seventeen years, they found 443 delinquents per 1,000 in the first mile unit, 58 in the second, 27 in the third, 4 in the fifth, and none in either the sixth or seventh. In the first two quarter-mile units of the central business district, over half the boys were brought into the juvenile court in an 18-month period.

Up to this point, however, this study serves only as a partial definition of the problem and as a preparation for a further approach. We have enough to form some hypotheses. We have certain regions characterized by an extraordinarily high delinquency rate, and at the same time there are regions in Chicago (not cemeteries, as Park has remarked) where there is no crime and no divorce. Unless an extremely large amount of bad heredity has been accumulated in the regions of high delinquency the explanation must be sought in the particular life-conditions in those regions.

It is already known that gang life is strongly developed in the regions of high delinquency, and that the delinquencies are largely group delinquencies. Shaw studied the cases of all boys brought before the juvenile court for stealing during a certain period and found that in 90 per cent of the cases two or more boys participated. One boy, in fact, laughed when the judge sentenced him to three months in Pontiac. He had been planning for this, since a sentence of this kind was a condition of full membership in his gang.

Twenty years ago, five thousand members of a Russian religious sect called the Molokans settled in Los Angeles. They resembled the Quakers somewhat in doctrine. They were all good people, and the old ones remained good. The children were good during the first years but have become progressively bad until at present about 90 per cent between the ages of eleven and eighteen have been before the juvenile court. The parents have become absurd and impossible to the children; the region has become a slum with a Mexican and oriental quota of population. The freedom of American children, the movies, etc., have had their influence.

I have presented these examples as research problems in the social process. The fact-finding surveys have disclosed the necessity of taking further steps to discover the causal relations between deviate behavior and given urban regions. The determination of causal relationships is preliminary to the introduction of purposive changes (reforms) in the social process, as it is in the material world. I will return to these examples later.

The mathematician, Poincaré, has thus described the basic procedure of analysis and of classification as approached by the natural sciences:

The most interesting facts are those which can be used several times, those which have a chance of recurring. We have been fortunate enough to be born in a world where there are such facts. Suppose that instead of eighty chemical elements we had eighty million, and that they were not some common and others rare but uniformly distributed. Then each time we picked up a new pebble there would be a strong probability that it was composed of some unknown substance. Nothing that we knew about other pebbles would tell us anything about it. [On the basis of likeness, we are able to form rules.] As soon as the rule is well established, as soon as it is no longer in doubt, the facts that are in conformity with it lose their interest. We cease to look for resemblances and apply ourselves before all else to differences, and of these differences we select first those that are most accentuated, not only because they are the most striking but because they will be the most instructive.[2]

In the social sciences the situation is not essentially different

[2] Henri Poincaré, *Science and Method*, pp. 17, 20.

from that in the natural sciences. The main difficulty at present is not that our behavior data are beyond the application of scientific method but that so few elements have yet been isolated, and that the experimental factors are producing a process of constant change in the materials we are studying. At any given moment, however, a set of rules (codes or standards) exists, and the deviations from these rules as represented by, let us say, the commission of crime are the material for our immediate study. The isolation of various behavior and experiential elements in this group, and their comparison with the recurrences of these elements in the non-deviating population is the further problem. The fact that our knowledge must of necessity be very meager until we have further fundamental research should not, of itself, be discouraging. It is, indeed, now admitted that even the physicist and chemist have a limited appreciation of their facts and that they are obliged to proceed (with considerable success) as though what they do not know does not exist.

In a good experiment in physics or chemistry, the influence of a given factor is measured by excluding all interfering factors. The change in the original material with the introduction of a specific factor can then be measured. Repetition of the experiment should give the same results, subject only to an experimental error. In the social field, if a factor has been discovered to be strongly associated with (for example) crime, in a given complex environment, its influence as a causative factor can be inferred only by excluding it in a situation in which all other factors are kept the same as in the original situation. But in experiments dealing with humans (or even animals and plants), interfering stimuli cannot be excluded, influence cannot be directly measured, and inferences as to causality become much less certain. Direct experimentation is here never clear-cut. So many other influences are brought to bear besides the one which it is intended to measure, that only by a widespread statistical comparison of various situations can any adequate inferences emerge. These inferences will never have the certainty of "laws"; they will always be in terms of probability. The better the experiment, the less dependent are the inferences on statistical manipulation. The impossibility of carrying on a strict experimentation in the social sciences is due also to our present inability to measure (or even adequately to recognize) the complexities of any given social situation or environment, and this renders impossible any equalizing of factors in two situations.

The inadequacy of research techniques in the social field may be illustrated by the attempts of criminologists to determine "criminal types." These studies have always assumed a marked differentiation of the criminal in some one respect from the rest of mankind. Thus, we have had theories of the criminal type as representing physical anomaly; all criminals possess these anomalies (exceptions are occasionally admitted) and mankind generally does not. Persons possessing these anomalies who have not committed crimes are "potential criminals," who will, presumably, commit the next series of crimes. We have had similar theories representing the criminal as the mentally abnormal type; for example, criminals are feeble-minded, and the non-criminal feeble-minded are potential criminals. Exceptions are rarely allowed, but it has been conceded that "There remain a few children of normal and superior intelligence whose delinquency must be accounted for in some other way."[3] Finally, we have theories asserting the typical criminal to be emotionally disordered (psychopathic).

All these attempts to define the criminal type assume some sharp differentiation of a group of mankind in their inherited tendencies or early conditioning, and assume further that the correlation between this sharply differentiated characteristic and the commission of crime is practically perfect. But when empirical checks of these assumptions have been made, the correlations were destroyed. Types have always seemed most clear-cut where only the deviating group has been studied, that is, where knowledge of the distribution of the typological characteristic among the general population is lacking. The tendency to idealize the general population where data do not exist has been observed time and again. It is necessary to mention only the experience with regard to the testing of the intelligence of

[3] I. H. Williams, "Delinquent Boys of Superior Intelligence," *Journal of Delinquency*, 1:34.

the draft army, where almost half the army would have been classified as feeble-minded had the same criteria previously applied to criminals been used. And when the same criteria were applied to draft army and criminals, no feeble-minded type emerged in the latter group. This has been the fate of all theories which have attempted to define a criminal type. A factor, the incidence of which in the general population is assumed to be slight, has been found to be preponderant among a group of criminals. It is, therefore, assumed to define a type generally or specifically related to criminality (that is, either *the* criminal type, irrespective of crime, or a particular type, such as the murderer). As data are accumulated regarding the incidence of this trait generally, it is found to be present in various groups of the non-criminal population. In other words, it has not been found that any trait or characteristic is the exclusive attribute of the criminal; he does not exist as a pure type.

These theories have, however, often contained a significant element. A correlation will be found to exist between a given attribute and criminal behavior, e.g., criminal groups will be found to have somewhat disproportionate numbers of persons of low-grade intelligence as compared with groups of the general population. The theory of type will not hold, but a factor of some etiological importance may emerge.

From concerning ourselves with a single factor, we pass to a consideration of a multiplicity of factors which may be involved, and the isolation of these factors from each other and the study of their inter-relationship become problems of fundamental importance. The method becomes that of multiple rather than single classification. Each variable must be considered in terms of other variables. The perspective must constantly be shifted from one factor of significance to other factors involved. In this way an estimate of the strength of a single factor may be secured, as well as the strength of several concomitant factors. The realistic approach to the criminal is in terms of concomitance of various factors (physical, mental, cultural) and their inter-relationship as compared with those of non-criminal groups. It is not a question of "all or none" of a given attribute being possessed by a criminal group and thus differentiating a type. It is rather a question of "how much" and "in what other relationships" this attribute exists in various groups of criminals as compared with various other groups.

I may suggest that research into behavior as related to the social process may take three general forms.

(1) Detailed accounts of the processes involved and the changes in behavior and attitudes occurring in radical situational changes for individuals and groups of individuals. These accounts would be in the nature of case histories and documentary analyses of the situations produced in the ordinary course of events by social change, by certain empirical therapeutic measures, etc. Immigration is one of the most satisfactory situations of the kind produced by or in society, as was noticed in the case of the Molokan colony in Los Angeles. The movement of populations from the country to the city, the slum areas in the city, the geographical culture areas, the varying culture configurations and behavior patterns of races and nationalities, are other examples. Empirical therapeutic measures are represented by foster-home placements, the experiments of Dr. Esther L. Richards[4] in moving psychopathic children from one family situation to another until adjustment was made, and those of Dr. Harry Stack Sullivan in promoting the association of psychopaths in groups among themselves. Detailed life histories of individuals reveal changed behavior as associated with situational change. These studies and documents have value both as focusing upon the totality of the processes involved in these changes (or rather the resultants of these processes), giving, so to speak, a behavior perspective, and as indicating what factors should be isolated for more careful investigation.

(2) The study and evolution of environment. The inadequacy of the measurement of environmental influences has been apparent in all studies which have purported to show the effects of change of environment. Most of these studies can claim to

[4] "The Significance and Management of Hypochondriacal Trends in Children," *Mental Hygiene*, 7:48–49.

have shown only that change in behavior was associated with a change in environment or situation. No adequate definition or measurement of the factors present in the new situations and absent in the old has been made. The sociologists, psychiatrists, and social workers have all attempted to indicate the factors associated with the change, but too often the determinations have been rationalizations. The attempts to quantify environment have been generally absurd. The Whittier scale is a composite of ratings of a home on the basis of necessities, neatness, size, "parental conditions" and parental supervision. The Minnesota scale consists of a detailed elaboration of material equipment with an amazing system of weighting, presumably on the basis of the degree of "culture" indicated by the possession of certain articles (alarm clock rated 1, mantel clock 2, grandfather's clock 3, etc.). Neither of these, nor any known attempts at composites, can be said to give any adequate picture of the environmental processes. Even those factors which can be readily investigated have received little attention, for example, the morphology of the family (that is, its composition with regard to age, sex, maturity, occupational and relationship range), income and expenditure, housing, and so on. Much record is needed simply to give a definition of environment in direct, quantitative terms.

(3) The development of a more accurate technique in observing and recording. The inadequacy of behavior recording is perhaps even more obvious. The recent development of observational techniques in the study of the social behavior of young children is throwing light upon the pitfalls in the way of reliable behavior records. The definition of the unit of behavior to be observed has been found to be a problem demanding much careful experimentation, in order to produce adequate control of the observer.

The work done by Dorothy Swaine Thomas[5] and her associates at Yale and Columbia represents a beginning in this type of research. They are developing observational studies in several

5   *Some New Techniques for Studying Social Behavior* (Child Development Monograph No. 1).

fields involving social interaction. They are also checking the observability of various units of behavior by repeated observations in the talking moving pictures. Their results indicate the types of units that can be evolved for accurate recording (physical contacts, verbal contacts, contacts with materials, etc.) in very small time intervals (five seconds). Factors making for unreliability in observational recording are being analyzed in detail. This work is laying a foundation essential for correlations between behavior elements and other factors in personality and environment, for until we are in a position to record behavior accurately, we cannot give credence to such correlations, however accurately these other factors may have been determined.

I am not suggesting that behavior can be adequately observed and recorded by the observational method or by statistical procedure. It appears, in fact, that the behavior document (case study, life record, psychoanalytic confession) representing a continuity of experience in life situations is the most illuminating procedure available. In a good record of this kind we are able to view the behavior reactions in the various situations, the emergence of personality traits, the determination of concrete acts, and the formation of life policies and their evolution.

There are undoubtedly insuperable difficulties in the way of perfecting the life record on the side of objectivity and reliability. It is introspective, the memory is notoriously treacherous, observation is defective, phantasy, fabrication and bias play large rôles. Court testimony is the best example of the difficulties encountered in securing a complete and objective narrative of past events. But this form of data is capable of improvement and systematization, and will have valuable applications when considerable numbers of life histories adequately elaborated are employed in a comparative way in order to determine the varieties of the schematization of life in varieties of situations. And it must be recognized that even the most highly subjective record has a value for behavior analysis and interpretation. A document, for example, prepared by one compensating for a feeling of inferiority or elaborating a delusion of persecution is as far as possible from objective reality, but the subject's view of the situation, how he regards it, may be the most important element for interpretation. For his immediate behavior is closely related to his definition of the situation, which may be in terms of objective reality or in terms of subjective appreciation—"as if" it were so. Very often it is the wide discrepancy between the situation as it seems to others and the situation as it seems to the individual that brings about the overt behavior difficulty. A paranoic person, at present in one of the New York institutions, has killed several persons who had the unfortunate habit of talking to themselves on the street. From the movement of their lips he imagined that they were calling him vile names, and he behaved as if this were true. If men define those situations as real, they are real in their consequences. The total situation will always contain more or less subjective factors, and the behavior reactions can be studied only in connection with the whole context, that is, the situation as it exists in verifiable, objective terms, and as it has seemed to exist in terms of the interested person.

Behavior analysis and interpretation will also be furthered through the development of the longitudinal approach to the life history. It is important not only to examine many types of individuals with regard to their experiences at various past periods of life in different situations, but it is important also to follow through groups of individuals into the future, getting a continuous record of experiences as they occur.

It is also highly important for us to realize that we do not as a matter of fact lead our lives, make our decisions, and reach our goals in everyday life either statistically or scientifically. We live by inference. I am, let us say, your guest. You do not know, you cannot determine scientifically, that I will not steal your money or your spoons. But inferentially I will not, and inferentially you have me as guest.

What is needed is a continuous and detailed preparation and study of life histories along with the available statistical studies, to be used as a basis for the inferences drawn. And these inferences in turn must be continually subjected to further statistical analysis as it becomes possible to transmute more factors into quantitative form. The case study method and the "natural history" method must not only precede the more scientifically acceptable method in order to produce realistic hypotheses and indicate what units should be defined and isolated; they must also be used as a general background of reference to the more limited statistical findings, which lead, as we have indicated, to inferences which must be constantly checked for validity against the large mass of material not yet analyzable.

Returning now to the examples of regional surveys, which disclosed a relation between behavior and specific urban areas, in order to understand the causal relationships it would be necessary to study the social influence of a given area of high delinquency on the juvenile population. And in order to do this it would be necessary (1) to make studies of the institutions and agencies exercising influence—home and family, school, church, boys' and girls' clubs, gangs, recreation centers, kind of work, commercialized pleasures, etc.; (2) to use a control group of non-delinquent boys and girls equal to the total number of delinquent boys and girls in the same region; (3) to equalize the factors in the two groups so as to make the data comparable and capable of qualification, comparing the individuals of the two groups, for example, with reference to intelligence, psychoneurotic responses, abnormal marital relation of parents (death, divorce, separation), nationality of parents, occupation of parents, educational background (including years in school and grade finished, kind of school attended, attendance in school, age at leaving school), occupational history, sex history, etc., and (4) to prepare detailed case histories and life histories of delinquents and non-delinquents as a means of judging the influence of the existing institutions and agencies.

Similar studies should then be made in various other selected regions of the same city and eventually in different cities. The urban regions and the different cities as wholes present very different cultural milieus. There is a different distribution and emphasis of influences. Rochester, for example, is strong in respect to schools and the visiting teacher movement, and weak on the side of the juvenile court, while Boston is particularly strong on the side of the juvenile court. Healy and Bronner, in their attempt to measure their successes and failures with delinquent children in Boston and Chicago, in each of which they had carried on work for ten years, found enormous differences. In Chicago the failures were 50 per cent, in Boston only 21 per cent.

The systematic comparison of regions and cultures would eventually be important in forming hypotheses and policies. While it will be possible and, in some cases, necessary for these researches to go on separately, it is desirable that all the problems of crime causation and prevention be viewed and studied together and simultaneously in given situations, regions, and populations; that the same individuals be involved from all the standpoints, and that different local areas be studied by the same methods and compared.

Eventually programs of the same kind should be carried out among selected racial and national groups, for example, the Italians, the Scandinavians, the Germans, the Russians, the Japanese, the Chinese, etc., with reference to determining the relation between behavior and social structure comparatively. Studies of this kind would be particularly rich in hypothesis-forming materials.

If there were time, I should like to make some concrete suggestions as to the method of approach in determining the social influence of certain concrete factors in the total situation as they are related to behavior, especially to deviate behavior. I have in mind such things as population factors, family organization and disorganization, economic factors, alcoholism and drug addiction, the newspaper and crime literature, and the motion picture.

I will mention, however, another item that seems to me of importance. It appears that the present academic and often rationalistic approach to problems relating to the social process is not of a type best adapted to understanding and controlling the social process, and that a more adequate type of approach has been developed by the great industrial organizations as, for example, the American Telephone and Telegraph Company and the General Electric Company. In these organizations problems are set by the central investigations, but "pure" research is often far behind the immediate needs of these problems. Therefore, chemists, physicists, and other specialists are assigned laboratory work in their own fields, with no immediate practical ends, but with the general purpose of speeding up the development of particular aspects of the field. If an institution were similarly organized for the study and control of behavior, it would naturally be limited in the immediate research set-up to those elements of behavior which have already been isolated by the separate disciplines. And it would be further limited by the imperfect methods of measurement existing in these separate disciplines. As a matter of immediate procedure, the best available techniques in the psychological, anthropometric, psychiatric, biochemical, economic, and social-behavior fields should be applied with equal care to the study of individuals and groups deviating in given ways from given norms. Preliminary explorations in which some single typological or other factor may seem worth investigating could be carried out on a more limited scale, for purposes of checking on possible factors that should be later incorporated in the larger studies.

It is obvious that the research program of an institution would be retarded by the slow development of techniques in each of the separate disciplines upon which it must draw. It would, therefore, be essential to turn the attention of investigators in this field to the investigation of elements which the institution considered important. The originating and co-ordinating agency would be the institution itself. Much of the wasted effort in typological studies in criminology has been due to the fact that an investigator who is familiar with his own technique applies it to a group of criminals, without any knowledge of criminal behavior or criminology. The investigators from the several fields should be essentially technicians who are able to apply their existing techniques in directions suggested by the staff of the institution and develop new techniques for application in these directions. For example, the institution might direct the attention of economists to problems of measuring labor stability and encourage specific development in psychology, physiology, sociology, and the other social sciences which would presumably prove of value to the eventual relation of elements in the field of criminal behavior.

It has been evident to you that in attempting to outline an approach to the examination of the social process I have had in mind the deviate behavior in anti-social lines. I have done this for the sake of concreteness. But there is a more comprehensive and normal type of behavior reaction going on every day before our eyes which has to do with the participation of the masses of the population, often whole populations, in common sentiments and actions. It is represented by fashions of dress, mob action, war hysteria, the gang spirit, Mafia, omertà, Fascism, popularity of this or that cigarette or tooth paste, the quick fame and infamy of political personalities. It uses language—spoken, written, and gesture. It is emotional, imitative, largely irrational and unconscious, weighted with symbols, and sometimes outrageous. It is capable of manipulation and propagation by leading personalities and the public print. Its results are commonly and publicly accepted definitions of situations. Its historical residuum constitutes the distinctive character of races, nationalities, and communities. In this region lies the psychology of the evolution of public opinion and of social norms. I am ready to believe that this is the social process which you would have chosen to have presented here at this time. But we are not prepared at present to do much more than rationalize about this larger social process. It would be necessary to break it up into special aspects, as I have attempted to indicate, and to make a long-time job of it. This would be possible if there were a redistribution of attention and money which would place behavior research on something like a parity with research in the biological and physical fields.[6]

[6] Dorothy Swaine Thomas, of Yale University, is responsible for the items relating to statistical procedure in this paper.

# The Bibliography of W. I. Thomas

"The Scope and Method of Folk-Psychology," *American Journal of Sociology*, 1 (January, 1896) : 434–45.

"On a Difference in the Metabolism of the Sexes," *American Journal of Sociology*, 3 (July, 1897) : 31–63, Ph.D. dissertation, University of Chicago; reprinted by the University of Chicago Press, 1897.

"The Relation of Sex to Primitive Social Control," *American Journal of Sociology*, 3 (May, 1898) : 754–76.

"Sex in Primitive Industry," *American Journal of Sociology*, 4 (January, 1899) : 474–88.

"Sex in Primitive Morality," *American Journal of Sociology*, 4 (May, 1899) : 774–87.

"The Psychology of Modesty and Clothing," *American Journal of Sociology*, 5 (September, 1899) : 246–62.

"The Gaming Instinct," *American Journal of Sociology*, 6 (May, 1901) : 750–63.

"Der Ursprung der Exogamie," *Zeitschrift für Socialwissenschaft*, 5 (1902) : 1–18.

"The Relation of the Medicine-Man to the Origin of the Professional Occupations," *Decennial Publications of the University of Chicago*, First Series, 4 (1903) : 241–56.

"The Sexual Element in Sensibility," *Psychological Review*, 11 (January, 1904) : 61–67.

"The Psychology of Race-Prejudice," *American Journal of Sociology*, 9 March, 1904) : 593–611.

"Is the Human Brain Stationary?" *Forum*, 36 (October, 1904) : 305–20.

"The Province of Social Psychology," *Psychological Bulletin,* 1 (October 15, 1904) : 392–93. Also in *American Journal of Sociology,* 10 (January, 1905).
"The Adventitious Character of Woman," *American Journal of Sociology,* 12 (July, 1906) : 32–44.
"The Mind of Woman and the Lower Races," *American Journal of Sociology,* 12 (January, 1907) : 435–69.
"Der Mangel an Generalisationsvermogen bei den Negern," *Zeitschrift für Socialwissenschaft,* 7 (1904) : 215–21.
*Sex and Society: Studies in the Social Psychology of Sex.* Chicago: University of Chicago Press, 1907.
"The Significance of the Orient for the Occident," *Publications of the American Sociological Society: Papers and Proceedings, Second Annual Meeting,* II (1907) : 111–24 (discussion, pp. 124–37, 136–37 by W. I. Thomas). Also in *American Journal of Sociology,* 13 (May, 1908) : 729–42, 754–55.
"The Psychology of the Yellow Journal," *American Magazine,* 65 (March, 1908) : 491–96.
"The Psychology of Woman's Dress," *American Magazine,* 67 (November, 1908) : 66–72.
"The Mind of Woman," *American Magazine,* 67 (December, 1908) : 146–52.
"The Older and Newer Ideals of Marriage," *American Magazine,* 67 (April, 1908) : 548–52.
"Eugenics: The Science of Breeding Men," *American Magazine,* 68 (June, 1909) : 190–97.
"Votes for Women," *American Magazine,* 68 (July, 1909) : 292–301.
"Woman and the Occupations," *American Magazine,* 68 (September, 1909) : 463–70.
"Standpoint for the Interpretation of Savage Society," *American Journal of Sociology,* 15 (September, 1909) : 145–63.
*Source Book for Social Origins: Ethnological Materials, Psychological Standpoint, Classified and Annotated Bibliographies for the Interpretation of Savage Society.* Chicago: University of Chicago Press, 1909; Boston: Richard G. Badger, 1909.
"Race Psychology: Standpoint and Questionnaire, with Particular Reference to the Immigrant and the Negro," *American Journal of Sociology,* 17 (May, 1912) : 725–75.
"Education and Racial Traits," *Southern Workman,* 41 (June, 1912) : 378–86.

"The Prussian-Polish Situation: An Experiment in Assimilation," *Publications of the American Sociological Society: Papers and Proceedings*, Eighth Annual Meeting, VIII (1913): 84–99. Also in *American Journal of Sociology*, 19 (March, 1914): 624–39.

"The Origin of Society and of the State," *Studies in Social Science*, 1 (No. 1). Chicago: Zalas Corporation, *ca.* 1915.

"The Persistence of Primary-group Norms in Present-day Society and Their Influence in Our Educational System," in *Suggestions of Modern Science Concerning Education*, by Herbert S. Jennings, John G. Watson, Adolf Meyer, and W. I. Thomas, pp. 159–97. New York: The Macmillan Company, 1917.

*The Polish Peasant in Europe and America.* With Florian Znaniecki. 5 vols. Boston: Richard G. Badger, 1918–20 (Vols. I and II originally published by the University of Chicago Press, 1918). Second edition, 2 vols. New York: Alfred A. Knopf, 1927. Reprinted, 2 vols. New York: Dover Publications, 1958.

*Old World Traits Transplanted.* With Robert E. Park and Herbert A. Miller. New York: Harper & Brothers, 1921. (A volume in the Americanization Studies, Allen T. Burns, director.)

*The Unadjusted Girl: With Cases and Standpoint for Behavior Analysis.* Boston: Little, Brown, and Company, 1923. Criminal Science Monograph No. 4. (Supplement to the *Journal of the American Institute of Criminal Law and Criminology*.)

"The Problem of Personality in the Urban Environment," *Publications of the American Sociological Society: Papers and Proceedings of the Twentieth Annual Meeting.* XX (1925), 30–39.

"The Behavior Pattern and the Situation," *Publications of the American Sociological Society: Papers and Proceedings, Twenty-second Annual Meeting.* XXII (1927), 1–13. Reprinted in *Personality and the Social Group*, edited by Ernest W. Burgess, pp. 1–15. Chicago: University of Chicago Press, 1929.

"The Configurations of Personality," in *The Unconscious: A Symposium* pp. 143–77. New York: Alfred A. Knopf, 1927.

*The Child in America: Behavior Problems and Programs.* With Dorothy Swaine Thomas. New York: Alfred A. Knopf, 1928.

"The Relation of Research to the Social Process," in *Essays on Research in the Social Sciences: Papers Presented in a General Seminar Conducted by the Committee on Training of The Brookings Institution, 1930–31*, pp. 175–94. Washington: Brookings Institution, 1931.

"The Comparative Study of Cultures," *American Journal of Sociology*, 42 (September, 1936) : 177–85.
*Primitive Behavior: An Introduction to the Social Sciences*. New York: McGraw-Hill, 1937.
"Comment by W. I. Thomas," in *An Appraisal of Thomas and Znaniecki's "The Polish Peasant in Europe and America,"* Social Science Research Council Bulletin 44, by Herbert Blumer, pp. 82–87; other comments, part 2, *passim*. New York: Social Science Research Council, 1939.

## Books and Articles on W. I. Thomas

Harry Elmer Barnes. "William Isaac Thomas: The Fusion of Psychological and Cultural Sociology," in *An Introduction to the History of Sociology*, edited by Harry Elmer Barnes, pp. 793–804. Chicago: University of Chicago Press, 1948.
Herbert Blumer. *An Appraisal of Thomas and Znaniecki's "The Polish Peasant in Europe and America,"* New York: Social Science Research Council, 1939.
Emory S. Bogardus. "The Sociology of William I. Thomas," in *Sociology and Social Research*, 34 (September-October, 1949) : 34–48.
———. "William I. Thomas and Social Origins," *Sociology and Social Research*, 43 (May, 1959) : 365–69.
Marvin Bressler. "Selected Family Patterns in W. I. Thomas' Unfinished Study of the *Bintl Brief*," *American Sociological Review*, 17 (October, 1952) : 563–71.
Ernest W. Burgess. "William I. Thomas as a Teacher," *Sociology and Social Research*, 32 (March, 1948) : 760–64.
Ellsworth Faris. "In Memoriam: William Isaac Thomas, 1863–1947," *American Journal of Sociology*, 53 (March, 1948) : 387.
———. "William I. Thomas, 1863–1947," *Sociology and Social Research*, 32 (March, 1948) : 755–59.
Gisela J. Hinkle. "The 'Four Wishes' in Thomas' Theory of Social Change," *Social Research*, 19 (December, 1952) : 464–84.
———. "Rejoinder to Volkart," *Social Research*, 20 (January, 1954) : 473–77.
Floyd Nelson House, "The Polish Peasant," in *The Development of Sociology*, pp. 283–90. New York: McGraw-Hill, 1936.

John Madge. *The Origins of Scientific Sociology*, chapter 4 and *passim*. New York: The Free Press of Glencoe, 1962.

Howard W. Odum. *American Sociology: The Story of Sociology in the United States through 1950*, chapter 8 and *passim*. New York: Longmans, Green and Co., 1951.

Robert E. Park, "The Sociological Methods of William Graham Sumner and of William I. Thomas and Florian Znaniecki," in *Methods in Social Science: A Case Book*, edited by Stuart A. Rice, pp. 154–75. Chicago: University of Chicago Press, 1931.

Edmund H. Volkart (ed.). *Social Behavior and Personality*. New York: Social Science Research Council, 1951.

——. "Aspects of the Theories of William I. Thomas" (reply to G. J. Hinkle's "The Four Wishes . . ."), *Social Research*, 20 (October, 1953) : 345–57.

Kimball Young (ed.). *Social Attitudes*. New York: Henry Holt & Co., 1931.

——. "William I. Thomas (1863–1947)," *American Sociological Review*, 13 (February, 1948) : 102–4.

——. *The Contribution of William Isaac Thomas to Sociology*. Evanston, Ill.: Student Book Exchange, n.d. (Appeared originally in *Sociology and Social Research*, 47, Nos. 1, 2, 3, and 4 [October, 1962; January, April, and July, 1963].)

Florian Znaniecki. "William I. Thomas as a Collaborator," *Sociology and Social Research*, 32 (March, 1948) : 765–67.